TRUMP
THE "CHOSEN ONE"

To Demetra,

A great boss and real friend from your best employee ever!

Bruce

Hope you like the book,

Mark Levin

TRUMP
THE "CHOSEN ONE"

The Road to Perdition

BRUCE M. FINE

& HENRY B. LEWIN

Columbus, Ohio

Trump: The "Chosen One"
The Road to Perdition

Published by Gatekeeper Press
2167 Stringtown Rd, Suite 109
Columbus, OH 43123-2989
www.GatekeeperPress.com

Copyright © 2020 by Bruce M. Fine & Henry B. Lewin
All rights reserved. Neither this book, nor any parts within it may be sold or reproduced in any form or by any electronic or mechanical means, including information storage and retrieval systems without permission in writing from the author. The only exception is by a reviewer, who may quote short excerpts in a review.

The cover design, interior formatting, typesetting, and editorial work for this book are entirely the product of the author. Gatekeeper Press did not participate in and is not responsible for any aspect of these elements.

ISBN (hardcover): 9780578687117
ISBN (paperback): 9781662901690
eISBN: 9781662901225

Be vigilant, oh liberty, for the crazed are everywhere.
Be sure, there is no certainty you'll find them only "there".
For danger comes from hatred deep, and God has understood
That evil uses hateful things disguised as something good.
They spread their plan of chaos now on those who would be free.
Beware of those who preach of God and listen to their pleas.
"Kill the Jews and infidels," is wrong and clear to see.
"Ban the Muslims!" "Build a wall!" That sounds the same to me.
Be careful of the "truth" they speak, and the hatred that is preached
For this is not the Word of God, nor lessons He would teach.
When sermons sow the seeds of hate and twist God's holy lines;
Fanatics follow just like sheep, with poisoned crippled minds.
They spread their lies; seduce the weak to that which is insane.
What evil grips the hearts of men, to delight in others pain?
It harbors hatred, death and fear for each and all to bear.
From those who think that they know God, and do evil
with a prayer.

   –John Henry Fairfax, from the Poem "September 11," copyright 2001

DEDICATION

Be the kind of woman that when your feet hit the floor each morning the devil says: "Oh crap, she's up!"

–attributed to Ingrid Bergman, actress

I just love bossy women. I could be around them all day. To be bossy is not a pejorative term at all. It means somebody's passionate and engaged and ambitious and doesn't mind leading.

–Amy Poehler, actress and comedian, 2011

WE LOVE STRONG, INDEPENDENT, CARING, SELF-ASSURED women. Our wives are perfect examples. To Mary Lou and Maria: we truly thank you for the encouragement, support, and inspiration you have given to this and all the endeavors we've engaged in. It is during times of crisis when people learn the most from each other. The more we learn, the more we grow. In many ways you have been our teachers as well as our companions. Darwin would be proud of the way you helped in our evolution. We dedicate this book to you, with love.

ACKNOWLEDGEMENTS

After the 2016 elections, there was a lot of talk. We talked with one another, with our wives, with our friends and our families. We had opinions and concerns. We also had a range of emotions, and not least some panic, dismay, fear, and disbelief. We came up with ideas, and probably a few conspiracy theories. At some point we started to see themes appearing in our rants, and our thoughts began to gel into some sort of cohesion. We wondered if, working together, the two of us could make sense of it all in writing. So we began. We did research. We wrote. We did more research. We talked. We wrote. We got to a point, maybe early 2019, when we were sure we were done, or close to it. Oh, were we wrong. Things kept happening. Trump kept tweeting. Like many Americans we could barely keep up with daily news and current events. So we did what we felt we had to do and we kept writing and revising, and revising more, and adding new materials in an effort to keep our book current with the times. More things were happening and it never settled down. We would most likely be writing this book ad infinitum if it were not for the editorial help of Tracy McLoone. We want to acknowledge Tracy's hard work and her unique set of knowledge encompasses politics, federal policy, current events, past events, culture, the English language, and grammar.

CONTENTS

DEDICATION..vii

ACKNOWLEDGEMENTS ix

INTRODUCTION THE WORLD OF TRUMP............................xv

CHAPTER 1 FROM SWAMP TO CESSPOOL................................1

CHAPTER 2 HIDDEN ENEMY..21
    Beware the Live Dragon...23
    Trump's Circus Act: Fool Some of the People 39
    Politics as Usual and Everything to Fear 60

CHAPTER 3 RELIGION AND MORALITY ... AND POLITICS........75
    Corruptions of Christianity 78
    What Would Jesus Do? 83
    A Moral and Religious People 88
    That Which is False and Dangerous 100
    Where There Is Hatred...108

CHAPTER 4 ECONOMIC PAIN AND GAIN 115
    Our Incomes are Like Our Shoes................................117
    Persuading the Sheep...120
    The Only American Principle 125
    A Judicious Hand 140

CHAPTER 5 BEWARE: THE REBIRTH OF FASCISM 147
    CONFUSION OF PRINCIPLES...149
    THE SECRET OF TYRANNY...157
    NOT FROM POWER OR RICHES, GRANDEUR OR GLORY...................160
    THAT ELITIST APPROACH TO GOVERNMENT 162

CHAPTER 6 THIS IS OUR DEMOCRACY 179
    THE VERY DEFINITION OF TYRANNY 181
    THE PESTILENCE OF FOREIGN INFLUENCE 189
    MONEY AND MORE MONEY, POWER AND MORE POWER 198
    SELL NOT VIRTUE TO PURCHASE WEALTH 204
    LIKE SELF-PRESERVATION, A DUTY TO GOD............................207

CHAPTER 7 CRISIS..215
    NO TIME TO LOSE 218
    THE BIGGEST THREAT 220
    NOTHING LEFT FOR YOUR CHILDREN...................................227
    BEING GOOD AND DECENT PEOPLE 230

CHAPTER 8 DON'T LET THE BASTARDS GRIND YOU DOWN..235
    EDUCATE YOURSELF 240
    WORLD NEWS: PAY ATTENTION...242
    JOIN FORCES (EVEN IF YOU CAN'T FORM YOUR OWN PAC) 243
    FIND YOUR MORAL COMPASS 245
    DON'T FORGET OUR PAST 247
    AND DON'T LET A BASTARD GRIND YOU DOWN 249

EPILOGUE WHERE ARE WE NOW, WHICH WAY IS OUT, ARE WE TOO LATE?..259

INTRODUCTION

THE WORLD OF TRUMP

> Educate and inform the whole mass of the people … They are the only sure reliance for the preservation of our liberty.
> —Thomas Jefferson, president and statesman, 1787

> This guy being the president, it's like there's a horse loose in a hospital. I think eventually everything's going to be okay, but I have no idea what's going to happen next. And neither do any of you and neither do your parents, because there's a horse loose in the hospital!
> —John Mulaney, comedian, 2017

WE ARE BEST FRIENDS. ONE OF US is a self-proclaimed Democrat, and the other leans independent. We don't agree on everything. We respect one another. We watched the results of the 2016 presidential election together. The outcome shocked both of us. One of us thought, "He's the newly elected president; let's give him the benefit of the doubt." To say the other was less optimistic is a bit of an understatement. We both wanted to believe we could rely on our nation's founding principles and on "the whole mass of the people",[1] in the words of Thomas Jefferson, to keep our leaders in check and things from going too far astray. It quickly became apparent that there are many people who, like us, did not need

---

1   Thomas Jefferson, "Letter to Uriah Forrest [with Enclosure], 31 December 1787", *Founders Online,* National Archives Founders Online, accessed September 10, 2019, https://founders.archives.gov/documents/Jefferson/01-12-02-0490.

the predictive powers of Nostradamus to see what was coming. After the election we heard comedian John Mulaney comparing a Donald Trump presidency to the dangerous absurdity of letting a horse run loose in a hospital: even if the level of destruction is uncertain, even if that horse can find a quiet place and more or less stay out of the way, there's likely to be some damage and probably some unpleasant surprises.[2]

Unfortunately, our initial concerns have been borne out and any benefit of the doubt turned into shock and dismay. In August 2019, President Donald Trump declared himself "the Chosen One" on camera, to the press, and therefore to the world. This moment disturbed us greatly, and we were not the only ones. Even though Trump claimed later to have said it in jest, his statement and the visual image he created spoke volumes about Trump's aggrandized view of himself. Even more troubling was the way that Trump was claiming the mantle of our savior and had been amassing the support of evangelicals and the Christian Right. We came to realize that it's not just that there was a proverbial horse loose in the hospital and we were waiting to see what would happen. We've been watching it happen. It is not good and it's no joke anymore. The damage is very, very real, and it is immense.

Donald Trump's claims that he acts for and in the best interests of the American people are deceitful. His deliberate defiance and lack of adherence to the rule of law is the first step in destroying our democracy and replacing it with a caste system where the top one percent of the economic pyramid holds almost everything—money, power, control of resources—and leaves everyone else too busy just trying to get by to do anything about

---

2 John Mulaney, "The Late Show with Stephen Colbert", CBS, June 9, 2017, https://www.cbs.com/shows/the-late-show-with-stephen-colbert/video/NNJLoCcCIRfef09e6cj_ip5l7oK34DmT/john-mulaney-trump-is-a-horse-loose-in-a-hospital-/.

it. As Americans and as people of faith, we must protect our democracy lest we lose it. We should not simply give lip service to our religious faith and allow others to distort it for their own monetary and political gains.

Writing this book is our attempt to help preserve the liberty that was so important to our founding fathers' philosophy of a nation. It is our response to the reality of the current health crisis and the toxic political, religious, and economic environment in which we now find ourselves. It is time to fight to take back our country. Many people have been lulled to complacency (the "someone else can fix this" approach) or are just too tired from the daily grind of making ends meet to know where to start—and that was even before the threat of coronavirus.

We wrote this book for those Americans who are the most adversely impacted by what's happening now both with our economy and in our society. Here's a hint, "those Americans" being affected? That's all of us if we ignore our values and don't pull our democracy out from the cesspool. We hope to convince our readers of the imminent need to be more involved in elections and civic life. If we want to have a planet left to live on and a truly free democratic nation, we no longer have the luxury of abdicating our civic responsibilities to the corrupt and greedy. The novel coronavirus (COVID-19) pandemic has made all of this enormously obvious. The "horse" itself is no longer our nation's primary concern. Instead, the chaos created by that horse allowed a national crisis to erupt with the spread of COVID-19, a microscopic invader with the potential to kill hundreds of thousands of Americans.

We can't yet know the total damage or the fallout from this pandemic, but we do know as we write this that our hospitals are overburdened, people are ill and dying, and the disease continues to cause harm, while we still lack adequate testing and supplies. The perfect incubator for the rapid spread of this invader was an ill-prepared, know-it-all, commander-in-chief who claims to know more about battle than generals, more about science than scientists, more about medicine than licensed MDs and nurses, and whose mind seems to shift with the wind. This "commander-in-chief" ignored numerous early warnings from his own intelligence community, even with updates presented to him daily and warnings as early as November, 2019 about the likelihood of a pending pandemic.[3] That horse in the hospital might just be a Trojan horse, with Americans like the duped Trojans—and we can see some Trojan leaders who stand to benefit from this chaos and destruction.

Our national security is far more vulnerable since Trump moved into the White House. If we want safety, fairness, pride and self-respect we must become active participants in our political system. We invite you to return to the words of Thomas Jefferson to keep in mind that the people—all of us, "are the only sure reliance for the preservation of our liberty."[4] Donald Trump is not "making America great again", unless you mistakenly think "great" is synonymous for racist and/or elitist. We must decide against becoming a nation of hypocrites and act accordingly. In this book we highlight power brokers of whom we need to be wary, including many people we have elected as our leaders, but also people who operate out of the limelight and behind the scenes. We hope this dialogue will engage honest men and women who want to help reclaim our democracy from forces of greed, hypocrisy, and self-interest. We unapologetically criticize the large portion of evangelical Christians and other religious leaders who have

---

3   Josh Margolin and James Gordon Meek, "Intelligence Report Warned of Coronavirus Crisis as Early as November: Sources", ABC News, April 8, 2020, https://abcnews.go.com/Politics/intelligence-report-warned-coronavirus-crisis-early-november-sources/story?id=70031273.
4   Jefferson, "Letter to Uriah Forest."

abandoned the teachings of Christ to support Donald Trump, despite Trump's unconscionably immoral behavior and policies. We also know that while white evangelicals make up a large and vocal portion of Trump's base, not all evangelicals can be painted with the same brush, and that some younger and more racially diverse evangelicals have been pushing back against the hypocritical image of a pious Donald Trump and against those religious defenders of Trump who positioned this morally bankrupt fraud as their "chosen one."

In the chapters that follow, we first address the all-consuming war against COVID-19 and critically review our government's preparedness and response under Donald Trump's watch. The next chapter discusses the self-serving hypocrisy of some of the religious right, and the related dangers to our political system. We then highlight the reasons for and the means to alleviate the huge income and wealth inequality in the United States. The next two chapters compare the rise of fascism in Germany leading to World War II to what is now transpiring in America and across the globe and discuss related damaging effects of elitism, and we delve into tyranny and the corrupting influence on our democracy of extreme concentrations of money and power. The following chapter documents the severity of the global climate crisis and the political and business forces working to undermine efforts to change.

Our final chapter, "Don't Let the Bastards Grind You Down", calls on Americans to plan for the future by educating ourselves, but also not to forget our past. With our nation's problems stemming from a significant lack of moral leadership, each of us must individually examine our own moral compass and work to restore morality as a basic tenet of our governance. We end with an epilogue that we hope captures some of the fallout of the rapidly unfolding events that were happening as we were writing—

and we did have to pick a point at which to tell ourselves to stop writing and start doing, and maybe even move on to other projects.

Unlike Donald Trump, we are not asking you to believe our claims on blind faith. We provide a wealth of documentation and resources that our readers can explore to learn more and come to their own decisions. There are places in this book where we make light of some of the absurdity occurring in our nation's politics, with sarcasm, wordplay, or hyperbole, because sometimes we needed the levity. We are fully aware that in the end none of these are laughing matters. It is a sad and sobering state of affairs that confronts us. This is not what we want for our country, and it is neither what our founding fathers envisioned nor consistent with our nation's core values.

We believe most writers borrow from one another by volleying ideas and building on opinions and perspectives. We wanted to frame the book with words and ideas that we as Americans commonly connect to our core values. Throughout the book we use words attributed to great writers, thinkers, executives, activists, and many others, to start chapters and sections; sometimes, the attributions are obvious. Other times nobody seems sure of the source of a commonly used quote. We've tried to provide the origin of each epigraph, and to let you know whenever we weren't sure ourselves. We hope the thoughts and data we offer will motivate those of you who feel indifferent or hopeless, or have become complacent, to get involved. We appeal to our fellow Americans to help protect and preserve our democracy by voting to replace the corrupt politicians who threaten it.

To those courageous patriots who have stepped forward and sounded the alarm about the lies, deceptions, false information and hateful rhetoric, our country owes you a debt of gratitude. As for the rest of us, our job is to hold our elected representatives accountable and to do so by voting. This is our small part to support that effort.

Humans are imperfect and from time to time we all harmlessly exaggerate, or forget things, or make inaccurate statements. However, the breadth and depth of the lying, greed and corruption coming out of this administration is threatening the very survival of our democracy. Those who base their arguments solely on propaganda and conspiracy theories rely on a disdain for civil discourse and the discrediting of proven data.

Much of our analysis is informed by the work and words of others: authors, journalists, politicians, and discussions with friends. We thank them for their vigilance to our democracy and belief in our freedom of the press. We thank those who came before us for their insights, tenacity, and courage to speak truth to power. We invite you to check the facts, think for yourself, and draw your own conclusions.

We trust the words contained herein will help mobilize Americans to engage against the very real threats to our way of life, and to reset our nation's moral compass to reflect the real values of the American people. That you will be motivated to vote for and hold accountable, politicians intent on repairing and re-establishing our international stature as a model democratic government and moral leader; reconnecting with our allies in democracy and taking a big step away from tyrannical leaders; insisting on a more equitable distribution of income and wealth in the United States; and re-engaging with renewed force in the fight to stem the threat of global climate change and pandemics before it is too late. We sincerely hope that you find this book worthy of your time and consideration.

CHAPTER 1

FROM SWAMP TO CESSPOOL

> I will Make Our Government Honest Again—believe me. But first I'm going to have to #DrainTheSwamp ...
>
> —Donald Trump @realDonaldTrump, Twitter, October 2016

> We found that Mussolini's government made a big point of draining literal swamps, as public works projects, and he did conduct mass firings of civil servants. In addition, Mussolini touted the metaphor of purification as a defining principle of his political philosophy.
>
> —Louis Jacobson, editor and political journalist, PolitiFact, 2018

TRUMP PROMISED IN HIS CAMPAIGN FOR president to clean and drain "the swamp", his term of insult to describe government in Washington, D.C. and beyond. It was part of his appeal to Americans who felt they were losing out on what they were due and wanted someone to blame. It was a catchy phrase and his believers loved it. Contrary to what Trump claimed he would do his actions have led to far worse conditions. Under Trump, the "swamp" turned into a festering mess. It is now a cesspool, dirtier and murkier than before, unable to sustain beneficial life forms, and with a huge influx of far more dangerous denizens of the deep that seem able to survive—even thrive—in this fetid political ecosystem. In her 2018 book, *Fascism: a Warning*, former Secretary of State Madeleine Albright likened Trump's campaign rally cry to Italian fascist dictator Benito Mussolini declaring he would drain swamps to improve the lives of the Italian people.[5] Journalist and veteran political fact-checker Louis Jacobson determined that Albright was more or less right (half right, per *PolitiFact*), except that Mussolini was being very literal: actually draining marshes in which malaria-causing mosquitos festered and putting in pumps and other infrastructure.[6] In that, Mussolini kept his word, for better or worse.

During the 2016 presidential campaign, Donald Trump shouted "drain the swamp!" more times than we care to count: he swore to clean up government, and make politics "honest." This was far from his only false claim or breached promise. Candidate Trump also promised the American people a far better healthcare system, a massively improved infrastructure, a much fairer tax structure and an epic return of manufacturing and high paying jobs. Despite his repeated declarations of success, he has yet to deliver on any of his campaign promises, at least not for most Americans. In fact, the only benefactors of his policies and executive orders are those at the very top of our country's wealth pyramid.

The tax bill that Trump endorsed significantly benefited the wealthy, while any gains in the bill to the middle class were wiped out by the elimination or reduction of existing deductions that would have directly benefited middle- and lower-income taxpayers. Nor has there been any meaningful infrastructure bill or jobs bill that has gone anywhere, much less passed and signed into law.

Alternative energy efforts are being defunded in favor of fossil fuels, foreign policy is in shambles, and elected representatives are turning a blind eye to their constitutional duty as a check-and-

---

5   Madeleine Albright, *Fascism: a Warning (HarperCollins, 2018).*
6   Louis Jacobson, "Madeleine Albright Compares Mussolini, Trump on Use of 'Drain the Swamp'", *PolitiFact,* May 9, 2018, https://www.politifact.com/factchecks/2018/may/09/madeleine-albright/madeleine-albright-right-about-mussolini-and-drain/.

balance to the executive branch. Now America is faced with the life-threatening coronavirus and its attendant financial consequences, which have been exacerbated by this president's abysmal leadership.

In the COVID-19 crisis, contrary to his own glowing review of his performance, Trump has shown incompetence of leadership on a level never before seen in our commander-in-chief. He appears incapable of believing that anyone knows more than he does. He doesn't seem to have a clue how to recognize (much less formulate) a strategic organizational plan to address the crisis that our nation faces, immediately and with longer-term fallout. As we write, this disease continues to ravage its victims young and old, taking over hospitals and care facilities. The lack of critical supplies is resulting in the infection of the nurses, doctors, caretakers, first responders and many others who are trying to help and keep our nation and its people functioning. Much of the damage is irreparable and it is only just begun—and that doesn't even get to the long-lasting effects on our economy, on small businesses, on people's jobs and incomes, on children's ability to learn, and much more, including things that we probably haven't imagined yet. All the while, Trump focused on finding a scapegoat for the lack of adequate testing capability, and it was no surprise that he tried to cast blame on Obama and only those governors who were Democrats.

Trump has contended throughout his presidency that "Do Nothing Democrats [sic]" in Congress are spending all of their time trying to get him removed from office rather than putting forward legislative proposals for his signature. We should all know better. The reality is that it is primarily Trump and Senate Majority Leader Mitch McConnell working in concert to hold up legislation and at the same time declaring that congressional Democrats are obstructionist.[7] It's an old political trick: "manufacture" your own

---

7   Blake Dodge, "Democratic Senators are Tweeting Photos of the Giant Pile of 'Dead' House-Passed Bills on Mitch McConnell's Desk", Newsweek, December 18,

bogeyman, put it out there, and then tell everyone it's the other side's fault. Why not put these pieces of legislation up for votes? The sad reality is it is not consistent with their agenda. Subsequently, there is no record—and Republicans, who may find themselves voting down helpful measures would then have to answer to their constituents and the American people. <u>No vote, no questions, no exposure.</u> By refusing <u>to bring legislation to the floor, McConnell is engaged in a deliberate obstruction of the system to avoid what he and the President do not like or want.</u> They then seek cover by blaming the lack of progress on everyone else and especially those do-nothing Democrats he keeps talking about.

Mistaken Identity

Our elected leaders should, in accordance with their oaths of office, put the needs of the country and the protection of citizens above all else. They should know and follow our Constitution as it defines our democratic republic. They should be moral. They should be courageous. They should be compassionate. They should be informed with actual facts, know what they don't know, and seek advice from wise counselors. We hope that the people elected to serve as our leaders possess the integrity and intestinal fortitude to put these things above party loyalty and self-interest. This is no longer an ideal we can count on. It is not what is happening. Self-interest seems to be today's motivation for many of the politicians and we deserve better. Unfortunately, we are getting further from this with every day of this presidency. In his article, "Coronavirus crisis underlines eight of Trump's failings as a leader", national security expert Peter Bergen, author, journalist and CNN national

2019, https://www.newsweek.com/democratic-senators-tweeting-photos-giant-pile-dead-house-passed-bills-mitch-mcconnell-desk-14780472019]

security analyst, lays out in a simple list how the crisis has highlighted Trump's remarkably bad leadership traits:[8]

- Doesn't do homework; consciously doesn't prepare and puts in the least possible effort.
- Believes he knows more than the experts—on any and all subjects.
- Trusts his own gut, when "going with your gut in a complex crisis when you don't do homework or listen to experts is not likely to produce relevant knowledge or coherent policy."
- Increasingly surrounds himself with a "team of acolytes"—people who won't challenge him (and gets rid of anyone who does).
- Lies and misleads extensively: "It is hard to believe a man who has made more than 16,000 false statements in his first three years in office."
- Blames the messenger "for news he doesn't like," such as when news organizations report accurate information, he blames them for the information.
- "The buck never stops at Trump's desk." He's a reverse Harry Truman: "If things are going well, he is always ready to take credit … If things go poorly it's always someone else fault. Paging Mike Pence!"
- Acts as a "divider-in-chief, not the uniter-in-chief. Now is surely not the time … to claim that the coronavirus is being hyped by crazed Democrats," and his effort, "to pass it off as a partisan issue is crass at best."

---

8   Peter Bergen, "Corona Virus Crisis Underlines Eight of Trump's Failings as a Leader," CNN, March 2, 2020, https://www.cnn.com/2020/03/02/opinions/trump-failings-coronavirus- opinion-bergen/index.html.

Make no mistake we believe: Donald Trump is a peril, not a patsy. From the moment Trump entered the White House he has been deliberately disrupting the delicate balance of our three branches of government. He has been undermining a democratic system that has survived and prospered, and been admired and respected around the world for over 240 years. His domestic and foreign policies are inconsistent, dangerously flawed, and constitute a serious immediate threat to our nation. He is "a clear and present danger," who has seduced much of the evangelical Christian right into overlooking his moral deficiencies with the promise of conservative judges and courts to overturn Roe v. Wade, and eliminate the right to reproductive choice. Those who close their eyes to this deception constitute a danger to us all for their willingness to support a man who would lead us into a national theocracy when in reality would create an autocracy with Trump as the leader. The following lists examples of the things he has done since entering office:

- Effectively disassembling the State Department and decimating its institutional knowledge as seasoned experts are forced out or leave in disgust, making real diplomacy with other nations practically impossible.
- Removing or forcing out experienced department heads and Cabinet officials throughout government, then filling the vacancies with "acting" replacements that seem inclined to acquiesce to his will.
- Repeatedly making public statements denying Russian interference in the 2016 elections despite all evidence otherwise that grows almost daily.
- At the same time not filling vacancies on the Federal Election Commission, leaving it without a quorum to investigate or enforce election violations, and making our

local, state and federal governments and electoral systems vulnerable to further hacking and intrusion from foreign entities.
- Continually promoting a Putin-endorsed Russian narrative that Ukraine, not Russia, interfered in the U.S. elections.
- Having his personal attorney, Rudy Giuliani, inappropriately intercede in official U.S. policy, including promoting a debunked conspiracy theory put forth by the Russians that the government of Ukraine was extorted by Trump's political rival for personal advantage in the upcoming election.
- Publicly requesting—and in private talks insisting—that the governments of Ukraine and China announce investigations against his political rivals in order to create a false narrative in service of his own personal and political gain.
- Continually criticizing, thus alienating, longstanding foreign allies of the United States.
- Creating and instigating situations in the Middle East (and elsewhere) that are opening doors to give Putin's Russia a stronger global foothold.
- Making outrageous claims about the North Atlantic Treaty Organization (NATO) and insisting our nation is being taken advantage of by our allies, which stokes fear and anger within and outside of the United States.
- Interfering with and obstructing congressional investigations into his actions, including refusing to turn over to Congress subpoenaed documents.
- Ignoring advice and warning signs regarding the novel coronavirus, thus leaving the United States ill-prepared to stem the spread of the virus.
- Implying COVID-19 was a "hoax" and the crisis fomented by Democrats.

- Abdicating his responsibilities as commander-in-chief by his failure to effectively lead a national pandemic response.
- Failing to provide adequate federal support to the states as well as to medical professionals to fight the novel coronavirus.

Trump's continual defiance of the rule of law and flagrant violation of our Constitution are decidedly not democratic. Rather, his actions mirror those of Russian leader and oligarch Vladimir Putin; a man Trump repeatedly expresses his admiration for. Keep in mind that Putin is a former agent of the KGB and has been presiding over Russia since at least 1999, keeping himself in office as president or prime minister for over two decades straight.

Many people dismiss Donald Trump's actions as nothing more than the moves of a novice political hack floundering through the complicated maze of being chief executive officer of the United States. We have a different perspective. We believe Trump is not a "checkers player" attempting a relatively simple game in the spotlight he seems to love so much. Instead, we see Trump as playing chess on a complex world board, and he's five steps ahead of where most people think he is. There is much more going on here than easily meets the eye, and it does a serious disservice to our country to simply characterize Trump as a "moron," as former Secretary of State Rex Tillerson reportedly did—only to be fired by Trump shortly thereafter.[9] In an interview with Bob Schieffer on December 7, 2018, Tillerson described his time working under Trump.[10] While Tillerson did not use the word "moron"

---

9   In 2017, as Secretary of State, Tillerson reportedly used this word to describe Trump during a Pentagon briefing, but at the time neither confirmed nor denied saying it. Within days Trump had ousted Tillerson from his cabinet post.
10   Rex Tillerson, "Rex Tillerson Reflects on Firing, Working for 'Undisciplined' Trump," interview with Bob Schieffer, *CBS This Morning,* December

in the interview, his opinion was clear: "It was challenging for me coming from the disciplined, highly process-oriented Exxon Mobil corporation, to go to work for a man who is pretty undisciplined, doesn't like to read, doesn't read briefing reports, doesn't like to get into the details of a lot of things, but rather just kind of says, 'This is what I believe'." We think Tillerson's assessment missed the mark.

The danger Trump presents goes beyond being undisciplined, failing to read briefing reports and dismissing details, and is not from a lack of common sense or intelligence on his part. We believe the real danger is that he lacks both integrity and morality. We are convinced that Trump has a definite plan and strategy: a self-serving, get-richer plan that is decidedly not grounded in the best interests of our nation. And he is using a relatively small and ill-informed portion of the electorate as a strategy to propagate his plan. The evidence of this is mounting as the list of Trump's suspect actions grows.

While we might be able to accept any one or two of these things as the acts of an ignorant bumbler, taken together this list is an indication of a deliberate dismantling of our safeguards both domestically and around the world. There is no obvious or even reasonable explanation that this is in our national interest, so why is Trump doing these things, and doing all of them?

Everything Trump is doing seems to benefit Russia, and, more to the point, Putin's vision for Russia. Trump is no moron. There must be something in this for Donald Trump. There is a reason that Trump wants to undermine NATO. There is a reason he allowed the Russian government to get a foothold in the Middle East. There is a reason he is erasing our institutional knowledge and berating our federal law enforcement and intelligence agencies responsible for safeguarding our nation. There is a reason why he

---

7, 2018, https://www.cbsnews.com/news/rex-tillerson-bob-schieffer-interview-houston-firing-trump-tweet-tillerson-insult-2018-12-07/.

is ignoring scientists and denying the inherent dangers of global warming. We think the reason just might be to create a new world order by controlling fossil fuel and global energy usage. Might Trump's vision be focused on dollar signs for his own benefit and not U.S. control for strategic purposes? This restructuring would take a perfectly executed game plan, and Putin is the master strategist who is perfectly positioned to execute it. Could Trump be a pawn on that chessboard, or a Russian asset? We may never know for certain, but just the prospect that we could even begin to see this as a possibility is frightening. We do know that attempts by anyone, including the U.S. Congress, to get to the facts about Trump's actions and financial records, are blocked at every turn.

As Americans we must start taking the threat of Donald Trump seriously. In the event that people have forgotten, the government of the United States does not belong to President Trump, nor is he above the law. Contrary to what Attorney General William Barr has suggested on several occasions, the president does not have unfettered power to do anything he wants.

False Prophets and Fear-Mongers

America has long stood as a beacon of decency in the world, yet we see a growing number of Americans disgusted by the state of our politics and fed up with our politicians pandering to corporate interests and wealthy donors. We know this from talking to our neighbors, friends and colleagues. We know from our regular engagement with a wide range of news sources. We know from numerous studies and polls with accurate, honest, verifiable research. We believe many of you find yourselves feeling the same way that we do: with an excess of information about what's wrong and no reliable map to get to what's right. We believe that America's current problems stem in large part from a lack of moral leadership, driven by corruption and greed that are the hallmarks of this egotistical, maniacal, narcissistic, fly-by-the-seat-of-his-(probably overpriced)-pants president.

We readily acknowledge that our political system is not perfect; it never was and never will be. There have been many times in our country's history when the divisiveness of our politics has been set aside so we could work for a common good, but sometimes we have needed a wake-up call. However, we firmly believe that the United States has the best system of government in the world. We also believe that while this system is not yet irreparably broken, the current state of politics has placed our democratic form of government in serious jeopardy. Because ours is a system of government "of the people, by the people, and for the people," President Abraham Lincoln 1863, the American people also are in jeopardy.[11] We are not surprised that Lincoln's words were a response to our nation's most violent division to date: The Civil War.

We know from history that divisions among the people of the United States, regardless of political and ideological philosophies, can be put aside when the dangers to our democracy and freedom are threatened by outside forces. The sinking of the Lusitania in 1915 rallied Americans to unite and support aiding European allies in World War I, even with the fractious party politics of the time. The bombing of Pearl Harbor on December 7, 1941 (the day of infamy), united the American people and political parties to stop the forces of aggression and end the travesties and atrocities being committed by the Axis forces of Nazi Germany, the militaristic Japan of Emperor Hirohito, and fascist Italy under Mussolini. The horrors of the September 11, 2001, terrorist attacks

---

11 Abraham Lincoln, "The Gettysburg Address", November 19, 1863, Abraham Lincoln Online, accessed May 1, 2020, http://www.abrahamlincolnonline.org/lincoln/speeches/gettysburg.htm.

in the United States shocked and then unified our seriously divided nation to rally as one people in compassion and strength to address the threat of global terrorism.

The greatest threat to our republic now is coming from within, from the deception and immorality of a corrupt domestic system driven by political and religious leaders who are more concerned about their own self-preservation and power than in doing what is right for the nation. These self-interested leaders are willing to make proverbial deals with the devil and look away, while U.S. election systems are hacked by malicious foreign interests and false, manufactured information is spread with abandon. They are seducing good Christians and other people of faith with a false narrative, claiming piety in one area while hiding their corruption and self-interest in another. The Scriptures are filled with warnings about false prophets. Do not be deceived.

Noam Chomsky, the American linguist, philosopher, historian, political activist and great mind of our time, said, "The smart way to keep people passive and obedient is to strictly limit the spectrum of acceptable opinion, but allow very lively debate within that spectrum of acceptable opinion and encourage the more critical and dissident views. That gives people the sense that there's free thinking going on, while all the time the presupposition of the system is being reinforced by the limits put on the range of the debate."[12] For the purposes of immoral leadership, this means that if you can't control the way someone votes you have to control the way they think, using fear tactics to convince people their options for action are limited. Then, these people will be more likely to vote however you want them to (including not voting at all). With enough money and a lack of morals, any one of us can have the

---

12   Noam Chomsky, *How the World Works* (Soft Skull Press, 2011).

power to convince a lot of people to believe just about anything we want, true or not.

It seems to us that not a day goes by where we are not subjected to fear tactics and demagoguery by some elected or appointed politician or religious leader. The ultra-wealthy spend vast amounts of money to disseminate misinformation through all forms of media. The day-to-day effect is that it becomes impossible to separate reliable information from out-and-out lies. This was evident in the 2016 presidential election, and has only snowballed into an avalanche since then. In this atmosphere we no longer look for heroes among our political or religious leaders. Because of the influence of money, many of those to whom we have granted the power to govern us, politically and spiritually, appear more interested in preserving their positions of wealth and power than safeguarding our rights and our Constitution from enemies both foreign and domestic.

We cannot give these leaders carte blanche and assume they will do what is in the best interest of the citizens and the nation. We must challenge these leaders and hold them accountable. It is our belief that the only means we have to secure our system from falling apart is to invoke our constitutional rights and act accordingly. The key word here is "act." We cannot just stand "idly by," as some of our greatest leaders, including Theodore Roosevelt, John F. Kennedy, and Martin Luther King, Jr., have warned.

In just a few months we face a decision about who will lead us in these uncertain times, but in pulling together to fight COVID-19, our nation's attention has been diverted away from the November 2020 election. Our natural inclination in times of war and crisis is to fully support our leader; but COVID-19 is not a conventional foe, and critically questioning the decisions of this president does not aid the enemy. Furthermore, being led by a person that many people suspect to be a narcissistic president is seriously exacerbating the problem. Trump is not leading our nation in fighting this epidemic. He is posturing. He is making contradictory and potentially harmful claims. He has made a very bad situation considerably worse, further jeopardizing Americans' health and financial stability. President Trump can't seem to help himself. To avoid this crisis becoming our "new normal", we need to oust these leaders who seem to be competing to dethrone Vice President Mike Pence as "sycophant of the year." We need our leadership to insist on truth and expose false narratives.

Who Really Pays the Price?

Although the U.S. electorate has been disrespected, mistreated and lied to by political parties for almost forty years, the Trump administration has taken disingenuous promises to a whole new level of absurdity and hypocrisy. Many promises have been made to the middle-class. But look carefully at who has actually reaped the benefits of the policies arising from those promises, and who is paying the price. The administration's claims of having created a healthy economy do not reflect the reality that millions of Americans are forced to live paycheck to paycheck, without being able to save, much less invest or have a financial security net. Many people need to work two or even three jobs just to provide for their families. Accounting for inflation, real wages have not risen in the past four decades. The 2017 tax cuts went largely to the richest taxpayers and dramatically expedited a forty-year trend of increasingly consolidating wealth and attendant power to the top of the wealth pyramid, as well as increasing the national debt to over $24 trillion. It should be noted that most of the interest on this debt will be paid for by middle-class taxpayers and our children, a burden that will be exponentially greater than the average, one-time $300 tax refund they were told they received. Workers and the middle class are paying dearly.

Now the effects of the novel coronavirus have wreaked havoc on our economy. There are an estimated 33 million Americans already jobless, the stock market has fallen to 23,724 from a high of 29,556 on February 12, 2020, a 20 percent drop, and 65,000 Americans have died, a number that may be over 200,000 before year's end. Most of this devastation could have been avoided had Trump listened to the experts and fought the virus head-on at the outset of the epidemic. Even in the middle of fighting the pandemic, Republicans ensured that the CARES Act relief package included tax breaks for those making $1 million or more a year. Tens of thousands of Americans probably died unnecessarily and our economy is in dire straits due to the president's lack of preparedness and undisciplined response to the pandemic.

American farmers also have borne the weight of this administration's false promises and questionable actions. Dairy is dumped and food is rotting in the fields as the shutdown has many people trying to feed their families. One might think the administration might formulate a plan to pay the farmers and mobilize an effort to distribute that food to those that are desperate to have it. No strategic thinking: just let the farms go into bankruptcy and the corporate interests can take them over. Yet many rural white Americans, including farmers, continue to support Trump. It is not only the administration's trade policies that are wreaking havoc for farmers and other Americans. Recently, the administration did everything in its power to suppress a government study showing the potentially apocalyptic effects of the global warming crisis and predicting devastating storms and flooding, fires, and crop failures. If allowed to continue, these conditions will culminate in global water and food shortages. Most of our politicians, at least the ones who understand science, are aware of this potential global catastrophe. So why aren't they doing more to make sure it does not happen? We think we have some idea.

In the United States, the people and groups pulling the strings for the conservative right have embraced two operating theories: "trickle-down faith" and "trickle-down economics." Both of these have surface plausibility and targeted appeal. Each proclaims that money, power, and decision-making are best left in the hands of an elite few, with the assumption that they'll always have the greater good in mind and therefore any benefits will "trickle down" to the rest of us. Trickle-down economics is a fairly well-known concept: tax breaks to the richest individuals and corporations with the assumption that they will put that money back into the economy, stimulating growth so that wealth will then "trickle down" to the middle and lower classes. So far, after decades of trying, it hasn't worked as promised, and the benefits just seem to flow right back up to the rich.

"Trickle-down faith" is a concept whereby God selects an elite few to rule over the rest of us. This promotes an elitist, totalitarian view, in which religious leaders dictate individuals' political alignment. Many Christian evangelicals espouse that to be a true Christian, a person must support a conservative political agenda, and to support progressive or liberal causes is evil and akin to dancing with the devil. By that flawed logic, if you are religious you must blindly support Trump, regardless of his words or actions and the impact of those on your neighbors. Yet, Jesus was considered a radical by most of his contemporaries because of his non-conformist views on power and wealth. Jesus did not promote a "trickle-down" faith in which wealth and power were the best indicators of a person's relationship to God and ability to lead others, and that material self-interest was a measure of high achievement.

One of our goals is to peel away the superficial and the "BS" to reveal the malevolence behind trickle-down economics and trickle-down faith. It is inaccurate to say that these just don't work. Instead, it is more accurate to say that they don't work as advertised: they do not in fact benefit all levels of society. They do, however, work as intended: to empower a set of hypocritical and ultra-rich elites who deem themselves the most pious and far superior decision-makers, and therefore more worthy of money and power than the rest of us. Interesting circular logic, give more to the elites because they have made sure that they already have the most. Even the phrase "trickle down" suggests that the wealthy are somehow above the rest of America in all respects, not just in how much money they have.

Saving Democracy

The two of us are not politicians or political pundits or academic theorists, but we know the current environment of polarization with its "us or them" mentality is toxic for civility and democracy. We are socially liberal and fiscally moderate. We don't feel that "liberal" is a dirty word; nor should "conservative" be, or at least not as it was before being co-opted by the politics of wealth and fear-mongering. Liberal does not mean a person is a socialist. It doesn't make someone a pornographer, child molester, rapist or moral degenerate. "Liberal" does not set someone apart from God or religion or faith. We don't believe that "moderate" means a person doesn't care or can't decide. We don't believe that our government should be in the business of legislating or favoring any particular form or practice of religion. We don't believe that God is so inept or out of touch as to need the intervention of self-proclaimed pious religious leaders forcing particular religious beliefs on others.

We do believe that by the Constitution of the United States and with our founding fathers' framework for representative democracy, as citizens of this nation we have the right—in fact, each of us has the obligation—to demand leadership from our politicians based on some measure of competence and a moral compass reflective of core American values. We believe these values reflect faith and what most firmly sustains us as individuals and as a nation:

> Faith in God, community and family—all of these in the many forms that make up our great diverse nation, and knowing that practicing any one religion, or even belief in God at all, is not a prerequisite for holding and practicing these values.
> Faith in the law and the Constitution—with knowledge of how we as a nation should adhere to these, and when they are being ignored.

We are not men with all-access passes through the halls of power, but our careers have provided us some opportunities to peek through the windows and, at times, to even stand inside the doorway. We've worked with Congressional leaders and heads of federal departments, corporate executives, and national nonprofits and advocacy groups. While some of these leaders have acted with honor and integrity, more often than not we have witnessed most trying to game the system in an effort to hold on to power and further their financial interests at the expense of things as important as public safety. Like many of you, we have been disgusted and distrustful of our government institutions, and at the same time want to trust and have faith in them. We are sick of being lied to and manipulated and patronized by self-serving leaders and elitist political institutions, but we keep on hoping and voting, and every now and then we are rewarded with a leader we can admire. Sadly, in the critical political climate we face, we are losing faith with the vast majority of our nation's leaders and it seems harder to find those who deserve admiration.

Our major political parties are indebted to big campaign donors. Once you see the actual amounts of money being funneled to our politicians by special interests, it's much easier to understand why these politicians loyally reward the ultra-rich with legislation favorable to their interests, often at the expense and without regard to the rest of us. The Center for Responsive Politics (CRP) is a non-partisan nonprofit organization, and its Open Secrets initiative provides to the public, free of charge, the federally required information reported on political donations to candidates and the origins of campaign contributions. This includes sizable donations from pharmaceutical companies, insurance companies, oil companies, trade and professional associations, individuals, and more. Even just a quick perusal of the OpenSecrets.org website reveals the level to which many politicians seem to be for sale to the highest donors. CRP tracks the effects of money and lobbying on elections and public policy with a mission of creating more educated voters, a more involved citizenry, and a more responsive government, regardless of what party is in power. It was founded in bipartisanship by former Senator Frank Church, a Democrat from Idaho who served from 1957 to 1981, and Republican Senator Hugh Scott of Pennsylvania who served from 1958 to 1977, and as Senate minority leader 1969 to 1977. Can you even imagine this kind of bipartisanship today?

The ability to buy politicians' votes was greatly increased as a result of a landmark Supreme Court decision issued on January 21, 2010, that largely ended restrictions on corporate spending on elections. This rollback of campaign finance restrictions was largely a Republican maneuver; the GOP saw the potential gains as more valuable than transparency or integrity in elections. The decision opened the door for practically unlimited campaign contributions from corporations by essentially treating a corporation like an individual for the purpose of campaign contributions. Thank you, Justice Clarence Thomas and the rest of the Citizens United "fan club" for deciding to define corporations as having the same rights as an individual and vastly increasing corporations' already gargantuan ability to influence policy toward their own interests. It is worth noting that Citizens United president David Bossie, friend of Trump minions Steve Bannon and Kellyanne Conway, was hired by Trump as a deputy campaign manager for the 2016 election, and is said to have introduced Bannon to Trump.

Taking all of these leaders out of the shadows and into the sunlight is a first step; if they are not allowed to operate in secrecy, we can more readily identify the real threats that they pose. It is difficult to map out the deliberately complex and confusing maze of deception to uncover who or what is really imperiling our political system, and to what end. If we can see more clearly what's eating through our democracy, value by value, maybe we can stop the rot at the source.

CHAPTER 2

HIDDEN ENEMY

> The greatest compassion is the prevention of human suffering through patience, alertness, courage and kindness.
>
> —Amit Ray, author, mediation master, and spiritual leader, 2015

> COVID-19 represents the single greatest inflection point that global society has experienced. How we manage through this pandemic and its aftermath will impact the course of humanity for decades to come."
>
> —Tom Golway, technologist, author, and entrepreneur, 2020

THE FIRST REPORTED CASE OF THE novel coronavirus (COVID-19) in the United States was in mid-January, 2020, in Washington State. The virus spread rapidly. In total disregard of the warnings and predictions by national security, medical and public health authorities around the globe, President Trump expressed denial about consequences and was dismissive of the dangers of this disease. By the first of May, the number of COVID-19 cases in the U.S. stood at over 1,092,000, with over 65,000 attendant deaths, excluding ancillary deaths.[13] The administration still has not put together a national policy or plan for testing.

This is arguably the most serious health crisis faced by

---

13   The recorded deaths due to COVID-19 somewhat underestimate the actual number of fatalities caused by the novel coronavirus. Many have died and been buried or cremated without ever being tested for COVID-19 particularly many of those who died in nursing homes or long-term care facilities.

the world since the black plague that killed half the population of Europe and the Spanish flu epidemic of 1918. Trump's focus through all of this? It seems to be on finding scapegoats. His administration's actions are seen by some as politically motivated, therefore petty and spiteful in this situation. If nothing else, they are just plain reckless. A major goal of this president seems to be to dismantle everything accomplished under former President Obama in order to feed his own voracious ego, regardless of the cost to the American people. How many people will die unnecessarily because of lack of preparedness and bad national leadership? Of one thing we remain certain: this "commander-in-chief" will blame everyone else for his administration's lack of preparedness for this predicted catastrophe.

Tom Golway, chief technologist at Hewlett Packard Enterprises and an expert on emerging technologies, described this crisis in a tweet as, "the single greatest inflection point that global society has experienced" (@readyforthenet, April 5, 2020). It is a critical time in which we as a nation and a world are facing deterioration if we fail to effectively manage and respond to this "new normal." Golway added that it is not enough to just manage effectively; we also have to consider how we are doing that. We take that to mean that morality matters now if we want to have a civil society in the future. As Americans we have trusted our leaders, no matter what their political leanings, are motivated to protect and preserve our republic and won't let it deteriorate by neglect or, worse, actively undermine it. Over the past three years we have been questioning if our trust had been misplaced. With this crisis we have our answer: Yes, it certainly has.

In times of war there will be instances of "friendly fire" in which soldiers are killed by their own troops when the intended target is the enemy. The reasons it happens include misidentification of the target, errors of judgement, or faulty materials, and its occurrence can often be traced back to mistakes or incompetence of those ultimately in charge, and conditions of arrogance of the leadership and refusal of those leaders to be accountable. The fight to control the COVID-19 pandemic is war against a hidden enemy. We are all targets, although this enemy more easily finds the poor, the sick, and the elderly, and the virus can be present in a person long before any symptoms appear.

On the front lines are doctors, nurses, first responders, hospital administrators, hospital staffs, scientists, police, firefighters and countless others risking their own lives every day of the war in efforts to save and protect the public. They go into the battle zone daily without necessary supplies and protections. They go not knowing if they will be a casualty themselves, or if by doing their duties they will cause their families to suffer. They are brave and are models of compassion who are working to prevent human suffering, "through patience, alertness, courage, and kindness," in the words of author and spiritual master Amit Ray.[14] Of course we try to avoid friendly fire, but the conditions of this war and absence of moral leadership from our chief executive makes that challenging. That is unconscionable to us.

Beware the Live Dragon

It does not do to leave a live dragon out of your calculations, if you live near one.

—J.R.R. Tolkien, writer and poet

On March 6, 2020, Donald Trump claimed the COVID-19 pandemic had been impossible to predict: "We're doing very well," Trump said at a White House press briefing, "But it's an unforeseen problem. What a problem. Came out of nowhere. But we're taking

---

14   Amit Ray, *Walking the Path of Compassion* (Inner Light Publishers, 2015).

care of it."[15] The record of evidence that belies every one of those claims is truly overwhelming, most of all that he could not have known it was coming and therefore could not have planned for it.

There had been predictions from global health and security organizations for years warning nations to prepare for an inevitable health pandemic, even more so in 2018-2019. The United States had held a strategic reserve of critical supplies in anticipation of such a crisis. There were warnings in 2019 specifically about the dangers of a coronavirus-like contagion. In 2016 the Obama administration had literally handed a global health crisis playbook to the incoming Trump administration. And it is just common sense: "It does not do to leave a live dragon out of your calculations, if you live near one."[16] The Trump administration completely left the live dragon out of their calculations for what 2020 would look like in America. It was as though Trump and his administration had no understanding of some of the most basic concepts of planning, business and management—and a common-sense meter below the empty level.

As we were writing this we could not yet know the outcomes and the totality of the fallout from this major health crisis, but already we could see that this pandemic pointed to leadership failures on at least two levels. First, general preparedness of our nation under Trump to face a health crisis of these proportions, or for that matter any national crisis. Second, and direr to most Americans in the spring of 2020, management of the COVID-19 pandemic, which we don't know whether to describe as a head-

---

15 "Remarks by President Trump at Signing of the Coronavirus Preparedness and Response Supplemental Appropriations Act, 2020", The White House, issued March 6, 2020, accessed May 5, 2020, https://www.whitehouse.gov/briefings-statements/remarks-president-trump-signing-coronavirus-preparedness-response-supplemental-appropriations-act-2020/
16 J.R.R. Tolkien, *The Hobbit* (Houghton Mifflin Harcourt, 2012 [George Allen & Unwin Ltd., 1937]).

in-the-sand approach or a chicken-with-head-cut-off style. No matter how you frame it, Trump's leadership in this crisis has been abysmal. He neglected to account for the "live dragon" that he had been warned was nearby and eying the United States.

An article in *The Atlantic* in March 2020 described Trump's leadership style in relation to the COVID-19 crisis:

> For his entire adult life, and for his entire presidency, Donald Trump has created his own alternate reality, complete with his own alternate set of facts. From our perspective, he has shown himself to be erratic, impulsive, narcissistic, vindictive, cruel, mendacious and devoid of empathy. None of that is news. The pain and the hardship the United States is only beginning to experience stem from a crisis that the president is utterly unsuited to deal with, either intellectually or temperamentally.[17]

This is not from a liberal journalist or a Democratic operative. These are the words of Peter Wehner, a veteran of the Republican administrations of Presidents Reagan, George H.W. Bush, and George W. Bush, and a fellow at the Ethics and Public Policy Center, a conservative-leaning think tank with the stated mission: "dedicated to applying the Judeo-Christian moral tradition to critical issues of public policy." We wholeheartedly agree with Mr. Wehner, we just wish he wouldn't sugar-coat his view of Trump!

As COVID-19 first entered the United States and started spreading rapidly and exponentially, our commander-in-chief made misleading statements with unconfirmed information that

---

17 Peter Wehner, "The President is Trapped", *The Atlantic,* March 25, 2020, https://atlantic.com.ideas/archival/2020/03/president-character-unequal-task/608743.

created confusion about safety practices, health standards, potential cures, U.S. national preparedness, and the severity of the virus. To pass COVID-19 off as a partisan issue, as Trump and his minions tried to do, seems obtuse and stupid at best; claiming that the coronavirus was being hyped by "crazed Democrats" would be humorous if not for the fact that Donald Trump actually has some of his followers believing it.

Throughout early 2020, President Trump attempted to keep America's expectations low by reframing the narrative of COVID-19, at one point indicating that a death toll of around 100,000 would be considered a victory. It seemed self-serving, if not crass. Were the number of dead to remain at or below that, he could then no doubt take a victory lap to proclaim himself a great wartime president and that if it were not for him, the death toll would have been much worse. The reality (i.e. outside Donald's alternate universe) is that with a competent leader the outcome would far likely have been better—and a competent president would not view 100,000 deaths as a victory.

By mid-April, with the number of cases growing, schools shut down, our economy tanking, the administration had neither released a national policy or plan for testing, nor provided necessary assistance to governors to facilitate testing in states and territories—and only about 1 percent of the population (3.3 million people) had been tested. COVID-19 was affecting 210 countries and territories around the world. The statistics were grim. Consequences were already daunting; hospitals were overwhelmed and people suffering from life-threatening conditions unrelated to COVID-19 not able to get health care. Major damage had been done to our economy. Many of the fight's foot soldiers lacked necessary life-saving supplies and protective equipment and had to make difficult choices about both personal and patient care.

How much would have been prevented with better planning and accountable, moral leadership?

Strategic and Tactical Planning

Trump touts himself as an exceptional businessman but he does not seem at all familiar with the concepts of strategic and tactical planning. Maybe that is why he has had to declare corporate bankruptcy six times. The burden of these bankruptcies fell on investors and others who had bet on Trump's business acumen. With the coronavirus pandemic, the American public is paying for Trump's failure in the basics of business and leadership with their livelihoods—and many have paid with their lives. There are a lot of people who concur with the Boston Globe's March 31 editorial in which the paper's editorial board condemned Donald Trump as "unfit for a pandemic" and said he has "blood on his hands."[18]

Strategy is the thinking process required to plan a change or to organize something. It defines the goals desired and how to achieve them. It can be a compendium of complex multi-layered plans devised for achieving preset objectives and may include tactical planning considerations. A strategic plan sets the overall goal and provides for the general idea on how to reach that goal. Its key components are: Where do you currently stand? Where do you want to be in the future? What would you like to achieve? And, who's responsible for each of those objectives? The Obama administration had a strategy for dealing with a potential pandemic.

Tactics are the actions necessary to carry out the strategy. The things to consider in a tactical plan are: What is the timeline

---

18   Brad Reed, "'Blood on His Hands': Brutal Boston Globe Editorial Declares Trump 'Unfit for a Pandemic'", *Raw Story*, March 31, 2020, https://rawstory.com/2020/03/blood-on-his-hands-brutal-boston-globe-editorial-declares-trump-unfit-for-a-pandemic.

for achieving these goals? Are there tools or resources necessary to accomplish these goals? And what specific actions need to be taken? It is clear Trump did not have the framework in place for a tactical plan to deal with COVID-19. Without clearly defined steps and responsibilities it can be difficult or even discouraging to tackle any problem particularly a massive problem like a pandemic. All of this is taught in the first year of business school, or can quickly be learned in running a business, and in business it is simple stuff and common sense. Perhaps Trump skipped class and was playing golf on the days they were teaching this at the Wharton School of Business.

Trump and his administration's lack of planning resulted in costly delays in preparing for and responding to the crisis— the shortage of testing kits, the woeful shortage of hospital beds and medical staff, the paucity of ventilators and other equipment and supplies including the inadequate number of PPEs for healthcare providers. The Trump administration even cancelled the maintenance contract for ventilators that were stored as part of the national strategic supply so many that were shipped to the states were useless. Should that be blamed on Obama as well, or did Hillary hide the maintenance contract in her server before it could be reinstated? Has anyone tried to blame Ukraine yet?

It wasn't until the very end of March that he finally heeded the warnings of Dr. Anthony Fauci and Dr. Deborah Birx, who are viewed as the two foremost pandemic experts in the country, and extended the "shelter at home" White House guidelines until March 30, 2020. President Trump prefers to listen to his gut, as Bergen noted, and his decisions are often knee-jerk reactions to whatever his gut says that day.

Even Fauci and Birx, Trump's own appointees, are not immune. Birx, the White House coronavirus response coordinator, made laudatory comments about Trump's handling of the crisis when she was introduced as part of the coronavirus task force on March 2, 2020. Birx has an impeccable record of accomplishments and a stellar reputation as one of the top infectious disease physicians in the world. We wish to give her the benefit of doubt that her public praise of Trump and stoking of his delicate ego was just her means of ensuring she would continue to have an opportunity to influence Trump's decision-making about this crisis. Fauci has also been somewhat circumspect. Fauci testified before Congress in mid-March that U.S. testing efforts were failing. He received heavy criticism from the president. On April 13th he walked back comments he made a day earlier that more lives could have been saved if the U.S. had acted faster. Fauci also may have thought he could do more good by playing Trump's game rather than risk being pushed out of the tent—Trump had retweeted twice on April 12, 2020 "Fire Fauci!" It is a dangerous game that Fauci and Birx are playing. If Trump prematurely declares the emergency over will Fauci and Birx raise their voices to protest? If so, will the public take the doctors' advice over Trump's? Both Fauci and Birx seem to show they have the courage of their convictions. Only time will tell if they will continue to show strength and to confront the president if necessary.

Trump has been accused of playing politics with the scarce resources necessary for states and communities to fight this deadly illness. On several occasions, Trump made statements that indicated he preferred only to deal with governors who treat him right, meaning willing to pay homage to him. These statements were undoubtedly intended to serve as a deterrent to anyone contemplating criticizing Trump, deserved or not. Resources from the federal stockpile of medical supplies seemed to be distributed based on a governor's deference to Trump rather than on the relative needs of each state. Most of our state governors responded admirably to the crisis. But there remains a need for a nationwide coordinated strategic plan, and to say that Trump has proven inept, or possibly just uncaring, is an understatement.

Having A Crisis? Find Someone to Blame

On March 13, 2020, President Trump declared a national emergency, making it his immediate responsibility to run the national disaster response to the looming crisis. On March 20, his message was: "It hit the world, and we're prepared and we're doing a great job with it, and it will go away, stay calm, it will go away." The president seemed unable or unwilling to pick a position: either he could not possibly have prepared the nation he leads for a crisis of this magnitude, or America was well-prepared to fight the pandemic and if everyone remained calm it would just go away. Neither position made sense.

By December 31, 2019, when the information was finally revealed to the public to confirm that this highly contagious virus was spreading and causing deaths in China at alarming rates, there had already been plenty of time for this microscopic invader to make its way around the world via unknowing travelers. It is unconscionable that the Chinese government kept the novel coronavirus outbreak in that country hidden from the rest of the world for over a month, costing other countries crucial time to prepare. However, intelligence reports and information from the World Health Organization (WHO) had been given to the White House earlier in December and as early as November. ABC News online reported on April 8, 2020:

> Concerns about what is now known to be the novel coronavirus pandemic were detailed in a November intelligence report by the military's National Center for Medical Intelligence (NCMI) according to two officials

familiar with the contents. …Analysts concluded it could be a cataclysmic event.[19]

NCMI is a component of the Pentagon's Defense Intelligence Agency. In December 2019 there were repeated briefings for policymakers and decision makers across the federal government and including the National Security Council (NSC) at the White House, according to the ABC News, and a detailed explanation of this looming problem appeared in the President's Daily Brief of Intelligence Matters (PDB) in early January.[20] More recent information suggests warnings were presented in the PDB even before that. "Intelligence officials' early alarms about possible pandemic went unheeded," was a headline on the front page of the *Washington Post* print edition on March 21, 2020:

> U.S. intelligence agencies were issuing ominous, classified warnings in January and February about the global danger posed by the coronavirus while President Trump and lawmakers played down the threat and failed to take action that might have slowed the spread of the pathogen, according to U.S. officials familiar with spy agency reporting.[21]

The *Post* article quoted a U.S. official speaking on condition of anonymity who had access to the intelligence reporting provided to members of Congress and their staffs and to officials in the Trump administration, describing the situation: "Donald Trump may not have been expecting this, but a lot of other people in the

---

19 Margolin and Meek, "Report Warned of Coronavirus."
20 Margolin and Meek, "Report Warned of Coronavirus."
21 Shane Harris, Greg Miller, Josh Dawson, and Ellen Nakashima, "Intelligence Officials' Early Alarms about Possible Pandemic Went Unheeded," *Washington Post*, March 21, 2020, A1.

government were—they just couldn't get him to do anything about it. ... The system was blinking red."[22]

Trump would have us believe that this was all the fault of the WHO, the international health arm of the United Nations. Trump seemed to be trying to convince America that because of what he deemed his timely decision to close our borders to travel to and from China he stopped the spread of the virus twenty-fold. "After his alleged moratorium more than 40,000 people were reportedly allowed to enter the United States from China without any testing being performed. Regardless, the novel coronavirus was already in the U.S. and was beginning to spread rapidly before imposition of the president's travel restriction."

If WHO misread the situation and failed to provide vital information that would have better contained the virus, the fact is that China clearly fed false and misleading information to WHO. To the best of public knowledge, WHO did not receive an intelligence agency report, nor do they have the capability of obtaining covert information on what is happening inside different countries. The White House did. In addition, WHO had a dozen employees of the Centers for Disease Control and Prevention (CDC) working with them in their Geneva headquarters. Without question this team would have warned CDC headquarters in Atlanta of the pandemic threat, and CDC would have then briefed the White House; CDC's role is to protect America from health, safety and security threats both foreign and internal and it is a major part of the U.S. Department of Health and Human Services (HHS). But still the president chose to ignore the information until it was too late for a crisis to be averted. Had he taken the time to listen to the experts, perhaps pressure could have been put on the Chinese government early on to help convince them to cooperate. It could not be clearer

---

22   Harris et al., "Intelligence Officials' Early Alarms."

that this president was informed of the danger and chose to dismiss the warnings.

Had it not been for the actions of many governors, mayors, local leaders, and experts in medicine and science who were willing to speak out and act to protect and save lives and communities, the losses would be even worse. That is true courage and a stark contrast to those who express willingness to sacrifice the old and vulnerable among us if it might save the economy. Had there been a proper, timely response when we were first attacked, the severity of our current situation would have been significantly lessened, the war shortened and the damage minimized.

The Trump administration had no legitimate reason why it failed to take precautionary measures ahead of time or at any time during the first three years of his presidency, such as restoring medical supplies in the Strategic National Stockpile. Instead, the Trump administration only recognized the shortages and their lack of planning after COVID-19 struck. Then they blamed Obama. Dear Mr. Trump, please understand that some of the people (your loyalists) you can fool all of the time, but some of us you can't fool at all. The Trump administration was warned from other quarters that the United States needed to be prepared for a pandemic. Crisis policy expert Michele Wucker pointed out on March 17 in the *Washington Post* that several warnings had been sounded publicly by epidemiologists and global policy experts in 2019 that the world was ripe for a pandemic and largely unprepared for one. Wucker highlighted just some of these: [23]

---

23   Michelle Wucker, "No, the Coronavirus Pandemic Wasn't an 'Unforeseen Problem': The Coronavirus Pandemic isn't a 'Black Swan.' It's a Gray Rhino", *Washington Post,* March 17, 2020. The article appeared in the *Post* Outlook section. Wucker is a Chicago-based strategist and author of *The Gray Rhino: How to Recognize and Act on the Obvious Dangers We Ignore* (St. Martin's Press, 2016).

- "The 2019 Global Preparedness Monitoring Board warned of the real danger of a fast-moving, lethal pandemic that could kill 50 million to 80 million people worldwide and destroy 5 percent of the global GDP."
- "'The United States and the world will remain vulnerable to the next flu pandemic or large-scale outbreak of a contagious disease that could lead to massive rates of death and disability, severely affect the world economy, strain international resources, and increase calls on the United States for support,' the Department of National Intelligence warned in its 2019 worldwide threat assessment."
- "In the fall [of 2019] the Center for Strategic and International Studies ran an eerily prescient pandemic simulation involving a coronavirus similar to the current one: around a 3 percent mortality rate, transmissible before symptoms showed and highly contagious."

Trump refuses to use facts or data and has resisted the advice of experts to inform his decision-making, and this global health pandemic was no different. Early on the president had pointed out that there were few, if any, cases reported in the United States, nor was the U.S. experiencing fatalities from the virus, so the threat did not warrant taking protective measures or shutting things down. At one point he even said cases were decreasing while they were in fact on the rise. If only the president would actually do his homework and read the material that is researched, written and prepared for him each day.

Why Didn't They Use the Manual?

After COVID-19 hit the shores of the United States, Trump alleged that the Obama administration was at fault for allowing the Strategic National Stockpile and other resources to remain bare.

That might make sense if it were happening in January 2017, but what about the intervening three years of Trump's rule? If you follow Trump's "logic," then it might be Obama's fault also that coronavirus testing protocols and kits were inadequate and didn't work in early 2020, or that the Obama administration bequeathed to Trump a failed and broken COVID-19 combat system. Fake News. For one, the test protocols and kits that didn't work would have had to be developed under Trump's administration, not Obama's: the novel coronavirus did not exist during Obama's tenure. In addition, if the shelves were actually empty when Trump took office, why didn't he have them restocked in 2017? Or 2018? Or 2019?

The funny thing (maybe not so funny) is that the Obama administration did, in fact, provide Trump with a playbook for dealing with a pandemic just like this one.

In 2014 when the Ebola virus broke out in West Africa, President Barack Obama composed a coordinated response to the growing crisis and appointed Ronald Klain, a former vice-presidential staffer to Joe Biden, to oversee the effort inside the White House. The Obama administration clearly defined the roles and budgets of the various agencies involved and placed incident commanders in charge in each Ebola-hit country and in the United States. Based on this experience, Obama set up a permanent monitoring and command group inside the White House NSC and another in the Department of Homeland Security (DHS). Both NSC and DHS followed the scientific and public health leads of the National Institutes of Health (NIH) and CDC, as well as advice from the State Department.

Under Obama, the NSC health unit created a pandemic preparedness manual: The Playbook for Early Response to High-Consequence Emergency Infectious Disease Threats and Biological Incidents. The playbook was completed in 2016, just before

Trump took office. The Trump administration declined to use the playbook, a fact reported in March 2020 by *Politico*[24]—which, by the way, included a copy of the playbook in their report in case the rest of us want to know what could have been done by the Trump administration. Trump literally had step-by-step instructions, or he would have if he'd bothered to do his homework. In the playbook Obama sought to lay the groundwork for a seamless, coherent response to avoid confusion and conflicting messages from federal officials. The playbook anticipated and provided instructions for managing many of the same roadblocks the Trump administration was facing in response to the COVID-19 outbreak, including lack of testing availability and persistent shortages of medical equipment and personal protective equipment (PPE) for healthcare workers.[25] As a further support that would have both helped the American people and the Trump White House, just seven days before Trump took office, Obama administration officials provided a simulation of an epidemic for incoming Trump administration personnel. It seems pretty clear to us that both the playbook and the simulation were ignored. Could it be because they originated in the Obama administration? Or might it have been because there was no musing about the possibility of people injecting disinfectants (Clorox, Lysol) to kill viruses? Perhaps the administration just thought it was incomplete without that information.

In the spring of 2018 the Trump administration fired and effectively dismantled the government's pandemic response chain of command, including the White House management

---

24   Dan Diamond and Nahal Toosi, "Trump Team Failed to Follow NSC's Pandemic Playbook", *Politico,* March 25, 2020, https://www.politico.com/news/2020/03/25/trump-coronavirus-national-security-council-149285.
25   Grace Panetta, "The Trump Administration Declined to Use an Obama-era Pandemic Preparedness Playbook, *Politico Reports", Business Insider,* March 26, 2020, https://www.businessinsider.com/trump-admin-ignored-obama-era-nsc-pandemic-prep-document-politico-2020-3.

infrastructure. The Trump White House also pushed Congress to cut funding for Obama-era disease security programs, including reducing $15 billion in national health spending and cutting the global disease-fighting operational budgets of the CDC, NSC, DHS, and Department of Health and Human Services (HHS). The government's Complex Crisis Fund, which existed to help prevent crises and promote recovery in the face of unforeseen challenges, was eliminated.[26] Trump claimed he didn't know anything about this dismantling of the federal pandemic response team, yet there is video of Trump explaining that decision, according to CNN political commentator and columnist S.E. Cupp.[27]

In May 2018 Trump ordered the NSC's entire global health security unit to be shut down and called for dissolution of the team inside the agency and reassignment of Rear Admiral Timothy Ziemer. In April 2018, John Bolton, then the White House National Security adviser, is said to have pressured Ziemer's DHS counterpart, Tom Bossert, to resign along with his team. Neither the NSC nor DHS epidemic teams were replaced. The disease-fighting cadres of the U.S. Public Health Service Commissioned Corps have steadily been eroded during the Trump administration, as officers who retire are not replaced. America's early warning systems were foolishly and inexplicably reduced.

The White House countered these criticisms saying there were no cuts, merely a reorganization to clarify responsibilities and increase efficiency and that nothing had fundamentally changed. In a *Washington Post* opinion piece on March 18, 2020,

26   Laurie Garrett. "Voice: Trump Has Sabotaged America's Coronavirus Response", *Foreign Policy*, January 31, 2020, https://foreignpolicy.com/2020/01/31/coronavirus-china.
27   S.E. Cupp, "America's Lack of Pandemic Preparedness is Unforgivable", Tribune Content Agency, April 1, 2020, in *Deseret News*, April 5, 2020, https://www.deseret.com/opinion/2020/4/5/21203537/pandemic-preparedness-disaster-government-america-president-trump-coronavirus-task-force-covid-19.

Tim Morrison, the former NSC senior director for counter-proliferation, confirmed the NSC had undergone a reduction-in-force and explained the cuts as "streamlining," while also claiming these cuts had "left the biodefense staff unaffected." Morrison's words, though, were quickly picked up and disseminated by right-wing media outlets. A March 18 blog post on one ultra-conservative website attempted to all at once validate Morrison's story, justify the cuts themselves, and then argue that nothing had changed with regard to the capability of our nation's pandemic response systems:

> The left, of course, does not think logically. Their solution to everything is more government, bigger government, more dedicated (and overstaffed) offices of this and that, and, naturally throwing lots of American taxpayers' money at whatever the perceived problem. More employees and more money are always better, even if the results don't support the premise. ... It's no wonder that Democrats and the media upon learning that overlapping offices and departments have been streamlined into one cannot comprehend that it has made the U.S.'s pandemic response stronger, not weaker. In fact, Morrison notes, since he left the NSC and staff cuts have continued, the biodefense staff has not been affected.[28]

Not true, said others who were directly involved. Former White House Pandemic Office Director Beth Cameron, who led the directorate under Obama, said that after the office had survived the first year of the Trump administration, she was, "mystified when the White House dissolved the office, leaving the country

---

[28] Fuzzy Slippers, "Media Hoaxes: No, Trump Did Not 'Disband' WH Pandemic Office, Cut CDC Work from '49 to 10' Countries, or Refuse WHO 'Testing Kits'", *Legal Insurrection,* March 18, 2020, https://legalinsurrection.com/2020/03/media-hoaxes-no-trump-did-not-disband-wh-pandemic-office-cut-cdc-work-from-49-to-10-countries-or-refuse-who-testing-kits/#more-312218.

unprepared for pandemics like COVID-19. …When this new coronavirus emerged, there was no clear White House-led structure to oversee our response, and we lost valuable time." She noted that even though the White House still has biological experts, "What's especially concerning about the absence of this office today is that it was originally set up because a previous epidemic made the need for it quite clear."[29] It gets worse. In February 2020 the *Los Angeles Times* reported that foreign policy veterans, "warn that the size and speed of [newly appointed NSC director Robert] O'Brien's cuts have left a vital part of the White House ill-equipped to respond to crises like the spreading coronavirus."[30] A March 14 AP News report quoted experts, including Fauci, former pandemic office staff members, and bipartisan members of Congress all wishing the office still existed in 2020 and wondering if the office had remained intact how much better the U.S. response to COVID-19 would have been.[31]

Fast forward to the first few days of May, 2020: over 1.09 million cases and 65,000 deaths; economic deterioration; and still no clear plan. There is an old adage: "You get what you pay for." For this, it wasn't enough.

Trump's Circus Act: Fool Some of the People

You can fool some of the people all the time, and all

---

29   Beth Cameron, "I Ran the White House Pandemic Office. Trump Closed It.", *Washington Post,* March 13, 2020, https://www.washingtonpost.com/outlook/nsc-pandemic-office-trump-closed/2020/03/13/a70de09c-6491-11ea-acca-80c22bbee96f_story.html.
30   Noah Bierman, "White House Quietly Trims Dozens of National Security Experts", *Los Angeles Times,* February 12, 2020, http://latimes.com/politics/story/2020-02-12/white-house-quietly-trims-dozens-of-national-security-experts.
31   Deb Riechmann, "Trump Disbanded NSC Pandemic Unit that Experts Had Praised", AP News, March 14, 2020, https://apnews.com/ce014d94b64e98b7203b873e56f80e9a.

the people some of the time, but you can't fool all of the people all of the time.

—attributed to both Abraham Lincoln, president, statesman and lawyer, and P.T. Barnum, showman, businessman and circus founder

Trump's refusal to take advice from anyone and his inability to develop a strategic plan to deal with the pandemic left his fragile ego exposed to criticism. Consequently, he did what he does best: project his ineffectiveness onto others. Rather than call our president a liar, we'll call it non-stop alternative "facts." Trump has the bully pulpit and he uses it to control the narrative, supported by world-class sycophants with enough credentials to add an air of credibility to his nonsensical claims, as though he's master of ceremonies of a three-ring circus. And it's not like he tries to hide it. Case in point, as reported in the *Los Angeles Times*:

> Six days before President Trump chose Robert O'Brien as his national security advisor in September [2019], the president said the job would be simple. "You know why it's easy?" Trump told reporters. "Because I make all the decisions. They don't have to work." As a key White House advisor, O'Brien clearly works—but he meets Trump's other job requirements: He avoids publicity, he gets out of the way on policy decisions, and he dismisses employees Trump views as meddlesome.[32]

We think he really does believe he can fool all of the people, all of the time—or at least enough of them—for his purpose, whatever that may be. It is telling that the famous adage is attributed to two of the nineteenth century's most remarkable men[33]: Abraham Lincoln, our president who effectively led our nation through the dire constitutional and social crisis of the Civil

---

32   Bierman, "White House Quietly Trims Dozens."
33   "You Cannot Fool All the People All the Time", *Quote Investigator*,

War, and P.T. Barnum, successful businessman and promoter of hoaxes that were meant to entertain us.

Trump in his daily "I'm the greatest!" press briefings habitually stated as fact that the U.S. was testing at a great pace, huge amounts of medical supplies had been shipped to the states, and medical equipment distributed. His words did not reflect the truth. What he did not say was that what was shipped and distributed was still woefully inadequate to meet states' needs, and supplies were painfully slow in being dispersed. Trump's information was not at all informative and, practically speaking, these declarations made governors' planning efforts far more difficult since they could not rely on the validity of the president's promises or truthfulness of his claims. The medical community had been counting on the administration to expedite delivery of critical equipment and supplies because of Trump's statements. His proclamations to the public instead framed a very different narrative from the one reported by most of the governors and the medical community—the people in the thick of it.

We needed a nationwide coordinated effort but without competent, honest leadership from the top, efforts were disjointed. Governors were left to fend on their own for their respective states. Because our president had abdicated his responsibilities, the price of ventilators increased from $25,000 to $50,000 each, as the states entered a bidding war with one another and the federal government for available ventilators. To overcome the lack of federal leadership several states banded together in consortiums to share equipment, supplies and staff on an as-needed basis. The president's narcissistic behavior and false narrative to maintain his base of support for the upcoming election left this war without a real commander-in-chief and the battlefield in complete disarray.

---

last updated December 11, 2013, accessed May 1, 2020, https://quoteinvestigator.com/2013/12/11/cannot-fool/ .

Cure or Snake Oil?

Dr. Anthony Fauci has advised six U.S. presidents on domestic and global health issues and pandemics, including HIV/AIDS. He was a principal architect of the President's Emergency Plan for Aids Relief (PEPFAR), a program that began under President George W. Bush that can claim to have saved millions of lives throughout the developing world. Fauci helped pioneer the field of immune regulation by making important basic scientific observations that underpin the current understanding of the regulation of the human immune response. You would think that with Fauci leading the administration's response, there would be widespread testing. During a congressional hearing on March 12, 2020 Fauci testified that the U.S. was failing in its coronavirus testing efforts: "The idea of anybody getting [COVID-19 testing] easily, the way people in other countries are doing it, we're not set up for that. Do you think we should be? Yes, but we're not." Obviously, the White House had covered up this problem, misleading the American public. As a result, this fundamental need still was unresolved after months of the virus spreading in the United States.[34]

There are no specific therapeutics approved by the Food and Drug Administration (FDA) to treat people with COVID-19. However, in a White House press briefing on March 18, 2020 and on innumerable other occasions President Trump has frequently touted a drug that has been around for a long time and has been very successful in the treatment of malaria saying that it has been approved by the FDA for the treatment of COVID-19. Fauci, NIH

---

34   Don Jacobson, "Health Official: Gov't has Failed to Give Easy Coronavirus Testing in the U.S.", UPI, March 12, 2020, https://www.upi.com/Top_News/US/2020/03/12/Health-official-Govt-has-failed-to-give-easy-coronavirus-testing-in-US/7841584031816/.

National Institute of Allergy and Infectious Diseases (NIAID) director and a White House coronavirus task force member, quickly stepped to the microphone and corrected our president. Fauci spoke truth to power. He explained that the efficacy of that drug has not been shown for COVID-19, it has many side effects (including heart attacks) and it is dangerous to base its potential value on anecdotes. The drug in question is chloroquine or in another formulation it is sold as hydroxychloroquine which is approved for the treatment of rheumatoid arthritis and lupus. Contrary to Trump's statement that it had gone through the approval process, FDA Commissioner Stephen Hahn said chloroquine had been approved for other indications, but it would still need to go through clinical trials. Dr. Hahn explained: "That's a drug the president has asked the FDA to take a closer look at as to whether an expanded use approach to that could be done to see if that benefits patients."[35]

On April 7, Mark Sumner wrote in the Daily Kos: "Drug pusher Trump has a share in the malaria drug he keeps overselling," explaining that Trump had a personal financial interest in Sanofi, the French drug maker that makes Plaquenil, a brand name version of hydroxychloroquine.[36] The White House claimed that the Sanofi stock was a minor part of a larger portfolio of stocks owned by Trump. Even if the president's financial interest was, in fact, not substantial, he should not promote a specific product. Since Trump has not been willing to release his taxes it has never been possible to determine the breadth and extent of his conflicts of interest.

---

35   Marisa Taylor and Aram Roston, "Exclusive: Pressed By Trump, U.S. Pushed Unproven Coronavirus Treatment Guidance", Reuters, April 4, 2020, https://www.reuters.com/article/us-health-coronavirus-usa-guidance-exclu/exclusive-pressed-by-trump-u-s-pushed-unproven-coronavirus-treatment-guidance-idUSKBN21M0R2.

36   Mark Sumner, "Drug Pusher Trump Has a Share in the Malaria Drug He Keeps Overselling for Coronavirus", *Daily Kos*, April 7, 2020, http://www.dailykos.com.drug-pusher-trump-has-a-share-in-the-malaria-drug-he-keeps-overselling.

Trump's shilling for this drug was driving up a gray market demand and making it difficult to acquire for those who need it now to treat rheumatoid arthritis or lupus. The FDA has since issued a hydroxychloroquine warning as studies have shown the risk of using the drug in the treatment of COVID-19. There are a number of drug trials in the U.S. and throughout the world to identify an effective treatment of COVID-19, but these are anticipated to take time. It may be a year or more before an effective medication is available.

In the meantime, it would be helpful for Trump to get out of the way and leave science to the scientists—a great number of innocent human beings are dying. But Trump never stops and gets more outrageous every day. The makers of Clorox and Lysol had to warn against ingesting or injecting cleaning products after Trump mused, with DHS science and technology head Bill Bryan, that it should be looked into as a treatment. In fact, Lysol's manufacturer warned that "Trump's suggestion is dangerous and 'under no circumstance' should disinfectant be injected in body."[37] Sadly, Birx looked pained but did not speak up to correct the president. Fauci was not in attendance at the press briefing. This is a prime example of how a little knowledge can be a dangerous thing. Trump may actually believe he knows everything about everything, but he is neither a scientist nor a medical doctor. It is possible that for Trump this is simply all about politics, and that making himself look good is so important that consequences to the public don't matter. It is also possible that he has a personal profit motive. If you have not realized by now, with Trump it is all about Trump, it is not about us.

---

37   Bess Levin, "Lysol Manufacturer Warns Trump is a Dangerous Moron, 'Under No Circumstance' Should Disinfectant Be Injected in Body", *Vanity Fair*, April 24, 2020, https://www.vanityfair.com/news/2020/04/donald-trump-lysol-coronavirus-warning.

Stupid People in Large Groups

"Never underestimate the power of stupid people in large groups," a helpful lesson attributed to comedian George Carlin, and it could not be stated more clearly.[38] In case you missed it, on April 15, 2020, Donald Trump's leadership was on display in Michigan, when the GOP coordinated an effort with Trump supporters to hold a mass rally in front of Democratic Governor Gretchen Whitmer's office to protest the state's shutdown. The protesters clogged the streets with so much traffic that first responders and essential medical personnel were unable to reach hospitals to respond to emergencies.

COVID-19 is extremely contagious, and each person who shelters in place can reduce the rate of infection substantially. It is estimated that on average a person infected with this virus generates two to two and a half new cases. Extrapolated out, it would not take long for the virus to spread across the country.[39] An article in *The Guardian* by Ian Sample on March 11, 2020 shed some light on the effectiveness of the mitigation measures in other countries: "China had 114,325 cases of coronavirus by the end of February 2020, a figure that would have been 67 times higher without intervention such as early detection, isolation of the infected, and travel restrictions."[40] The analysis concluded that if the mitigating measures had been imposed three weeks earlier the

---

38 See for example, "10 Best George Carlin Quotes of All Time", *Screen Rant*, November 7, 2019, https://screenrant.com/funniest-top_george-carlin-quotes-ever-comedy-stand-up/

39 Morgan McFall Johnsen and Holly Secon, "The Average Coronavirus Patient Infects at Least 2 People, Suggesting this Virus is Far More Contagious than Flu", *Business Insider*, March 17, 2020, https://www.msn.com/en-us/health/medical/the-average-coronavirus-patient-infects-at-least-2-others-suggesting-the-virus-is-far-more-contagious-than-flu/ar-BB11byhL .

40 Ian Sample, "Research Finds Huge Impact of Interventions on Spread of Covid-19", *The Guardian,* March 22, 2020, https://www.theguardian.com/

number of cases could have been reduced by 95 percent, and if the measures had been implemented two weeks earlier, two-thirds of the infections would have been avoided.

The Michigan rallies and similar events in other states tell us volumes about Trump's loyal followers: they are willing to go out into the public, without questioning and without hesitancy, and expose themselves and their families—and subsequently thousands of other people—to the risk of contracting COVID-19. This also suggests something about our president: he values re-election over the lives of American people. In the numerous two-hour-long press briefings that are supposedly about fighting the pandemic, how many times has anyone heard Donald Trump express sincere empathy for the victims of COVID-19? We wonder how much of a spike in novel coronavirus cases that stunt in Michigan is going to create.

We could at least have lowered our risk with immediately ramping-up of testing. The U.S. had tested only 1 percent of our population as of April. Many scientists asserted that to get a real handle on the spread of the virus we needed to test 70 percent, or 231 million people, before we could make an informed decision; that would mean an additional 228 million. Despite Trump's claims that we were conducting massive testing, the rate was only about 150,000 people a day. At that rate it would take four years to reach our goal, and with this limited data it would be a massive, unwarranted risk to open everything back up. Obviously, we as a nation—and the officials on whose shoulders this falls—would have to make decisions based on less data. The longer we maintain mitigating measures the more we reduce the risk. Trump is largely responsible for causing this situation. He couldn't fix it by ignoring it, but he certainly could try.

---

world/2020/mar/11/research-finds-huge-impact-of-interventions-on-spread-of-covid-19.

Trump did not put in place the mitigating policies to stem the spread of the virus—to close schools and businesses and for individuals and families to shelter in place. They were ordered by state governors and city and county leaders. It stands to reason that the president would therefore lack the authority to lift them: he cannot order American businesses to open or people to go return to their workplaces. However, many people in Trump's support base followed his prompts and decided to ignore the mitigating measures in defiance of state and local authorities. Several Republican governors also followed the president's lead.

Not surprisingly, Trump had initially promoted Easter Sunday, April 12, 2020, as the day to lift the bans and thus fill all of America's churches. In that he was playing to his evangelical backers. Jerry Falwell is one of the nation's foremost evangelical leaders and president of Liberty University, a conservative Christian evangelical school in Lynchburg, Virginia. He is a coronavirus conspiracy theorist and in an interview on March 13, 2020, on Fox & Friends said that, "overreaction to the threat is really an attempt to make President Trump look bad," and suggested that the virus is a bioweapon concocted by North Korea and China to target Trump.[41]

Against all common sense, not to mention state guidelines, Falwell partially re-opened Liberty University on March 30, 2020, including some dormitories, welcoming back 1,900 students. As of the first of April, a dozen students reportedly had COVID-19 symptoms and one had died. It seems that Falwell and other pro-life Republicans would rather endanger and potentially cause the

---

41   Grace Panetta, "During 'Fox & Friends' Interview, Jerry Falwell Jr. Suggests the Coronavirus is a Plot to Hurt Trump and says Liberty University Will Continue to Hold In-person Classes", *Business Insider,* March 13, 2020. https://www.businessinsider.sg/jerry-falwell-jr-suggests-coronavirus-is-plot-to-hurt-trump-2020-3.

deaths of tens of thousands of Americans than for the government to borrow money to subsidize payrolls, even with interest rates near zero.

The "commander-in-chief", the guy who claims he has "total authority", who "as president can do anything he wants" did not utter a word or intervene in any way. In fact, he encouraged the civil disobedience with his tweets. He publicly sent messages to several Democrat governors throughout the U.S. to "liberate" their states from the shelter-in-place rules, inciting civil unrest and defiance of state laws. Included in his never-ending messages were calls to the public that their second amendment rights were being threatened. This had police forces in cities throughout the nation concerned about the increased threat of violence as in some places heavily armed neo Nazis and militiamen joined the protestors.

A major factor that exacerbated this crisis is that our president lacks a moral compass. Trump seems to be solely about Trump. His concern seems to be singularly focused on getting reelected at any cost regardless of the consequences to American's lives. Trump has been under pressure from business leaders, Senate Republicans, conservative economists and newscasters to quickly remove the social distancing guidelines—get America back to work. On March 23, 2020 during a White House briefing Trump announced: "America will again be open for business—very soon," and, "We cannot let the cure be worse than the problem itself," and announced his target date for everything to reopen as April 12.

The "cure" in this case was mitigating the spread of the virus through social distancing and sheltering at home. The "problem" was that without this cure we would not be able to catch up and get ahead of this virus, thus many more people would die. Finally adhering to the advice of Fauci and Birx, on March 30, Trump extended the White House guidelines to April 30, but still continued his calls to open up the economy well before the experts indicated it might be safe. To be sure, sheltering at home watching the steady rise in the number of infections and related deaths and worrying about where the next source of income will come from is extremely difficult, especially for the millions of Americans living paycheck to paycheck. Our government must do what is needed to support the American people. However, we feared that requests for this much-needed support were falling on deaf ears in the Senate, and that a majority of wage earners would be faced with a decision whether to put food on the table or protect themselves and their loved ones from exposure to the virus. Now some states are in effect forcing people to return to work by cutting off unemployment assistance.

Dead People Don't Work

It is irresponsible and shows a great lack of foresight to open up the economy and send people back to work and school without isolating who has the virus and who is likely to spread it. We need a much larger sample size than is available. If the economy is opened up without planned safety measures we will be making our future a crap-shoot at best. We think Nefraya (@Nefraya, March 26, 2020) said it best in a tweet: "Dear Republicans, dead people don't work and dead people don't buy things. And survivors have long memories." We have not gotten ahead of the novel coronavirus. The state governors are anxious to do the testing but adequate supplies are not available. There is little doubt premature abandonment of the mitigating measures will result in a significant uptick in COVID-19 cases and attendant deaths.

The numerous forecasts of the projected number of COVID-19 cases and fatalities were all heavily dependent on key assumptions, with the amount of testing accomplished at the top of the list. Other factors included: support provided to frontline healthcare professionals; public response to stringent mitigation measures; and whether federal or state governments would force premature lifting of mitigating measures. There are several manufacturers/suppliers of test kits, each with their own set of reagents (the mix of chemicals used for these tests) for their particular device. But in this pandemic the entire world has been competing for test kits and the attendant reagents, and reagent supplies are low or have run out.

The obvious and logical—and perhaps the only—effective and efficient way to meet this U.S. need is for President Trump to use the Defense Production Act (DPA) to open the supply chain and the administration to oversee the production and distribution of the kits and requisite chemicals; the governors do not have the power to do that. However, even under the DPA and in full production mode, manufacturers would still not be able to catch up in time to meet the pressing need.

The earliest forecasting models predicted a death toll of 1.5-2.2 million people, assuming that the United States would not undertake any mitigating measures. On March 31, 2020, at a White House press briefing, Trump, with Fauci and Birx, announced that, assuming the United States did everything it could as a nation, the best-case scenario indicated national fatalities of 100,000 to 240,000. By April 15, just two weeks later, 32,700 Americans had already perished and the end was not in sight. The University of Washington's Institute for Health Metrics and Evaluation (IHME) predictive model forecast that COVID-19 would take 60,308 lives in the United States by August 4, 2020, and a forecast from The COVID-19 Tracking Project survey conducted April 13-14 was very close to that.[42] These were optimistic estimates that assumed

---

[42] Jay Boice, "Experts Think the U.S. COVID-19 Death Toll Will Hit 50,000 by the End of April", FiveThirtyEight: Science and Health, April 17, 2020. https://fivethirtyeight.com/features/experts-think-the-u-s-covid-19-death-toll-will-hit-50000-by-the-end-of-april/.

mitigation measures would remain in place and would largely be adhered to for some time.[43] The death toll would be far less had we been prepared and implemented mitigation procedures earlier when it was first clear we would be facing this deadly virus.

If the mitigating measures in place end up being lifted or not fully enforced too soon, many more who could be spared will instead suffer. Yet several red-state governors were either refusing to shut down their economies or were ordering the reopening of their states, and some were encouraging public protests. In states that were shut down, some people, with verbal support via text messages from the president, were defying state laws and gathering publicly and without protective gear. By April 30 the number of deaths was over 65,000. Anyone with symptoms should be tested and the results made available immediately, but without more testing there is no accurate means to estimate the infection rate.

With the disease spreading rampantly, Trump and his ultra-conservative followers had started calling for everyone to return to work in early March, claiming the potential economic devastation would be far worse than some people dying, particularly if older people were disproportionately represented. It has been suggested that the elderly are no longer productive, thus a financial strain on the rest of society. Further, that could save on social security costs—a boon if you hate those entitlement programs? What would Jesus say about that? Larry Kudlow, Trump's chief economic advisor, told Fox News on March 25 that the U.S., "may need to make 'difficult trade-offs'."[44] The "tradeoffs" he referred to are

---

43   Peter Szekely, "Adherence to Social Distancing Spurs Dip in Projected U.S. Coronavirus Deaths", Reuters, April 18, 2020, https://www.reuters.com/article/us-health-coronavirus-usa-forecast-idUSKBN2200AW. The IHME advised states not to relax distancing and protective measures until achieving an infection rates of less than one per million of population.

44   Justin Wise, "Kudlow Says US Will Have to Make 'Difficult Tradeoffs' on Coronavirus: 'Cure Can't Be Worse Than Disease'", *The Hill,* March 23, 2020, https://

humans: our grandparents, our mothers and fathers, our children, siblings, friends.

Difficult Leap (without a Net)

We understand that at times a few must be willing to sacrifice for the many. It may feel cold and callous, and we are fully aware that human lives are not merely statistics. However, we do understand Larry Kudlow's logic, and the way it was presented publicly misrepresents the facts and what the numbers mean. It was a challenging leap of logic that, when shown to the public, became a casualty of oversimplification. We as a nation have very difficult decisions to make, but what Kudlow set up is a false dichotomy. It is not simply a choice of the economy versus fatalities. Instead, we stand to lose both, and we have woefully inadequate data to determine the level of risk we face.

What would make more sense is a public policy to massively increase the level of testing over the status quo of 150,000 people a day. A plan to test and identify individuals who could safely return to the workforce could be done in significant numbers, but impossible without the administration's cooperation. It helps to explore the trade-offs alluded to by Kudlow if we want to understand why.

People may have higher or lower perceptions of risk that do not equate to the actual statistical risk. Oftentimes people view themselves as invulnerable—they are worried about others but feel that it won't happen to themselves or their loved ones. But it can and it does. There is no economic standard for the value of a life. However, when looking at the risk/reward trade-offs that people make with regard to their health, economists often consider the

---

thehill.com/homenews/administration/489064-kudlow-says-us-will-have-to-make-difficult-trade-offs-on-coronavirus.

value of a statistical life, which is the value placed on changes in the likelihood of death, not the price someone would pay to avoid certain death. It is an economic value used to quantify the benefit of avoiding a fatality. It is a statistical term for the cost of reducing an average number of deaths by one. Knowing the value of life is useful for cost-benefit analyses for decision-making, especially for public policy. Simply put, if the costs outweigh the benefits, the proposed initiative is not worth pursuing.

Keeping the mitigating factors in place to fight the further spread of COVID-19 comes at a huge cost to our economy. How can we weigh the benefits of opening up our economy now against the cost of the increased number of deaths that would occur if we abandon the shelter-in-place regimen before we've gotten in front of the spread of the virus? In the United States the value of a human life is calculated at approximately $10 million for the purpose of decisions regarding public safety. Added to the cost of the increased number of fatalities would be the estimated costs of the increased number of non-fatal illnesses and the increased strain on our already over-burdened hospitals and healthcare system.

If re-opening the economy prematurely results in an additional 2 million infections and 100,000 more fatalities, the massively increased strain on an overwhelmed system will be devastating, the total estimated costs could exceed $2 trillion. However, that analysis minimizes the actual risk. If we do open up our economy too early and people begin dying at a rate of 2,000 or more each day again, economies will need to close down again. It would be a lose-lose result and could plunge the U.S. into a depression. The distinct possibility of that happening rendered Kudlow's characterization of the problem as premature, and not a decision to be made at that point: it was an oversimplification that as publicly stated provided false hopes. The United States first needs massively more COVID-19 testing to determine what could be done to mitigate the death rate and revive our economy. However, contrary to the advice of experts some states have elected to go ahead and open their economies anyway.

Ringling Brothers and Barnum & Bailey Presents: Trump's Circus

In March and April, the social situation was, "…about 95 percent of America's population, or about 306 million people, under some form of lockdown."[45] At that time, Fauci predicted this might be necessary for several more weeks at least. On April 4, Trump yet again in his White House briefing stressed the need for America to get back to work soon, something he was demanding virtually every day. As of April 15, the president vehemently was claiming he had absolute power to order states to reopen offices and businesses. That is inaccurate, to say the least; it is unconstitutional under the Tenth Amendment. And it is only one of many, many statements made by Trump that have invited reactions ranging from disbelief, to anger, to confusion, and more disbelief. It was like a political and social circus, but one with a very strange ringmaster. One more indication of a desire to create an autocratic system with him at the helm.

Criticism of this circus came not just from elected officials who were Democrats, or left-leaning media outlets, but from voices across the political spectrum. Many were recognizing that the problems America was facing were the result of a lack of national leadership. The president's handling of the COVID-19 pandemic was a spotlight in which an array of problems was revealed. For

---

45   "8 Times World Leaders Downplayed the Coronavirus and Put Their Countries at Greater Risk for Infection", *Business Insider*, April 11, 2020, https://www.businessinsider.in/slideshows/miscellaneous/8-times-world-leaders-downplayed-the-coronavirus-and-put-their-countries-at-greater-risk-for-infection/slidelist/75098071.cms.

those of us who had been aware of this all along, it felt like more of the same, only worse. For others, it was truth made clear: the emperor was in fact not wearing any clothes. The hoax was out in the open. Here we offer our readers a sampling of some of the most egregious instances of Trump's 2020 circus tricks.

- "Trump Says U.S. Has Coronavirus 'Totally Under Control'" as one headline put it after Trump appeared on CNBC's *Squawk Box* on January 22, just one day after the CDC confirmed the first U.S. case of coronavirus in Washington State. Trump said he was not at all concerned about the possibility of a pandemic.
- A January 31 *Foreign Policy* magazine article by Laurie Garrett declared: "Trump Has Sabotaged America's Coronavirus Response", and, "the United States has never been less prepared for a pandemic."[46]
- On February 25, Chris Cillizza for CNN's *The Post* wrote: "Donald Trump seems to know very little about the coronavirus. Most of those thoughts are either wrong or factually questionable—or at least optimistic or at worst misleading."
- Nancy Cook and Matthew Choi reported for *Politico* that on February 28, "President Trump tried to cast the global virus outbreak as a liberal conspiracy intended to undermine his first term, lumping it alongside impeachment and the Mueller investigation. He blamed the press for acting hysterically about the virus…he downplayed its dangers saying against expert opinion it was on par with the flu."
- Also, February 28, David Knowles of *Yahoo News* reported:

---

46   Laurie Garrett is a former senior fellow for global health at the Council on Foreign Relations. She was awarded the Pulitzer Prize for Explanatory Journalism in 1996 for a series in *Newsday* chronicling the Ebola virus outbreak in Zaire.

"Trump calls coronavirus 'hysteria' the Democrats new 'hoax'."[47] Knowles added that, "On that same day then acting White House Chief of Staff Mick Mulvaney called coronavirus 'hoax of the day' at an appearance at the Conservative Political Action Conference." We do not think that narrative really worked out for the president.

Wait. There's more. A BBC News "Reality Check" team kept tabs on Trump's misleading or false statements and published a summary of their analysis on March 26:[48]

Trump's view: "The U.S. has done a very good job on testing. When people need a test, they can get a test." The Reality Check Team noted that Trump said this on March 25, but in early March 2020 the White House had conceded that the United States did not have enough testing kits to meet this crisis. Even though testing did increase, the best estimates at the time indicated only 1 percent of our population had been tested. Some health centers reported problems with the kits they did get. But states were not receiving very many, and America heard from governors, mayors, and healthcare providers that there were in fact very few test kits available to them. As of March 11, per capita the United States had carried out 26 tests for every million residents, far less than other countries. How much less? The United Kingdom: 400 tests per million. Italy: 1,000 tests per million. South Korea: 4,000 tests per million.[49] There is legitimate concern that the virus may have spread as quickly and widely as it has in the U.S. because so few tests were carried out early in the manifestation of the disease. The

---

[47] David Knowles, "Trump Calls Coronavirus 'Hysteria' the Democrats' 'New Hoax'", Yahoo News, February 28, 2020, https://news.yahoo.com/trump-calls-coronavirus-hysteria-the-democrats-new-hoax-011312448.html.
[48] Reality Check Team , "Coronavirus: Five Trump Claims Fact-Checked," *BBC News,* March 26, 2020, https://www.bbc.com/news/world-us-canada-51818627.
[49] Reality Check Team, "Five Trump Claims."

reality is that instead of doing more testing and better testing, the United States was playing catch-up from way behind since the start.

Trump's view: "Very soon we are going to come up with a vaccine." The reality is that when Trump made that comment on March 7, he probably had no idea how soon a vaccine would be developed, much less become available. The BBC's reality check was that scientists were working hard to develop a vaccine, testing in animals was underway and possible testing in humans later in the year, but that many scientists had stated that unless we got extremely lucky it would be at least 12-18 months before a safe, effective vaccine became available.[50] Optimism can be helpful, but in this case, presenting false hope and downright lies is literally hazardous to our health.

Trump's view: "Last year 37,000 Americans died from the common flu. Nothing is shutdown [sic], life and the economy go on…Think about that." Yet again, *BBC* noted, reality diverges from Trump's March 9 statement. The best CDC estimates of deaths from the flu in the United States between October 2019 and February 2020 was 34,157, and if we're talking about the flu that might be within reason. However, COVID-19 is not the flu. It killed two times that number in three months, and research, including from WHO, indicated COVID-19 has a significantly higher mortality rate than the seasonal flu.[51] Moreover, the threat of COVID-19 is not yet contained by vaccines or immunity from previous outbreaks. Making matters worse, the ongoing shortages in our healthcare system are already negatively impacting patient care during the epidemic, there are a large number of seriously

---

50   Reality Check Team, "Five Trump Claims."
51   The death rate from flu is on average about 0.1 percent. On March 3, 2020, WHO reported the novel coronavirus death rate based on all confirmed cases that had resulted in death as 3.4 percent worldwide; by April it was 6.7 percent.

ill patients in care, and the death rate likely to continue to rise in coming weeks.

There has been widespread criticism of Trump's "handling" of this crisis and people from a range of political views now questioning his leadership viability. In the conservative *National Review,* writer and political commentator Mona Charen zeroed in on what Trump was doing wrong amid the burgeoning coronavirus pandemic:

> In a serious public health crisis, the public has the right to expect the government's chief executive to lead in a number of crucial ways: by prioritizing the problem properly, by deferring to subject matter experts when appropriate while making decisions in informed and sensible ways, by providing honest and careful information to the country, by calming fears and setting expectations, and by addressing mistakes and setbacks. … Trump so far hasn't passed muster on any of these matters.[52]

Lamenting Trump's handling of the crisis, Charen decried the electorate of 2016 for "voting for a malignant narcissist who had never served anything other than his own bottom line."

From CNN's Chris Cillizza:

> What we've seen from the start of the coronavirus has been a relentless focus on himself and how he is being perceived by the public rather than a prioritizing of the broader common good. To borrow a phrase from my friend and colleague Chris Cuomo, a public health

---

52   Mona Charen, "After This, Voters Will Take Their Responsibility Seriously", *National Review,* March 13, 2020, https://www.nationalreview.com/2020/03/after-this-voters-will-take-their-reponsibility-seriously.

emergency like this one requires putting the 'we' in front of the 'me'—and with each passing day the President makes clear he is either unwilling or unable to do that.[53]

A *Washington Post* article on March 22, 2020 had the headline: "Trump's lagging response widens rift with city and state leaders" and pointed to:

> the growing gulf between the White House and officials on the front lines of the pandemic underscored concerns in cities, states and Congress that Trump does not have a coherent or ready plan to mobilize private and public entities to confront a crisis that could soon push the nation's health-care system to the brink of collapse.[54]

At the state level the displeasure did not just come from Democrats. Larry Hogan, Republican governor of Maryland and chairman of the National Governors Association, said on CNN that, "Without the tests we really are flying blind, we're sort of guessing about where the outbreaks are and about what the infection rate and the hospitalization rates are." Hogan said that Trump's claims that getting access to testing was no longer an issue was "just not true."[55]

---

53   Chris Cilizza, "What National Review Nails about Trump's Poor Performance on Coronavirus", CNN, March 11, 2020, https://cnn.com/2020/03/11/politics/national-review-donald-trump-coronavirus/index.html.
54   Robert Costa and Aaron Gregg, "Trump's Lagging Response Widens Rift with City and State Leaders", *Washington Post*, April 1, 2020.
55   Julia Hollingsworth, Adam Renton and Joshua Berlinger, "Maryland Governor Says People Who Violate Stay-At-Home Order Could Face Jail Time", CNN, March 31, 2020, https://www.cnn.com/world/live-news/coronavirus-outbreak-03-31-20-intl/h_750746956a84f74f1ef39e6303e79aa2.

Politics as Usual and Everything to Fear

> Such is the immense difference between a country which has morals and one which is corrupted. The former has everything to hope and the latter everything to fear.
>
> —Goveurneur Morris, founding father and Federalist, 1794

COVID-19 is like living with a monster too small to see but so large we can't contain it. Schools, restaurants, bars, movie theaters, concerts, casinos, dance studios, pool halls, gyms, sports events, retail stores, airlines, cruise ships, and most other businesses were closed. On the ground, real patriots responded. There were hundreds, perhaps thousands, of stories of Americans joining this effort. Homebound workers and students were making personal protective equipment (PPE) and medical equipment to alleviate shortages. Retired medical professionals returned to work, and volunteers assisted hospital staffs. Restaurants and service workers were donating unused food and supplies to those who most needed it. These are true American heroes who deserve our undying gratitude. As founding father Gouverneur Morris, a staunch supporter of having a strong central government to support the confederation of states, wrote to George Washington, morals matter in times of crisis. Morris was comparing the American revolution—a country with morals to what he saw happening in France—corruption.[56] As a nation with morals, at least we hope we still do, we should not leave states to fight among themselves for resources and rely on piecemeal efforts of available citizens.

With the volume of help required to fight this war, federal leadership and assistance is necessary, and while private individuals

---

56 Gouverneur Morris, "To George Washington from Gouverneur Morris, 12 March 1794," *Founders Online,* National Archives, accessed April 30, 2020, https://founders.archives.gov/documents/Washington/05-15-02-0282.

and companies stepped up, it is not enough for the government to just call on private industry to aid in the pandemic response effort by manufacturing masks, ventilators and other requisite supplies and equipment.

Had Trump maintained the infectious disease staff that was in place under President Obama we would have been better prepared for the pandemic. An independent, bipartisan panel formed by the Center for Strategic and International Studies in 2018 concluded that lack of preparedness was so acute in the Trump administration that: "(The) United States must either pay now and gain protection and security or wait for the next epidemic and pay a much greater price in human and economic costs." Prophetic!

We do wonder whether even if there were a separate directorate under Trump, as during the Obama administration, it would have actually made things any better. It wasn't as if Trump was not warned about the impending crisis, early on and in real time. As we've already noted, the intelligence community and CDC had already told the Trump administration that China was lying about the severity of its situation and it was highly likely if not almost certain that the United States was at risk. And the Trump administration's "reorganization" of that mission reminds us of something we once heard: a bad reorganization is like a spastic colon, and this fits that description. Perhaps Trump saw it as saving a few million dollars in government salaries in order to help offset the billions of dollars in tax cuts given to Trump's billionaire buddies.

Trump's decision to scale back the bureaucracy ended up costing American taxpayers trillions of dollars and tens of thousands of lives, not to mention the loss of jobs, education, and so many other things. Still, in every daily coronavirus briefing we never fail to hear from President Trump what a wonderful job he and his task force are doing, how his fast action and intuitive response have saved perhaps millions of lives. These "briefings" are nothing more than self-aggrandizing campaign rallies put on at taxpayer expense. America is paying for Trump's circus, and that is a hoax if there ever was one.

The probability of a global COVID-19 pandemic was envisioned as far back December 2019. If Trump was truly not aware of the impending crisis, then he should have been, but it is our perspective that he simply chose to put his head in the sand and ignore it, thinking or hoping it would just go away. Had his administration recognized the significance of this clear and present danger and planned ahead, it could have bought time and helped stem the spread of the virus.

Typically, Senate Majority Leader McConnell blamed the Democrats for the administration's lack of preparedness and slow, disjointed, feeble response. McConnell claimed the White House and Republicans in Congress were preoccupied because of the impeachment hearings. The credulity of Trump supporters is beyond comprehension. It is hard to accept that there are so many gullible people in the world. Most of us would need some very strong antacids to swallow McConnell's malarkey. (Note to Joe Biden: we like that word, too.) Had the Republicans been honest and done their jobs in the Senate trial, we may well have avoided this crisis, or at least diminished the negative effects.

Some of us intend to hold the president and Senate Republicans responsible for their malfeasance and incompetence as commander-in-chief and legislators. Presidents are in office to deal with crises. The longer Trump remains in the Oval Office the more danger our nation will face. The coronavirus in all likelihood will return. Under this administration, it is doubtful that the United States will be better prepared, and there will be other dangers in our nation's future. How would this out-of-control megalomaniac respond to these potential threats? The ability to competently respond to a crisis and direct the production and distribution of essential resources to battle a national epidemic has been clearly shown to be beyond the capability of this president.

Trump developed a narrative that the federal government serves as only a back-up to the states in this fight. In his campaign-style coronavirus briefings he has attempted to elevate his presidential standing by referring to himself as a "wartime president." He wants to have it both ways. He wants to maintain a position from which he can blame state governors if things worsen, and if things improve he could swoop in after the crisis has passed and claim victory for himself, claiming that because of his swift and decisive leadership millions of lives were saved. Whom to believe? The President of the United States who claims he knows more about everything than virtually anybody and lies to the public an average of 100 times a week? Or the governors and medical professionals on the front lines and Fauci and the other true experts on the coronavirus? There is no panacea in this decision for us. The longer the mitigating measures are in place the more likely it is that more workers will lose their jobs and face very difficult financial dilemmas. The government has a responsibility to provide until the siege ends. Remember, "of the people, by the people, for the people"?

Politics should be shelved during this pandemic. Meanwhile, Trump continues to blame it all on Nancy Pelosi and the Democrats. The president and political conservatives have increasingly agitated to end the mitigating measures meant to buy time and save lives. How many more people could die if we do it too early? Many of our conservative brethren have pushed the narrative that health experts are part of a deep-state plot to hurt Donald Trump's reelection efforts by keeping the United States shut down as long as possible and further damaging the economy—and there are people out there who actually believe that. That narrative is contemptable. According to far-right political reasoning, we guess we would have to add medical professionals, scientists, every news outlet except Fox, universities, all Democrats, Republicans Larry Hogan and Mitt Romney, and anyone else who criticizes "the chosen one," and then just keep adding to the ever-growing "enemies of the state" list that Trump seems to have compiled. Ever hear the expression "Everyone is wrong except you and me and I'm not so sure about you"? From our perspective, America's doctors, nurses and other healthcare professionals and hospital staff who have unselfishly fought on the front lines of this war should be given consideration for sainthood. They have increased our faith in mankind. To them we say: God bless every one of you, we will be forever grateful.

A word of caution is in order. Based on preliminary data, it has now been suggested by several doctors and scientists that the novel coronavirus may cause a number of hidden health problems, some of which may not surface until much later. If this is accurate these problems may affect not only the people who became seriously ill from the disease but also those who were infected but asymptomatic. Making matters worse, as many as 33 million people may have lost their health insurance coverage when they lost their jobs due to the economic fallout of this crisis.[57] If Republicans get their way, who is to say that insurers will not categorize these maladies as pre-existing conditions when people are seeking new health insurance coverage? Food for thought while the administration is in court trying to completely undo the Affordable Care Act including the pre-existing condition exemption.

---

57   Mayra Rodriguez Valladares, "Over 35 Million Americans Are Now Out Of Work And Millions More Will Join Them", Forbes, April 30, 2020, https://www.forbes.com/sites/mayrarodriguezvalladares/2020/04/30/over-35-million-americans-are-now-out-of-work-and-millions-more-will-join-them/#26dcfd656b7e.

Stimulating the Rich

Congress passed a $2 trillion stimulus package on March 25, 2020 to alleviate the financial suffering. The stimulus was delayed as Republicans in the Senate lobbied for more of the money to go to big corporations with few constraints on how the corporations would be allowed to use the federal funds. Since they required 60 votes in the Senate for passage and the Democrats refused to cave in to the Republican demands, the Senate Republicans did not prevail. Speaker of the House Nancy Pelosi stated that Democrats had turned the proposed bill, "...on its head. From trickle down for corporate America to bubble up for workers."[58] Consequently, the final bill included assurances that the industries that did receive funds must not lay off workers and are not permitted to use the federal money for stock buybacks to raise their stock prices and provide increased salaries and/or bonuses for corporate executives.

These corporations employ millions of American workers and the bailouts are necessary. It is interesting, or maybe hypocritical, that Republicans do not consider these corporate bailouts as an exercise in socialism, despite their declared criticism as "socialist" any proposals that would ensure universal health care (like every other industrialized nation) and other safety nets for at-risk and needy Americans. Further, Trump had said he did not want to deploy the DPA to help in this crisis because he considers such actions to be socialist. By that definition it is socialist to help American workers and provide a safety net for the neediest individuals in society, but giving money to corporations is not. As a sidebar, the original Senate version of the stimulus package reportedly would have benefited Trump's personal business ventures.

---

58   Pelosi said this in an interview with Rachel Maddow on *The Rachel Maddow Show* (MSNBC) on April 5, 2020.

After signing the $2 trillion stimulus bill (CARES Act) Trump declared that he did not consider the restrictions on how corporations are allowed to use that money as mandatory, but rather suggestions. Democrats insisted on the creation of a new inspector general (IG) to ensure that the White House did not improperly distribute taxpayer money; Trump said he would not comply with the portion of the CARES Act that requires an existing IG to oversee this emergency fund—including the $500 billion corporate bailout fund Treasury Secretary Steve Mnuchin controls. In a signing statement, Trump wrote that he would not permit a new IG to issue certain reports to Congress "without presidential supervision," explaining, "I will be the oversight." He was again asserting that he is above the law and can do what he wants without congressional oversight.

As a clear indication of this administration's ongoing corruption and greed being boundless, on April 7, President Trump fired the coronavirus funds watchdog Glenn Fine, acting Department of Defense IG.[59] This is all the more reason to quickly step up the Congressional Oversight Commission. Fine is an attorney who over the years has been described as "a model inspector general."[60] The removal of Fine will allow Trump to put in place an IG who could be expected to do the president's bidding. Absent oversight and with $500 billion to play with, he would be able to reward friends and/or himself handsomely, and punish enemies. Unless the Congressional Oversight Commission can stop this, it could be like a private auction; let the bidding begin.

---

59   Glenn Fine is no relation to the author of this book Bruce Fine.
60   David Badash, "Trump Fires Respected Acting Defense Department Inspector General to Remove Him as Coronavirus Funds Watchdog", *The New Civil Rights Movement,* April 7, 2020, https://www.thenewcivilrightsmovement.com/2020/04/trump-fires-widely-respected-acting-defense-dept-inspector-general-to-remove-him-as-coronavirus-funds-watchdog/.

A CARES 2 package was being prepared as we wrote this. Democrats were said to be looking to include measures to: extend unemployment aid and small business assistance for several additional months; authorize another round of direct checks to taxpayers; help hospitals, health care workers, farmers, first responders, and education programs; and assist smaller cities and communities that may have been shortchanged. The Republicans reportedly had agreed to include money in the bill to boost the overwhelmed healthcare system. Republicans also would be calling for more corporate aid. House Speaker Nancy Pelosi would no doubt revisit the need for more funding for the states to aid in the November 2020 elections.[61] Under the circumstances we would not hold our breath waiting for that to happen: it is not in Republicans' self-interest.

Warning from Wisconsin

Republicans have worked to suppress the votes of Black, Latino, Native American and young voters. Trump recognizes that lower voter turnout benefits Republicans and that mail-in voting does not. In a few White House press briefers, Trump claimed that "mail-in ballots are corrupt." There is no real or even substantial evidence for this.[62] Here's some impressive hypocrisy: the president and first lady requested mail-in ballots from Florida for the November 2020 election.

The Wisconsin primary election on April 7, 2020 shows

---

61   Erica Werner and Mike DeBonis, "Worried That $2 Trillion Law Wasn't Enough, Trump and Congressional Leaders Converge on Need for New Coronavirus Economic Package", *Washington Post*, April 6, 2020, https://www.washingtonpost.com/us-policy/2020/04/06/trump-democrats-coronavirus-stimulus-trillion/.
62   The only case of a problem with absentee voting occurred in a North Carolina congressional election in 2018 that was overturned by the state after an investigation suggested that a Republican political operative had improperly collected and possibly tampered with ballots.

just how much Republicans are willing to use any means possible to skew an election to their favor, including capitalizing on the pandemic. In a special session of the legislature, Wisconsin refused to postpone its primary election. Democratic Governor Tony Evers then issued an executive order delaying in-person voting from April 7 until early June. State Republicans quickly challenged the governor's emergency action by filing a motion with the state supreme court. The conservative-leaning bench blocked Evans' order in a 4–2 decision. A lower court ruling had extended the deadline for absentee ballots by six days. The U.S. Supreme Court reversed that lower court ruling. The vote was along ideological lines. The court's ruling did not specifically address the COVID-19 threat.

There was a severe shortage of election volunteers for the Wisconsin primary due to the novel coronavirus. As a result, only five polling locations out of the 180 that historically operate on election days were open in Milwaukee. Consequently, the wait time to vote in Milwaukee and elsewhere was one-and-a-half to two hours. A television clip showed a black woman being denied the right to vote because she got to the line two minutes late. She had just finished her shift as a hospital nurse fighting COVID-19.

Daniel Kelly, the incumbent Wisconsin supreme court judge who was appointed by Republican Governor Scott Walker in 2016, was defending his seat against local circuit court judge and former prosecutor Jill Karofsky. The election was intended to be non-partisan, but Kelly received a glowing endorsement from President Trump, while both Joe Biden and Bernie Sanders backed Karofsky. Wisconsin is poised to clear more than 200,000 voters from its rolls, and this race was the focal point of the fight between Democrats and Republicans about delaying the election. Kelly and Karofsky have differing ideologies. Journalist Patrick Marley, who covered this race for the Milwaukee Journal-Sentinel, reported that

Kelly had written a decision that the city of Madison could not ban guns on buses, argued that the U.S. Supreme Court decision legalizing same-sex marriage undermined democracy, compared abortion to murder, and praised a decision that upheld Act 10, the 2011 law that scaled back collective bargaining for public workers. Karofsky had said she believes there are constitutional ways to put restrictions on guns, supports same-sex marriage, considers abortion to be a matter between a woman and her doctor, and backs collective bargaining."[63]

Karofsky won handily (55 percent to Kelly's 45 percent), which cut into the conservative majority on Wisconsin's Supreme Court and might prove crucial as the court weighs the case about purging the voting rolls. This Republican ploy did not work, but their attempt to steal an election put thousands of Wisconsin voters and other residents in harm's way.

The stakes are even higher for the November 2020 national elections. If the pandemic continues to keep people at home through November 3 in parts of the country, states will need money to support mail-in voting, expand early voting and online registration, and increase safety for in-person voting. The Republicans agreed to only $400 million of the $4 billion requested by Democrats under the CARES Act. The Brennan Center for Justice estimated states would need $2 billion to adequately prepare for elections this year.[64] Trump and many congressional Republicans argued that

---

63   Patrick Marley, "Liberal Jill Karofsky Wins Wisconsin Election, Defeating Conservative Justice Daniel Kelly," *Milwaukee Journal Sentinel*, April 13, 2020, https://www.jsonline.com/story/news/politics/elections/2020/04/13/wisconsin-supreme-court-election-results-daniel-kelly-vs-jill-karofsky-conservative-liberal/2983933001/.

64   Jack Brewster, "Senate Stimulus Bill: Democrats Wanted $4 Billion in Election Assistance - They Got $400 Million", *Forbes*, March 25, 2020, https://www.forbes.com/sites/jackbrewster/2020/03/25/senate-stimulus-bill-democrats-wanted-4-billion-in-election-assistance---they-got-400-million/#5acd234151f4.

the Democrats were trying to pack the CARES Act with unrelated legislation for political benefit. Nancy Pelosi, though, indicated on April 7 that the fight was not over, declaring of the Democratic Party on MSNBC's *Rachel Maddow Show* "We don't agonize, we organize."

However, without sufficient funding to ensure a fair election, there could very well be a constitutional crisis serious enough to endanger our democracy. Because Trump minimized the dangers of COVID-19, and because his echo chamber, Fox News, broadcast the same message to its unwitting viewers, Republicans would be more likely than Democrats to vote in person. Insufficient funding to support the election process might result in voter suppression, which would benefit Trump's reelection. Alternately, if insufficient funding results in perceived problems during the voting process and Trump loses, he would very likely claim corruption and/or fraud and ask for legal redress from the Supreme Court to declare the election invalid. In that event, a large number of Republicans would likely lose their seats, so invalidation of the election would be in their perceived self-interest as well and many would most assuredly support Trump.

If the Supreme Court were to rule against Trump's request to invalidate the election, it is possible he would not accept that decision. In that case Trump would no doubt be supported by many Republican elected officials at all levels of government. He has already successfully ignored congressional oversight, dismantling the separation of powers clause of the Constitution. Why would anyone think he would behave different with the judiciary? We wonder how the U.S. attorney general might respond to that; at the time of this writing, that was William Barr, a vital player in Trump's "sycophant symphony." Would Barr—or any Trump attorney general—support Trump essentially declaring martial law and continuing to occupy the White House? If that seems absurd, look at what this self-proclaimed "Chosen One" has already done to our nation's institutions of government. No doubt there would be people who would offer to assist Trump in his quest to stay in the Oval Office.

This is all conjecture in May 2020. But while our nation's attention was, as it should have been, focused on the war against COVID-19, those of us not on the front lines used some of our idle time at home to reflect on how we arrived in this surreal place and how we can as a society ensure a far brighter, more secure future. COVID-19 rapidly and dramatically changed our way of life. The war against this virus can be compared to a track meet—it includes both a sprint and a marathon. Our team didn't even enter the sprint competition and our marathon grew much longer and over far more difficult terrain. This is not a football game where in the end it doesn't matter if you score a touchdown before the final whistle and win 28–27 or you crush it during the whole game and win 28–0, because a win is a win. Victory in this pandemic will be based on minimization of fatalities.

No matter what news outlet we followed we were confronted with daily updates on the number of people who have been infected and the attendant number of deaths. News on the financial front was also frightening. Once the crisis subsides and America returns to work, it will take time for our economy to fully recover and we do not just mean a rise in the Dow Jones Industrial Average. Most Americans do not benefit from the stock market. Some businesses have already succumbed to the effects of our economic shutdown. Our unemployment rate rose dramatically in April; the figures suggested a rate of 17 percent, up from 3.5 percent before the pandemic. Experts projected dire unemployment rates for a year or more to come.[65] In March 2020, James Bullard, President of the

---

65   "United States Economic Forecasts 2020-2022 Outlook", *Trading*

Federal Reserve Bank of St. Louis, warned that as the coronavirus spreads, unemployment could hit 30 percent during the second quarter of the year.[66] To counter that it seemed logical to endure and starve out the virus by limiting our exposure. The shutdown was essential to win the war and economically bounce back.

Our country's lack of rapid response belies Trump's claims that the United States was fully prepared. His claims that he couldn't have known and his attempts to rewrite history and blame anyone else for his failures as commander-in-chief are indicative of a lack of moral and competent leadership. Friendly fire is not the only internal problem we might be facing in this war. We will win this war, but not without collateral damage, or unintended harm inflicted on civilians and innocent people in the course of war. It is something that effective moral leaders strive to avoid. The cost of the arrogant leadership of this administration and president is in the form of the loss of lives of many more civilians than was necessary.

President Trump took to providing daily updates on the status of the administration's efforts concerning the coronavirus, but the *Washington Post* called those updates "a risk to public health," and in the words of media columnist Margaret Sullivan: "These White House sessions—ostensibly meant to give the public critical and truthful information about the frightening crisis—are so far working against that end. Rather they have become a daily stage for Trump to play his greatest hits to captive audience members."[67] Trump used these briefings as a substitute for the campaign rallies

---

Economics, accessed April 20, 2020, https://tradingeconomics.com/united-states/forecast.

66   Steve Matthews, "Fed's Bullard Says U.S. Jobless Rate May Soar to 30% in Second Quarter", Bloomberg News," March 22, 2020, https://www.bnnbloomberg.ca/fed-s-bullard-says-u-s-jobless-rate-may-soar-to-30-in-2q-1.1410501.

67   Margaret Sullivan, "The Media Must Stop Live-Broadcasting Trump's Dangerous, Destructive Coronavirus Briefings", *Washington Post,* March 21, 2020,

he could no longer stage because of the public health risks posed by the coronavirus. He was joined on stage by Vice President Pence, who spent much of his time at the podium spewing propaganda about the president's masterful handling of the pandemic. Trump in turn would spend an hour or two in public self-aggrandizement. He spread propaganda while working for his own partisan political benefit. It was a naked attempt to portray himself as a wartime president bravely leading the nation through a tumultuous time, as if he were imagining himself as a Franklin Delano Roosevelt of the twenty-first century. A better way to frame this circus show is in these words of Margaret Thatcher, former Prime Minister of Great Britain: "Being powerful is like being a lady. If you have to tell people you are, you aren't."[68]

They say God does not give us anything we cannot handle. We will beat COVID-19 and we will rebuild our economy. But we have some questions. First, how many lives must be lost needlessly before we reach that point? Second, and just as important, how will we as a nation handle the recovery and any other crises to come?

---

https://www.washingtonpost.com/b8a2a440-6b7c-11ea-9923-57073adce27c_story.html.

68   Lucy Hutchings, "Margaret Thatcher's Most Famous Quotes," *Vogue* UK, April 8, 2013, https://www.vogue.co.uk/gallery/margaret-thatcher-most-famous-quotes.

CHAPTER 3

RELIGION AND MORALITY ... AND POLITICS

> For I was hungry and you gave me food, I was thirsty and you gave me something to drink, I was a stranger and you welcomed me, I was naked and you gave me clothing, I was sick and you took care of me, I was in prison and you visited me.
>
> —The Gospel of Matthew 25:35–36

> When the government puts its imprimatur on a particular religion it conveys a message of exclusion to all those who do not adhere to the favored beliefs. A government cannot be premised on the belief that all persons are created equal when it asserts that God prefers some.
>
> —Harry Blackmun, U.S. Supreme Court Justice, 1992

When President Donald Trump declared himself "the Chosen One" on camera, to the press, and therefore to the world, we were horrified. There was a very strong odor coming from the swamp the day Trump declared himself divinely anointed and above the law, with a right to act however he likes, without question. Although Trump later backtracked and claimed he hadn't been serious, his actions since then evidence he actually feels otherwise. Supreme Court Justice Blackmun explained his views about church-state separation in a 1992 school prayer case. He stated, "government cannot be premised on the belief that all persons are created equal when it asserts that God prefers some."[69] As the words of Christ make clear in the Gospel of Matthew, it is right and moral to meet the basic needs of all individuals, no matter who they are. Donald Trump seeks a grant of authority based on authentic faith, but he does so without feeling the need to live within any of the moral tenets of that faith—not the kind of separating of church and state that our founders planned.

Presidential politics, like much of the Bible, highlights a contest between hope and fear. Donald Trump excels at stoking fear and anger into public discourse on any important topic. He incites divisiveness at every opportunity to intentionally thwart any open and honest debate. Simply appealing to our better angels and expressing hope that things will get better is not enough to counter the erosion of the core principles of our governance that Trump is spearheading.

Trump's actions have challenged the principle of church-state separation, and the policies and actions being implemented by his administration are in direct conflict with the gospel of love—the overarching Christian principle that love for one another shown by living a moral and compassionate life as Jesus did, reflects God's love for mankind. Our nation's founders were largely Christian men who wanted to retain for our nation the values of Christianity, at least in some form. At the same time, and after extensive argument among those with differing opinions, our founders decided against endorsing any one religion in order to ensure that religious leaders would not unduly influence politics, deem some people less "equal" than others because of their faith, or form a religious elite class.

Who do we want to be as a nation? Our country's strength

---

69   Lauren Stein, "Justice Blackmun is Remembered for His Defense of Religious Liberties." Jewish Telegraphic Agency. March 4, 1999, https://www.jta.org/1999/03/04/lifestyle/behind-the-headlines-justice-blackmun-is-remembered-for-his-defense-of-religious-liberties.

has always been in our moral compass. The core values that have historically made the United States a beacon to the world, parallel the teachings of our religions: love thy neighbor as thyself; faith hope and charity; give us your poor and downtrodden – just a sample of some that are kind of important to us. The Gospels of the Bible tell of the true "chosen one," Jesus, practicing compassion and care for others: shared social responsibility. This was reflected in choices about our government made by our nation's founders. America was not to be a nation ruled by fear and unquestioning bowing down to a ruler claiming divine right, so a fundamental founding principle of the United States is the separation of church and state, provided for in our Constitution. The general principle was written by Thomas Jefferson and passed by the Virginia General Assembly on January 16, 1786, preceding by five years the First Amendment protections for freedom of religion.[70] The principle was based on Jefferson's own philosophy that no man should be compelled to support any religious worship or ministry, nor be punished or burdened or suffer in any way because of religious opinions or beliefs. It is not because of total agreement that this made its way into our Constitution. When the religious sects of Jefferson's day realized that their particular beliefs could be isolated or disfavored if the state were to endorse any one set of religious beliefs over others, they became quiet about seeking a state religion, and the right to worship without interference from the state or any government was adopted as a foundation of U.S. democracy.

The Bible equates the Ten Commandments as the laws of liberty; if you are curious, take a look at Exodus 20:2.17, or Deuteronomy 5:6. The commandments define love as

---

[70] Virginia Historical Society. "Thomas Jefferson and the Virginia Statute for Religious Freedom." Virginia Museum of History and Culture, accessed April 3, 2020, http://www.virginiahistory.org/collections-and-resources/virginia-history-explorer/thomas-jefferson.

the foundation of all Godly relationships. Obeying God's commandments and practicing love are irrevocably linked in God's eyes. The Commandments are a guide for what we do, how we think, and how we live; they are keys to a successful and happy life. We know that for most of us, there are some things that are easier to follow than others, but we still know the difference between right and wrong. The Commandments are not multiple choice; they are equally important and work in unison with one another. As with the rights and responsibilities granted by our Constitution, in order to live morally, you can't choose just one or two and ignore the rest.

The glaring inconsistency between Christian doctrine and actual public policies emanating from Trump and his administration is no accident, nor is it due to any lack of understanding on his part. As a skilled opportunist, candidate Trump immediately recognized his chance to grasp hold of the religious conservative right by promising—and delivering—a list of potential Supreme Court nominees believed to be favorable to reversing Roe v. Wade, and thus fulfilling the Christian right's most sought-after objective. Any other principles of Christian faith be damned.

Corruptions of Christianity

> To the corruptions of Christianity, I am indeed, opposed: but not to the genuine precepts of Jesus himself. I am a Christian in the only sense in which He wished anyone to be; sincerely attached to His doctrines in preference to all others.
>
> —Thomas Jefferson, U.S. President and statesman, 1803

Thomas Jefferson confirmed his commitment to Christianity in a letter to his lifelong friend and confidant Dr.

Benjamin Rush.[71] Jefferson's words were a response to accusations by the religious zealots of his day, that he was inadequately Christian to be a suitable leader in the new nation. The infusion of religious dogma into the political agenda is not a new concept. Jefferson, an astute politician and philosopher, was a staunch advocate for democracy and freedom. He recognized the hypocrisy in the religious politics of his day and the attempts by religious and political leaders to capitalize on their self-professed godliness to sway trusting congregants to unquestioningly follow their lead. Jefferson understood the dangers of codifying a religion into the law and articulated his understanding and insight of those dangers in a bill he submitted to the Virginia Assembly on January 16, 1786:

> All mighty God has created the mind free... all attempts to influence it by temporal punishments or burden, or by civil incapacitations tend only to beget habits of hypocrisy and meanness. And are a departure from the plan of the holy author of religion, who being Lord over both the body and mind, yet chose not to propagate it by coercions on either, as was His almighty power to do, but to expand it, by its influence and reason alone.[72]

These were—and still are—sound words to be heeded by all who would impose religion into our law and our democratic form of government. These words should also be remembered by those who are vigilant in protecting against this kind of imposition. The religious demonization of Jefferson and the Democratic Republicans by the Federalists sorely tested our nation's foundation, and it is not

---

71 Thomas Jefferson, "From Thomas Jefferson to Benjamin Rush, 21 April 1803," *Founders Online*, National Archives, accessed April 3, 2020, https://founders.archives.gov/documents/Jefferson/01-40-02-0178-0001.

72 Thomas Jefferson, "A Bill for Establishing Religious Freedom, 18 June, 1779", *Founders Online*, National Archives, accessed April 3, 2020, https://founders.archives.gov/documents/Jefferson/01-02-02-0132-0004-0082.

unlike what we see happening today. At the turn of the nineteenth century, the major political factions were the Federalist Party led by George Washington and John Adams; and the Democratic Republican party led by then-Vice President Jefferson. Religious zealots attempted to firmly implant into the government a highly conservative Christian-based political philosophy. But mixing a single religious philosophy with government makes for a lousy cocktail, and some of the finest political minds in our history found it unpalatable. Fortunately for our country's religious freedom, in 1801 the electorate firmly rejected the Federalist agenda. It is one thing to practice religion and live by your faith's set of values; it is another to coerce others by limiting their opportunities unless they say they believe as you do.

    Within the first month of Trump's presidency, civil rights attorney Rachel Tiven, former president of Lambda Legal, warned that Trump's erosion of the separation between church and state was "an invitation to theocracy. It is the privileging of some religions over others, and an invitation by members of those religions to flaunt the law."[73] We agree, and we want to keep sounding that warning. Religions should work together in harmony. Ecumenism, which seeks unity among all the world's Christians regardless of differences, has its roots in several religious groups that crossed national barriers in the mid-nineteenth century. William Temple (1881–1944), Archbishop of Canterbury, famously said while the world was still under the shadow of World War II that ecumenism was, "the greatest new fact of our era." After centuries of separation and hostility, Christians had begun to capture the simple biblical truth that the people of God in the body of Christ must exemplify

---

73   Juliet Eilperin and Sandhya Somashekhar. "White House Considering Action on Religious Freedom That Critics Warn Could Lead to Discrimination", *Washington Post,* February 2, 2017, http://www.washingtonpost.com/631ea41a-e8ee-11e6-bf6f-301b6b443624_story.html.

in the world how God gathered people together from the ends of the earth to witness a new humanity, as described in the Gospel of Mark 13:27. Temple believed that church–state separation did not mean churches should remain silent and not act on social issues, but there is no indication he believed that churches should take over politics.

The fact is that the religious right provides foot soldiers for the GOP and Trump's agenda has a profound implication for Republican ideology beyond issues of religious freedom. Politicized religion provides a substrate of beliefs that rationalize, at least in the minds of its followers, all three of the GOP's main lines of power: wealth concentration, control of worship, and culture wars. Democracy and liberty can be lost to a nation of religious zealots. Don't get us wrong, we do not resent the fervently religious people of the world who exercise their freedom of speech and hope to convince others to believe as they do. Our objection is when they attempt to legislate a specific religious belief by calling for opt-out provisions from compliance with federal policy and regulations on the basis of religious dogma, as Trump and his administration have crusaded.[74] In addition, at the National Prayer Breakfast in Washington, D.C., in February 2019, Trump also vowed to eliminate the ban on political support by tax-exempt ministries that was enacted in 1954 to maintain the separation of church and state.

The danger here is that permitting such exceptions opens the floodgates to government acceptance of discrimination based on sex, sexual orientation and gender identity—and that's just a start—poorly masked as claims of "freedom of religion." Individual rights are threatened when religion is forced upon the people in the guise of government policy. Be it a woman's right to manage her own reproductive cycle, or a same-sex couple wanting a wedding

---

[74] Trump stated his support for the First Amendment Defense Act, as well as signing Executive Order 13798, "Promoting Free Speech and Religious Liberty."

cake from a business that is open to the public, allowing religion to infiltrate our government is to, "beget habits of hypocrisy and meanness," in Jefferson's words.

Moreover, acceptance of these kinds of policies or laws upends existing and often hard-earned protections for individuals and communities, including for LGBTQ individuals, family planning, abortion and reproductive rights. Human Rights Campaign President Chad Griffin stated that the "opt-out" provision, "reads like a wish list from some of the most radical anti-equality factions."[75] Trump's Executive Order 13798 prohibits penalizing or denying tax benefits to any person or organization who believes, acts or declines to act in accordance with certain religious/social beliefs, including (but not limited to): marriage is or should be recognized as the union of one man and one woman, sexual relations are properly preserved for such a marriage, male and female and their equivalents as referring to any individual are immutable and biological sex determined by anatomy, physiology, or genetics at or before birth, and a human life begins at conception. That E.O. 13798 is titled "Promoting Free Speech and Religious Liberty" makes us wonder what Donald Trump actually thinks about freedom and liberty.

We can't bring the dogma of our respective religions into the public domain or government (e.g. prayer in public schools). But we do not have to, nor should we, abdicate our individual religious beliefs to actively be involved in politics. To the contrary, we should be guided by those core values in everything we do, including selection and support of our leadership.

---

75 Miguel Granda, "Religious Liberty Should Not Be Violated", *The Reporter*, March 31, 2017, http://mdcthereporter.com. *The Reporter* is the student newspaper at Miami Dade College.

What Would Jesus Do?

> Somehow, I get puzzled when I see so many Christians living in luxury and singing, "Jesus, I my cross have taken, all to leave and follow Thee, ... It seems to me there's an awful lot of trouble in the world that somehow wouldn't exist if all the people who sing such songs went and lived them out. I suppose I don't understand. But what would Jesus do?
>
> —Charles Sheldon, minister and author, 1897

"What would Jesus do?" is more than a modern Christian motto stamped on a bracelet. In the late nineteenth century, Congregationalist minister and author Charles Sheldon used these words in his novel, *In His Steps: What Would Jesus Do?* They are spoken by a man who is homeless because of economic hard times. He is outside a church listening to the music coming from within, but he is not permitted to enter because of his low social standing and appearance.[76] His words highlight the hypocrisy of people who profess a set of values but don't seem to live by them. A person who can only feel that they stand tall if someone else is on their knees, is a shameful excuse for a human being—and it is certainly not what Jesus would do. Demonizing people for their race or ethnic affiliation, sexuality or gender identity is abhorrent. Donald Trump, however, does just this. He incited hatred, fear and racism to mobilize his base for the 2016 election. His presidential campaign was fraught with demonization of racial and ethnic groups and smears against women. Trump opened the floodgates for angry and fearful people to commit racist and hateful acts. Racist fanatical groups across the globe were emboldened by Trump's victory.

---

76 Charles Sheldon, *In His Steps: What Would Jesus Do?* [Advance Publishing, 1898]. Project Gutenberg, posted August 11, 2009, http://www.gutenberg.org/ebooks/4540/4540-h/4540-h.htm.

Under the guise of stemming excessive "political correctness," the man in the most powerful political position in the world incited a resurgence of overt racism, sexism and xenophobia as acceptable behavioral norms. Welcome to the Trump cesspool.

On December 13, 2016, Trump's transition team announced that Stephen Miller would serve as senior advisor for immigration policy. Miller is said to be the chief architect of Trump's anti-Muslim travel ban and his horrifying policy separating migrant and asylum-seeking children from their families. In November 2019, *Hatewatch,* an online publication of the Southern Poverty Law Center (SPLC) that monitors activities of the radical right, published a blog post by Michael Edison Hayden exposing the racist source materials that have influenced Miller's vision of American immigration policies. "In the run-up to the 2016 election, [Miller] promoted white nationalist literature, pushed racist immigration stories …", which included white nationalist websites, a white-genocide themed novel, xenophobic conspiracy theories and eugenic-era immigration laws that Adolf Hitler lauded in *Mein Kampf.*[77] The SPLC had acquired more than 900 emails sent from Miller to writer Katie McHugh of the far-right website *Breitbart News*, in 2015 and 2016. The emails were leaked by McHugh and became the basis for an expose that showed Miller's enthusiastic push for the views of white nationalist media including American Renaissance, VDARE and the far-right conspiracy website *Info Wars*, and promotion of the French novel *The Camp of the Saints*, a racist work of fiction popular with neo-Nazis. The emails showcase the extremist, anti-immigrant ideology that undergirds the policies

---

[77] Michael Edison Hayden, "Stephen Miller's Affinity for White Nationalism Revealed in Leaked Emails", *Hatewatch, Southern Poverty Law Center, November 12, 2019,* http://www.splcenter.org/hatewatch/2019/11/12/stephen-millers- affinity-white-nationalism-revealed-leaked-emails.

Miller has helped spawn as an architect and contributing member of the Trump Administration.

This anti-immigrant, white supremacist rhetoric is clearly designed to create or awaken deep-seated mistrust and hatred. Find an enemy and focus their attention on the enemy so they don't see what you're doing. This is an old trick that worked for lots of fascist leaders and dictators. Sowing this kind of discord among the brethren in our opinion is not in keeping with the tenets of most Christian faiths. And engaging in such action, especially to promote oneself in an election, constitutes an immoral act.

If that were it, we might be able put most of the blame for Trump's racist and xenophobic rhetoric on Miller. Unfortunately, there's more. Richard Spencer is arguably the most notorious white nationalist in America. He is also an ardent supporter of Trump. He helped build the "alt-right" movement and was a central figure in that 2017 "Unite the Right" rally in Charlottesville where a woman was killed by a neo-Nazi who accelerated his car into a group of counter-protestors. Spencer also heads the National Policy Institute (NPI), a white nationalist organization. At NPI's 2016 annual conference in Washington, DC, anti-immigrant activist Peter Brimelow gave a speech titled, "Trump's America." Brimelow is the author of the book, *Alien Nation: Common Sense about America's Immigration Disaster* and founder of the anti-immigrant website VDARE which warns that America is being polluted by people who are nonwhite, Catholic or Spanish-speaking immigrants. Miller knew both Spencer and Brimelow while an undergraduate at Duke University. Miller and Spencer were members of Duke's Conservative Union, a politically focused student organization. Spencer told *Mother Jones* magazine in October 2016, "It's funny no one's picked up on the Stephen Miller connection. I knew him very well when I was at Duke. But I am kind of glad no one talked about this because I don't want to harm Trump."[78] Spencer knew that Miller's association with the group had the potential to harm Trump politically. Spencer's comments are indicative of what is known in the law as "consciousness of guilt." The attitude of the white supremacist groups should be morally repugnant to all people of conscience.

In an audio recording released in November 2019 by former Breitbart editor Milo Yiannopoulos, a voice Yiannopoulos alleges to be Spencer's is heard spewing an anti-Semitic, racist rant: "Little f*****g kikes, they get ruled by people like me. Little f*****g octoroons!" and, "[M]y ancestors f*****g enslaved those f*****g pieces of s**t! I rule the f*****g world! Those people get ruled by people like me!" So much for Spencer's image as a dignified conservative intellectual; he is just another ranting bigot; ignorant, crude, and hate mongering.

Yiannopoulos, for his part, is British by birth and worked to bring white nationalism to American mainstream attention under an O–1 "extraordinary ability" temporary worker visa. He was editor of Breitbart until being forced out after making controversial statements about pedophilia. Miller has denied any relationship with Spencer or Brimelow. We're sure Miller would want to emulate his idol, Donald Trump, so he certainly wouldn't lie. In any case, Miller stands as a primary example of Trump's "cleaning up the swamp" by replacing it with a cesspool. Just as Jefferson recognized the hypocrisy of practicing political opportunism counter to proclaimed religious beliefs, so should we.

Most of Trump's Christian right supporters have not wavered even in the face of his most unchristian policies. Why? It seems to us that they are not guided by true Christian principles of

---

[78] Josh Harkinson, "Meet the White Nationalist Trying to Ride the Trump Train to Lasting Power", *Mother Jones,* October 27, 2016, http://www.motherjones.com/politics/2016/10/richard-spencer-trump-alt-right-white-nationalist/.

faith, hope, charity, love and forgiveness; but merely following their true instincts accepting Trump's lip service. How have the teachings and lessons of the most influential messengers and prophets of the world's faiths been lost in the hypocrisy of practice? How do people fail to understand the great message of love delivered by Abraham and Moses, Confucius, Mohammed, and Jesus? Where is the Gandhi, or King, or Mother Teresa, or Tutu of this century? We must all do much better to extinguish this blight on American society. We cannot continue to allow people like Trump to divide us. We can, and must, help all Americans get a fair shake. It is not a simplistic "them or us." We are all "us." More than six million Muslims live in the United States. For our non-Muslim readers and those who try to legislate out of fear of an entire religion by painting all believers with the same broad brush, ask yourself how many Muslims you know. Maybe getting to know some is what Jesus would do.

"We need not think alike to love alike," said Ferenc David, founder of the Unitarian Church and its first martyr. Reverend David wrote the "Patent of Toleration" issued in 1781 by Habsburg Emperor Joseph II. The patent extended religious freedom to non-Catholic Christians allowing Protestants to immigrate to Austria and hold jobs. There's no firm count of how many religions there are, but a good estimate seems to be approximately 4,200. A religion comprises a set of beliefs, values and practices, and believers are bound by their faith, which they show in their practices and actions. We are not trying to dictate to anyone how they should define what their religion is or what it should be. But we do know that ignorance breeds contempt.

Trump is doubling down and using the same racist rhetoric and divisive tactics for his 2020 campaign as he did for 2016. Will these tactics have the same impact especially since evangelicals have achieved a solid conservative majority on the Supreme Court? Will evangelicals stick with Trump in 2020? How many evangelicals will demand a return to a more civil discourse, moral leadership, policies consistent with Christian beliefs, and an end to the bigoted, racist rhetoric? We can just wait and see, or we can call out these hypocritical views and hope that some evangelicals will remember that they are Christians and try to live and act and vote accordingly.

A Moral and Religious People

> Our Constitution was made only for a moral and religious people. It is wholly inadequate to the government for any other.
>
> —John Adams, U.S. President and statesman, 1798

John Adams, our nation's second president and first vice president, understood that our system of government only works if there is general agreement that people will act morally, be truthful, and follow our basic social contract that, while founded in Christian faith beliefs, also assures that church and state remain separate and government not be bound to any religious law. The famous quote by Adams about "a moral and religious people" can on its own appear be a big "well done, founders!" for the trust they put in our future, and a pat on the back for modern-day Americans for managing to behave morally enough that our Constitution still works. We suggest taking a look at Adams words in context. In a letter to the officers of the Militia of Massachusetts, Adams wrote:

> But should the People of America once become capable of that deep ... simulation towards one another and towards foreign nations **which assumes the language of justice and moderation while it is practicing iniquity and extravagance,** and displays in the most captivating manner the charming pictures of candor, frankness and sincerity while it is rioting in rapine and insolence: this

country will be the most miserable habitation in the world. Because **we have no Government armed with power capable of contending with human passions unbridled by ... morality and religion.** Avarice, ambition, revenge or gallantry, would break the strongest cords of our Constitution as a whale goes through a net.[79] *[our emphasis]*

Adams was warning that hypocrisy is possibly the most dangerous threat to democracy. If we want to keep our system and freedoms, we can't allow deceitful leaders who pay lip service to our values and laws but don't feel they need to follow them. Our Constitution is not equipped for authoritarian government because it is based on common agreement of what is good and right. Accepting immoral people as our leaders means we risk becoming, "the most miserable habitation in the world." Trump's defenders appear to be more worried about their own political futures than protecting their country. This denigrates the oaths they took for the offices they hold. These actions cannot be classified as minor missteps or jokes or a series of novice misunderstandings.

It is worth reminding ourselves that the president and our elected representatives have sworn an oath of office to protect and defend the Constitution against all enemies foreign and domestic. Assumed in this oath is that they will also not become one of those enemies. With what we can see in the Trump cesspool, Adams was right on target. Unfortunately for us, now, the bad odor of hypocrisy wafting up from the cesspool is strong, and even when people are willing to get close enough to try to see what is going on, it is hard to see through all the muck.

Each of us can decide for ourselves what we want our

---

79   John Adams, "From John Adams to Massachusetts Militia, October 11, 1798", *Founders Online,* National Archives, accessed March 20, 2020, https://founders.archives.gov/documents/Adams/99-02-02-3102.

relationship with God to be. Every individual must live their life in accordance with the standards and morality they choose, whether based in faith or religion, or some other secular set of social beliefs. One thing that has confused us, though, is how so many people who claim to be pious Christians seem to have abandoned their Christian beliefs in favor of a person who clearly lacks the attributes of what most would consider a moral individual. One would think a moral person, especially one occupying the White House as our nation's leader, would exemplify a measure of decency consistent with the teachings of most Americans' core values. *Washington Post columnist Richard Cohen has written about the paradox of Trump and the religious right. Back in 2018, before much of the information about Trump's duplicity was made public and well before his impeachment, Cohen wrote an opinion piece critiquing some "knee-jerk" reactions to Trump's behavior, both pro and con. He noted that the pro-Trump reactions are more lasting and far more dangerous:*

> There is such a thing, we are told, as Trump Derangement Syndrome. It is an ideological version of a speech disorder, which causes certain people to denounce Trump in obscene ways. It has come over the likes of Robert De Niro and, when it came to Ivanka Trump, Samantha Bee. It has prompted others to call Trump a traitor, which is a slanderous accusation too often used for crass political reasons. Sen. Joseph McCarthy called the Roosevelt–Truman administrations "20 years of treason."
> Yet, the more dangerous variant of the syndrome is the willingness of most Republicans to support Trump no matter what. One of the first outbreaks of this occurred in the 2016 South Carolina Republican primary, which Trump won handily. He did so running against fellow Republicans, not the reliably useful Hillary Clinton. **He even swept the evangelical Christian vote, beating such**

> staunch conservatives as Sen. Ted Cruz (Tex.) and Ben Carson, both of whom have been married only once. The thrice-married Trump, in vivid contrast, had run casinos and exchanged countless smirky remarks with Howard Stern. *His piety was in question.* [80] [our emphasis]

Cohen questioned evangelical Christians' continued support of Trump despite numerous ways that Trump's actions seem to be in direct opposition to these Christians' stated values, including: accusations of sexual abuse and harassment by numerous women; paying off at least two women for their silence regarding his extramarital affairs; exchanging joking comments about harassing behavior with radio host Howard Stern; being recorded on a video, later revealed by *Access Hollywood,* bragging about being able to get away with grabbing women by their genitalia; belittling the wartime torture of Republican Senator John McCain, an American hero; referring to impoverished nations as "shithole countries;" praising heartless dictators and demagogues including Putin and North Korea's Kim Jong Un; and, his response to the May 2017 white supremacist rally in Charlottesville, Virginia, during which counter-protester Heather Heyer was killed by a neo-Nazi, validating the neo-Nazi movement by saying, "You also had people that were very fine people on both sides" of the protest that day. All we can say is, wow, that's some list, and not even close to complete.

A particular problem for this president is the commandment Thou Shall Not Bear False Witness, which is a prohibition against lying. Unfortunately, it appears that many evangelical Christian leaders and their followers have lost their moral compasses and fail

---

80 Richard Cohen, "Why People Like Trump", *Washington Post,* July 23, 2018, https://www.washingtonpost.com/36514540-8ea2-11e8-bcd5-9d911c784c38_story.html.

to find that the repeated flagrant violation of this commandment is any indication of Trump's complete lack of honesty and moral conscience. According to the *Washington Post* Fact Checker (Glenn Kessler, Salvador Rizzo, and Meg Kelly), in Trump's first three years in office, he made 16,241 verified public false statements, inaccuracies, and/or deliberate misrepresentations.[81] No one is perfect, we all speak an occasional exaggeration, or a small omission to keep from hurting somebody's feelings. However, Trump's lies are not to spare other people from pain or embarrassment, but instead to promote his own agenda and personal self-interest. Even considering just those lies that the public can actually verify, President Trump averages more than fourteen lies a day. The really sad part is that Trump lies even when there doesn't seem to be any reason for it. Maybe he just likes practicing "the art of the lie," as author Rick Cusick describes in his book, *The Art of the Lie: From Satan to Trump*.[82] Trump's behavior is pathological and dangerously seems to draw from the "big lie" concept in Adolph Hitler's *Mein Kampf*:

> … in the big lie there is always a certain force of credibility; because the broad masses of a nation are always more easily corrupted in the deeper strata of their emotional nature than consciously or voluntarily; and thus in the primitive simplicity of their minds they more readily fall victims to the big lie than the small lie, since they themselves often tell small lies in little matters but would be ashamed to resort to large-scale falsehoods. It would never come into their heads to fabricate colossal

---

81   Rebecca Klar, "Fact-checker Counts 16K False, Misleading Claims by Trump in Three Years", *The Hill*, January 20, 2020, https://thehill.com/homenews/administration/479041-fact-checker-counts-16k-false-misleading-claims-by-trump-in-three.

82   Rick Cusick, *The Art of the Lie: From Satan to Trump* (Trine Day, 2018).

untruths, and they would not believe that others could have the impudence to distort the truth so infamously.[83]

After three years in office, there is substantial evidence based on the president's words alone that should compel Trump supporters, or at least those supporters who claim to be moral and religious, to reconsider their loyalty.

We have been particularly dismayed by Trump's repeated inappropriate comments that objectify and in cases sexualize his own daughter, Ivanka. A story in *Cosmopolitan* magazine catalogued some of these statements, which, taken together, are especially repellent.[84] On the Howard Stern Show in 2003, Trump said of Ivanka, "She's got the best body." The following year Trump agreed when Stern described Ivanka as, "a piece of ass." In 2006 Trump appeared on the television show The View alongside Ivanka, and said of his daughter: "… she does have a very nice figure. I've said that if she weren't my daughter, perhaps I'd be dating her." The November 2016 *Cosmopolitan* article reported that according to BuzzFeed, a draft of an article by political columnist Richard Cohen for the Washington Post in 1995, when Ivanka was only 13, featured a quote from Trump in which he asked an unnamed associate "Is it wrong to be more sexually attracted to your own daughter than your wife?" The report says that line was removed from the column shortly before publication.[85] We don't know if Trump's statements were attempts to be provocative and generate publicity,

---

83 Susan Ratliffe, ed., *The Oxford Dictionary of Quotations* by Subject (Oxford University Press, 2000).
84 Helin Jung, "Donald Trump Once Allegedly Asked If It Was 'Wrong' to Be 'Sexually Attracted' to Ivanka. The Line was Reportedly Deleted from a Washington Post Column Before Publication", *Cosmopolitan*. November 22, 2016, http://www.cosmopolitan.com/politics/a8353161/donald-trump-sexual-attraction-ivanka-trump/.
85 Jung, "Trump Once Allegedly Asked."

or just show his deep-rooted moral turpitude. Regardless, all would agree that such statements are deplorable and not something that a normal father would say about his own daughter.

Morality in most instances has a direct correlation to our religious texts, such as the Bible (Christian), the Torah (Judaic), the Koran (Islam), Tripitaka (Buddhist), the Vedas (Hindu), and the Upanishads (Hindu/Indian philosophy). In the Bible's Old Testament, the Book of Proverbs provides the basic principles of a good Christian life. It describes seven sins the Lord abhors: "six things doth the Lord hate: yea seven are an abomination unto Him." (Proverbs 6:16–19). These are a proud look; a lying tongue; hands that shed innocent blood; a heart that devises wicked plans; feet that are swift in running to evil; a false witness who speaks lies; and, one who sows discord among brethren. A credible argument can be made that, as president of the United States, Trump may be in the "abomination" category, and we have just a few of many possible examples to explain why.

A Proud Look

Pride in this sense is a "me-first" spirit and a lack of respect for others. When our hearts are prideful, we don't credit God or feel the need to follow rules. We mistreat people, looking down on them and thinking we are entitled to more than others. That it is acceptable to denigrate other people, whether in jest or mean spiritedness. To us one of the most egregious examples of Trump's overdeveloped sense of pride occurred on July 28, 2016 at a campaign rally in North Carolina during which Trump mocked reporter Serge Kovaleski by performing an unflattering impression of him. Kovaleski suffers from a congenital joint condition that affects his movement and speech. Trump pointedly flopped his own right arm with his hand at an odd angle and mockingly imitated

Kovaleski's speech pattern. This is but one example of Trump's many instances of abhorrent behavior demonstrating his "proud look" when comparing himself to others. We initially wanted to counter Trump's insulting behavior by mocking his own misplaced vanity, but we decided not to stoop to his level.

A Lying Tongue

"The Donald" committed more than 16,000 documented falsehoods in his first three years in office, and continues to do so. The count just goes up and up and up. Trump lies every day in one form or another, averaging between fourteen and fifteen public lies per day. We do not have enough paper to list all of them, but if you can stomach it, check out *The Washington Post* online database of Trump's falsehoods or the Poynter Institute's PolitiFact initiative, "All False Statements involving Donald Trump."[86] Just know that his lying knows no bounds: he tells lies about everything. About people he knows and doesn't know, about things he has said publicly, about events that happened and were witnessed by other people, even about the weather! He bears false witness and destroys lives. To say that this is reprehensible is an understatement. Many of his lies are direct illustrations of the five other deceitful things that the Lord despises.

Hands That Shed Innocent Blood

Trump's policies have separated children from their asylum-

---

86   Glenn Kessler, Salvador Rizzo, and Meg Kelly, "President Trump Has Made 15,413 False or Misleading Claims Over 1,055 Days", *Washington Post,* December 10, 2019, https://www.washingtonpost.com/politics/2019/12/16/president-trump-has-made-false-or-misleading-claims-over-days/; and, "Donald Trump", PolitiFact, Poynter Institute, accessed January 3, 2020, http://www.politifact.com/personalities/donald-trump/.

seeking parents at our southern border and not ensured they will ever be reunited. It has been well documented that the treatment of these immigrants and asylum seekers has been deplorable. According to the government's own reports at least seven of these children have died while in U.S. custody, reportedly as a result of neglect. The president's policies concerning immigrants and his fearmongering statements at rallies and press conferences, have stirred up the crazies. Horrifying acts of hatred such as the killing of Hispanics in public venues and the murder of Jewish worshippers in their synagogue are unconscionable. Considering Trump's hiring of immigrants, documented and otherwise, in his hotel and golf course businesses, we believe he probably has never cared about an influx of immigrants as long as they provided him with cheap labor. We further believe his current stance against granting asylum to immigrants is just political pandering to his base for re-election purposes. People are being treated inhumanely and dying for Trump's self-interest, and he does not seem to care. We are aware that our nation's borders need to be protected and can't be freely open, but we see no justification for the immigration policies implemented by this administration that promote cruelty and inhumane treatment of people who are willing to leave everything they know and have to save their families.

A Heart That Devises Wicked Plans

Trump exhibits a propensity to incite violence with his demagoguery and hateful rhetoric. In a number of Trump's earlier rallies, he suggested to his supporters that they punch dissenters out and not worry about it—he'd pay the legal fees. At a 2016 campaign rally he shouted to the crowd that perhaps a Black Lives Matter protester should have been roughed up. To put innocent people's lives at risk simply to win an election is beyond the pale of decency and certainly outside the bounds of any Christian belief or philosophy that we know of. He has incited "crazies" to send bombs to harm his detractors and political critics. After the number of times this has happened, Trump should be fully aware that every time he spouts off his inflammatory rhetoric about a given group or person, he encourages these targeted attacks. These "wicked plans" that incite people to violence should not be the behavior of a man who suggested that when elected he would uphold the rule of law as our president is sworn to do. We won't get started here on Trump's "wicked plans" leading to his impeachment, that's another chapter in this book.

A False Witness Who Speaks Lies

We consider Trump's treatment of former FBI Director Andrew McCabe one of the worst cases of Trump's bearing false witness and telling lies about a fellow human. The president had McCabe fired from his position as FBI director just 48 hours before McCabe's pension for his years of government service would have gone into effect. McCabe's mistake was doing the job he was sworn to do rather than doing what Trump wanted him to do. McCabe initiated the investigation into Russian interference in the 2016 presidential election—the investigation that Trump continues to call a "hoax," a fabricated story by partisan "deep state" operatives from the Democratic Party. Talk about false witness! There are truthful, reliable witnesses who have attested that Trump not only knew about the Russian interference in the 2016 election, but that he allegedly told the Russian ambassador that he didn't have a problem with it. While it may not be so out of the ordinary for a person to try to get even with someone who is pointing out their inconsistencies and potential wrongdoing, it is not permissible under the law in this situation, and it is not behavior befitting our nation's leader. It is also not very Christian, although Christian conservatives don't seem to notice. Trump has even tried to get Attorney General Barr to file criminal charges against McCabe. To date, Barr has had three sets of investigators trying to come up with something. So far, they can't seem to find anything to charge him with, although the word is that they're still trying. In addition, on April 3 Trump fired the inspector general for the intelligence community, Michael Atkinson, for having the audacity/integrity to do his job and follow the law. Atkinson, as was his duty, had informed lawmakers about a whistleblower complaint about President Trump's dealings with Ukraine. The complaint triggered impeachment hearings last fall.

Trump has reportedly also had Barr open up a new investigation into Hillary Clinton's emails and retroactively re-classified them as "top secret" communications three years later. An obvious attempt to charge that classified emails were sent using Clinton's personal computer even though they were not "top secret" at the time they were sent. This is a shell game. It is like paying off a debt to someone using marked bills, and then using those marked bills as evidence to claim that person stole the money from you. Bearing false witness?

One Who Sows Discord Among His Brethren

Among Trump's many discord-sowing declarations are: "Ban the Muslims;" Hispanic asylum seekers and immigrants "are invading our country" and are "rapists and murderers; "Go back to the shithole countries you came from and do something there;" "Democrats hate our country;" "Any Jew who votes for a Democrat is a traitor to Israel;" "She's a low-IQ person;" and, the horrifying and infamous, "When you're a star you can do anything you want with women—grab them by the pussy." All of these are incendiary, not to mention insulting, sexist and bigoted. They are designed to promote fear and hate. Trump is a leader with no moral compass. We find it astounding that a man of such deplorable character was elected to the presidency. Throughout his tenure as president, Trump's response to criticism has been to deflect it by sowing confusion and doubt about any and all allegations. He is a tyrant in a nation founded in opposition to tyrannical rule. Remember that it was the debunked "birther" conspiracy which claimed Barack Obama had been born in Kenya and thus was ineligible for the presidency that began the political career of Donald J. Trump. Even after that was shown to be a complete fabrication, Trump continued to push for political advantage with the bigots of the world.

Feet That Are Swift in Running to Evil

Trump shows no moral qualms or judgment in seeking relationships with leaders of the world who are known to be cruel dictators and untrustworthy allies. He has been "swift" in his running to establish ties to world leaders whose practices are abhorrent to democratic values and the basic tenets of Christianity. Trump has courted and repeatedly praised authoritarian leaders and despots who oppress their people, silence their opponents and rule by intimidation, including Putin, Kim Jung Un, and Turkey's President Tayyip Erdogan.

For more on this, please refer to the ultimate authority on the subject matter of morality and Christian values: Scripture, starting with Romans 12:19, Psalms 37:8, Proverbs 14:29 and 15:1, Ephesians 4:26-27, Colossians 3:8, and James 1:19-20). God gave us free will. It is time for the soul-searching to begin. Question authority, for too long we have failed to challenge self-serving, ungodly religious and political leaders many of whom have garnered great wealth and power as a result. As American poet and philosopher Ralph Waldo Emerson said, the enduring importance of civic engagement to making sure we have moral leadership is "that the punishment which the wise suffer who refuse to take part in the government, is, to live under the government of worse men."[87] This is where we are now, suffering under the governance of "worse men."

That Which is False and Dangerous

> In our country there are evangelists and zealots of many different political, economic and religious persuasions whose fanatical conviction is that all thought is divinely classified into two kinds—that which is their own and that which is false and dangerous.
> —Robert H. Jackson, U.S. Supreme Court Justice, 1950

Justice Robert Jackson sat on the U.S. Supreme Court from 1941 until his death in 1954. His words above about evangelists and zealots were a warning against seeing the world as only "us" and "them," and defining the people we label "them" as, by nature, wrong or evil. He was clearly troubled and concerned with the adverse effects that demagoguery and isolation of any particular group may have on society. Justice Jackson knew what he was talking about. His statement was made in the wake of World War II and the damage caused by fascism's propaganda machine and the rise of communist totalitarian states. He was appointed to be the U.S. Chief Counsel for the prosecution of Nazi war criminals in the Nuremburg trials. In his opinion regarding free speech, Jackson said: "The choice is not between order and liberty. It is between

---

87   Ralph Waldo Emerson, *The Works of Ralph Waldo Emerson*, in 12 vols. Fireside Edition (1909), Online Library of Liberty, The Liberty Fund, accessed December 20, 2019, http://oll.libertyfund.org/titles/86.

liberty with order and anarchy without either. There is a danger that, if the court does not temper its doctrinaire logic with a little practical wisdom, it will convert the constitutional Bill of Rights into a suicide pact."[88]

From our perspective, it is not only the president's moral turpitude that alarms us, but also that of the political leaders, evangelical leaders and others who enable this president by turning a blind eye and acquiescing to the deception Trump inflicts on the nation and the world. Is this the "suicide pact" that Jackson warned us about? We view these enablers as hypocrites, especially when they rationalize their positions, directly or implicitly, to claim that people who have a different cultural background or sexuality are violating the word of God because of their differences and therefore need to be restrained, restricted and/or punished.

How many people viewed the altered videos or received emails or social media notifications with false claims about former Secretary of State and Senator Hillary Clinton and her position on abortion? Like a ripped feather pillow released to the wind, once loose, you can never take it all back. At the September 2016 Texas Tribune Festival held in Austin, GOP Senator and presidential candidate Ted Cruz publicly claimed that Clinton, "Supports unlimited abortion on demand, up until the moment of birth, including partial-birth abortion, with taxpayer funding," a gross misstatement and intentional distortion of Clinton's views. Just a month before the election, an article in *Rolling Stone* asserted that vice presidential candidate Pence's allegation during a televised debate that Clinton supported so-called "partial birth" abortions was, "… inaccurate because 'partial birth' is a term made up by (anti-choice) activists to make abortions seem gruesome."[89] In the article, political reporter Bridgette Dunlap noted the cruelty of pro-

---

88   Terminiello v. Chicago, 1949.
89   Bridgette Dunlap, "Mike Pence's Casual Cruelty on Abortion at the VP

lifers, and Pence in particular, in deploying the term to describe all late-term abortions, when actually the procedure is, "usually performed when something has gone terribly wrong," and the term vilifies women who are often facing the loss of a wanted pregnancy. The article clarified the law and Clinton's position: "States are free to ban abortion after viability which occurs at about 24 week's gestation—and they do. That's been the law for over 40 years and that's what Hillary Clinton supports." But the misinformation had already been televised, the damage done.

    That's just one of many examples of the deceit, lies and obfuscations conducted in the 2016 election cycle, much of it done through social media and the Russians to assist Trump's election. These facts were proven by the information in the Mueller Report and confirmed by U.S. intelligence agencies. Yet Trump continually denies this, and even three years later is attempting to redirect blame away from Russia and onto the Ukrainian government. Once again, we ask ourselves why the president would do this and why "we the people" are letting it happen.

    All of us should ask: Has Mr. Trump ever exhibited braggadocio, misogynistic, narcissistic or maniacal tendencies, or is he simply a man who practices the teaching of "love thy neighbor" as you would a porn star, playboy bunny, Miss America contestant, or strange woman on an airplane? We should question why this is the person that many of the Christian right have designated their "Chosen One," and why many Christian evangelists deem him "savior" for the world. We have a serious problem with this. It's remarkable that even with all of the information available, many professed Christians do not question Trump's behavior and in the minds of many Trump supporters, none of this really matters. After all, Trump has declared himself, "The Chosen One," others have

---

Debate", *Rolling Stone*, October 5, 2016, https://www.rollingstone.com/politics/politics-features/mike-pences-casual-cruelty-on-abortion-at-the-vp-debate-119955/.

accepted that, and at the very least, he's the one the evangelicals have chosen to lead our nation. And for those people who have chosen to follow "The Donald," we know in our heart of hearts that the good Lord and Savior, Jesus, is right there with you, every step of the way, as you pave the way to the pearly gates of hell. Our greatest concern, though, is that many of you are trying to drag the rest of us right along with you. The two of us assuredly do not want to go that route, and that is a big reason we have written this book.

For our generation, the acceptance of the kind of deceit we are witnessing among political and religious leaders is referred to as "drinking the Kool-Aid." For those of you in younger generations not familiar with the term or its origin, allow us to provide you with a few facts about the phrase—and at the same time a lesson on the dangers of false prophets. Jim Jones was an ordained preacher, faith healer and cult leader. He was ordained by two faiths: the Independent Assemblies of God, and the Disciples of Christ. Jones later launched his own organization called "The People's Temple," in the 1950s. In 1976 he left the United States with many members of his congregation to live in a jungle commune in the small South American country of Guyana. In 1978 there were media reports of human rights abuses in The People's Temple. U.S. Representative Leo Ryan of California led a delegation of reporters, a camera crew, and relatives of temple members to the commune to investigate. After an attempt on Ryan's life and while he and his delegation were attempting to leave the commune and board planes to return to the United States, they were fired upon by Jones' security forces. Ryan and four others in the delegation were killed. Jones then coerced a mass suicide of 918 cult members by telling them to drink cyanide-poisoned Kool-Aid (or some other powdered drink mix); of the 304 children who died, most likely drank the Kool-Aid without really understanding what they were doing. Anyone who refused to drink the Kool-Aid was shot under Jones orders. This is the danger of following the immoral leadership of false prophets.

Jones did not come out of nowhere, and before The People's Temple, Jones had kept company with some widely known Christian evangelists with large followings. In 1956, Jones had organized a mammoth religious convention and shared the pulpit with Reverend William M. Branham, a healing evangelist and religious author highly revered as the more famous Reverend Oral Roberts. Roberts, for his part, is known for trying to extort money from his parishioners by telling them that God was going to call him home if he wasn't able to raise two million dollars, and it was rumored that he wanted the money to buy a jet for his personal use. We don't think he got the money, and God apparently changed His mind and decided He didn't want him to come home after all. We do not see these as the actions of true Godly men.[90]

Many evangelicals have been disillusioned by previous presidents including Jimmy Carter, Ronald Reagan and George W. Bush. Why? It is because those presidents did not deliver on reversing the downward trajectory of evangelism. American culture has not been trending towards alignment with the conventional conservative evangelical beliefs. To the contrary, the approvals of same-sex marriage and support for women's reproductive rights and legal abortion have increased, while membership in religious institutions and specific religious affiliations are steadily falling. Many evangelicals ultimately aligned with Trump in the 2016 election because they needed a change, deciding that as flawed as Trump's character is, politically he was preferable to Hillary Clinton. It has been widely reported that 81 percent of

---

90 For more information on Jones and the People's Temple, see the 1978 *New York Times* article, "Jim Jones: From Poverty to Power of Life and Death," and the 2007 *American Experience* documentary, "Jonestown: The Life and Death of People's Temple."

all evangelicals voted for Trump, but that figure is somewhat misleading and actually represents only older, white evangelicals. Since 59 percent of white evangelicals voted, it means about 48 percent of all white evangelicals voted for Trump – although they do make up a large and influential proportion of President Trump's base of support.[91]

Not all evangelicals support conservative Republicans. A small number of progressive evangelicals have campaigned for issues usually aligned with liberal causes and social justice, such as criminal justice reform, a living wage for workers, and ending predatory lending. Many younger evangelicals have parted ways from their mainstream on issues such as immigration. This group is more racially and economically diverse than evangelicals overall, and generally younger than the bulk of those who support Trump. Unfortunately, these evangelicals with a social conscience are far from a majority. Only about 20 percent of young evangelicals did not vote for Trump, and evangelicals generally remain a very solid voting block committed to the GOP agenda and willing to support Trump.

It is a matter of conjecture whether Trump sincerely speaks for conservative evangelicals or is just mouthing the talking points they want to hear. Let's just call it a co-dependency. For the most part many evangelicals dispensed with demonstrating any hint of personal Christian values and instead seem focused on trying to reverse the decline of evangelical influence on American culture. These evangelicals eye a potential cultural transformation to a culture in which there's no room for liberal beliefs. Reproductive rights are a serious issue for both pro-choice and anti-abortion

---

91   Many sources have stated that 81 percent of evangelicals voted for or support Trump. But that figure actually represents the percentage of self-identified white, born again/evangelical Christians who voted for Trump over Clinton in 2016, and equates to only 48 percent of all white evangelicals in the United States.

advocates, with little, if any, chance for compromise. For single issue voters, abortion rights can be one of the most powerful determining issues. The evangelicals have gained two conservatives on the Supreme Court and hope that the court will reverse Roe v. Wade and make abortion illegal again. We believe it is for this reason alone that most evangelicals and pro-life voters are willing to overlook Trump's serious flaws and questionable morality.

"Mike Pence's Secret Christian Empire is now in Charge of Public Health", was the headline of an article in *Raw Story* on March 6, 2020:

> The most unnerving aspect of the government's response (to COVID-19) so far has not been Trump's gibberish. He is in over his head and it shows, as usual. And we know from his response to Hurricane Maria and other natural disasters that his only concern in a crisis is his own political well-being. But I wouldn't have expected to hear the director of the CDC, Robert Redfield, laud Trump like a Fox news pundit. … Redfield is well known for recommending measures that were considered extreme even within the Reagan administration, including the forced quarantine of AIDS patients. He later had a financial interest in an HIV vaccine that didn't work, but he continued to push.[92]

The U.S. Surgeon General, Dr. Jerome Adams, is also a member of the COVID-19 task force. He is closely connected to Vice President Pence. Adams previously served as the Indiana state

---

92   Heather Digby Parton, "Mike Pence's Secret Christian Empire is Now in Charge of Public Health," *Raw Story*, March 9, 2020, https://www.rawstory.com/2020/03/mike-pences-secret-christian-empire-is-now-in-charge-of-public-health. Originally published in *Salon* as, "Is the Christian Right Now in Charge of Public Health Inside the Trump Administration?", March 9, 2020, https://www.salon.com/2020/03/09/is-the-christian-right-now-in-charge-of-public-health-inside-the-trump-administration/.

health commissioner. According to Ms. Parton, he was intimately involved in the response to the HIV outbreak in Indiana, where Pence refused to authorize a needle exchange program until a large number of people had died, in some people's opinion, unnecessarily. Trump appointed Adams surgeon general and appointed his anti-science vice president, Pence, to head the novel coronavirus task force. Redfield and Birx are both evangelical Christians and have been involved in the Children's Aid Fund International which lobbies for abstinence-only sex education for teens around the world. It is not preposterous to think that Pence is of the opinion that COVID-19 is simply God's will, that prayer alone is the only answer.

To be clear, Birx, Redfield and Adams all have impeccable medical credentials and an abundance of relevant experience to qualify them for their positions on the task force. But, as Heather Parton points out, it is obvious that Trump wants the team of Fauci, Birx, Redfield and Adams to cover up his own ignorance and incompetence, which is totally at odds with what these team members must know is best for the health of the American public. And even they have been vilified by the conservative press. A March 28 post by Dave Hodges on *The Common Sense Show* called Fauci, "far and away the most dangerous figure in America today."[93] A few days later on *Gateway Pundit* (tagline: "We report the truth and leave the Russia-Collusion fairy tale to the Conspiracy media"), Jim Hoft criticized Birx, albeit oddly: "Is Dr. Birx, the doctor with the scarf, a voice of reason or another Deep State doctor pushing economic disaster and suffering? ... Her past unfortunately

---

93   Dave Hodges, "Fauci's Research Fraud Endangers Every Life In America and Will Lead to the Complete Collapse of the Economy," *The Common Sense Show*, March 28, 2020, https://thecommonsenseshow.com/conspiracy-health-martial-law/faucis-research-fraud-endangers-every-life-america-and-will-lead-complete-collapse-economy.

provides the answer."[94] The "past" that Hoft referred to pointed to a *Washington Post Magazine* article which noted that Birx's husband had worked for President Clinton and that Birx had been President Obama's global AIDS coordinator – a position she also held in the Trump administration.[95] Having any connection to Clinton or Obama might be a kiss of death in the Trump circus tent.

Does the subculture of evangelical Christians clustered around the vice president truly believe that Trump is "The Chosen One" blinding them to communicate honestly with the American people about this crisis? Early on, as the crisis was evolving that appeared to be the case. Now, it appears more likely that they have been tolerating Trump's inane utterances to at least remain inside the tent to try to sway the president's opinions. It is difficult to say.

Where There Is Hatred

Lord,
Make me an instrument of your peace;
Where there is hatred, let me sow love;
Where there is injury, pardon;
Where there is doubt, faith;
Where there is despair, hope;
Where there is darkness, light;
Where there is sadness, joy.
O Divine Master,

---

94   Jim Hoft, "EXCLUSIVE: Dr. Birx's Connections with the Clinton Foundation and Obama Unfortunately Indicate Conflicted Loyalties", *Gateway Pundit*, March 31, 2020, https://www.thegatewaypundit.com/2020/03/exclusive-dr-birxs-connections-with-the-clinton-foundation-and-obama-unfortunately-indicate-conflicted-loyalties/.

95   Emily Bass, "Can Deborah Birx Save Us?" *Washington Post Magazine*, March 26, 2020, https://www.washingtonpost.com/magazine/2020/03/26/can-deborah-birx-save-us-coronavirus/.

Grant that I may not so much seek
To be consoled, as to console;
To be understood, as to understand;
To be loved, as to love;
For it is in giving that we receive.
It is pardoning that we are pardoned,
And it is in dying that we are born to eternal life.
Amen.

—Anonymous, "The Prayer of Saint Francis"

We are not holy men nor rabbis nor priests, but we are men of faith. We believe that our God will judge each of us on what we have done to improve the lives of others. We are all responsible for fortifying the moral compass of our beloved nation after three years of hateful rhetoric and actions. We do not hate Donald Trump and instead we do our best to hear and take to heart "The Prayer of Saint Francis." Nobody knows for sure who wrote this prayer, but it appeals to our best selves and urges us to fight our worst instincts with some positive thinking and forgiveness. We have no affiliation with a specific church or religious group, but to us this prayer has universal appeal for hope. We love our God and believe in His/Her sons Jesus Christ, Moses, Abraham, Mohammed, Confucius, Buddha, Gandhi, and His/Her daughter Mother Teresa. We believe the God of Abraham, Ishmael, Isaac, and Moses is the same God of Mohammed, Jesus and Buddha. Allah is a name to use for "he who has no name." As such, we are all ultimately accountable for any injury or wrongdoing we inflict on any of the children of His/Her creation.

When Trump turned his head and looked into the sky and declared, "I am the chosen one!" we wondered exactly what the evangelical and Christian right thought about his declaration. We wondered if it even mattered to anybody! After all, Trump might be right in some way. On November 24, 2019, on Fox News, Energy Secretary Rick Perry affirmed, "President Trump, you are the Chosen One."[96] The politically minded Christian right has, essentially, chosen Donald Trump to represent their pet causes. They have chosen him to be their savior of their close-held belief that abortion rights and the Roe v. Wade decision must be overturned at any and all costs, regardless of the sacrifice of our democratic values or the consequences to our democracy and individual rights. It appears some Christians believe that ensuring a conservative Supreme Court willing to get rid of reproductive rights is worth overlooking a significant number of not-so-minor departures from Christian theology.

In the words of Elie Wiesel: "The opposite of love is not hate, it's indifference. The opposite of art is not ugliness, its indifference. The opposite of faith is not heresy, its indifference. And, the opposite of life is not death, its indifference." That quote is from a speech given by Wiesel, an American novelist, political activist and a Holocaust survivor who received the Nobel Peace Prize in 1986 in appreciation of his universal condemnation of violence, hatred and oppression.[97] The Nobel committee praised Wiesel as a "messenger to mankind." Indifference is to do nothing and not care about what is happening. We don't give spiritual guidance, but our advice is based on our own faith, morality, and principles. And so, we advise: Do not be indifferent; Question political leaders and religious authorities. Find out what they really stand for and what they truly believe. Do not be deceived. The Kool-Aid rhetoric has been mixed

---

96   Eugene Scott. "Comparing Trump to Jesus, and Why Some Evangelicals Believe Trump is God's Chosen One", *Washington Post*, December 18, 2019, http://www.washingtonpost.com/politics/2019/11/25/why-evangelicals-like-rick- perry-believe-that-trump-is-gods-chosen-one/.
97   Elie Wiesel, "The Perils of Indifference", speech given at The White House, April 12, 1999, video, http://youtu.be/JpXmRiGst4k.

and is being doled out to a lot of thirsty people. Please, don't drink this "Kool-Aid!!!!"; don't drink the Clorox or Lysol either!

God created mankind in his/her own image and likeness. So, you don't have a problem with punishing, torturing or killing God's creations? Good Lord, where does it stop!!! Hate the Blacks, hate the Jews, hate the Catholics, hate the Mormons, hate the Muslims, hate the Pentecostals, hate the Mexicans, hate the brown people, hate LGBTQ people, hate the poor, and hate the rich if they don't agree with you. What books are you reading that say this is right? Who are you listening to that encourages such hate? Make no mistake; we are in a fight for the soul of the United States. Practicing bigotry, racism, misogyny is not among the desirable traits of anyone who represents those who truly practice the faith of the world's major religions in their diverse forms. This is a difficult time for religion. Many righteous Christian leaders are especially dismayed by how many in their ranks have rallied behind Trump despite the fact that Jesus is very clear on how we are supposed to treat people different from ourselves, and in support of Trump's hateful statements and actions that are just the opposite.

Most clergy are sincere, moral, spiritual men and women, and it appears there are still some spiritually minded evangelical Christians who are willing to speak out to defend the tenets of the faith. Recently, there is evidence that some evangelicals are turning away from the immorality of Mr. Trump. Mark Galli, editor in chief of the evangelical magazine *Christianity Today* and a respected biblical scholar, declared in a December 19, 2019, editorial: "The president of the United States attempted to use his political power to coerce a foreign leader to harass and discredit one of the president's political opponents. This is not only a violation of the Constitution, more importantly, it is profoundly immoral."[98]

---

98   Mark Galli. "Trump Should Be Removed From Office", *Christianity Today*,

Galli argued that given the magazine's position on the behavior and impeachments of Presidents Nixon and Clinton, it would be inconsistent in its Christian views if it supported Trump:

> To the many evangelicals who continue to support Mr. Trump in spite of his blackened moral record, we say this: Remember who you are and whom you serve. ... That he should be removed, we believe, is not a matter of partisan loyalties but loyalty to the Creator of the Ten Commandments. ... [T]he whole game will come crashing down on the reputation of evangelical religion and on the world's understanding of the gospel. And it will come crashing down on a nation of men and women whose welfare is also our concern.[99]

We hope that this condemnation of the president has started a discussion among evangelicals concerning whether they are damaging their own religious values and credibility. While it is highly unlikely that much of President Trump's evangelical base will be swayed by Galli's editorial, even if only a small number of Trump supporters split off it could deprive him of another term. *Christianity Today* is one of the most influential publications for evangelicals, and has criticized Trump and his policies on immigration in the past. The editorial in *Christianity Today* has advocated for Trump's ouster. This public statement reveals that there is discontent among a growing number of evangelical Christians who can no longer justify the cost to their moral conviction for making a deal with this "devil."

Beyond politics, we are truly indifferent to what happens to Donald Trump as a fellow man. Once he is evicted from the White

---

December 19, 2019, https://www.christianitytoday.com/ct/2019/december-web-only/trump-should-be-removed-from-office.html.
99   Galli, "Trump Should Be Removed."

House we do not care if he takes remedial reading classes; we do not care if he gets intensive, long-term psychiatric treatment; we do not care if he is able to avoid jail (well, we are trying not to care); we do not care if he tweets his way back to Florida and declares bankruptcy six more times. "Because power corrupts, society's demands for moral authority and character increases as the importance of the position increases," as the words of John Adams warn us.[100] We really don't care where he goes as long as he doesn't stay in the White House.

---

100   Attribution unconfirmed but see: "John Adams", MetroWest Daily News, last updated March 16, 2017, https://www.metrowestdailynews.com/special/20170316/john-adams.

CHAPTER 4

ECONOMIC PAIN AND GAIN

We continue to recognize the greater ability of some to earn more than others. But we do assert the ambitions of the individual to obtain for himself a proper security, a reasonable leisure, and a decent living throughout life, is an ambition to be preferred to the appetite for great wealth and great power.

—Franklin Delano Roosevelt, president (1935)

There's class warfare, all right—but it's my class, the rich class, that's making war, and we're winning.

—Warren Buffett, business magnate and philanthropist, 2006

TRUMP AND THE REPUBLICANS IN CONGRESS are running their 2020 campaigns in large part on the professed strength of the U.S. economy (before the dramatic downturn as a result of the novel coronavirus) but the reality is that only the wealthiest 10 percent reap the benefits of the stock market. Trump will claim that he and only he will be able to restore our economy to its pre-COVID-19 glory. In fact, for most Americans our economy was far from glorious.

Warren Buffett, who in 2019 was third from the top of the Forbes 400 list of wealthiest Americans, is aware that the existing tax structure benefits the wealthiest at the expense of everyone else, calling it "class warfare" initiated by the rich. (In 2006 Buffett was number two on the list). The rest of the population is being fed a line of propaganda, and forced to eat it. Yes, there will always be some people who can and do earn more than others, as President Franklin Roosevelt noted at the height of the Great Depression, but in saying this he was also making the distinction between wealth and greed. In this chapter we show the enormity of this inequality, the timetable over which it has occurred, the effects, and the government's role in all of this.

The income and wealth inequality in the United States that has existed for a long time is rapidly getting worse under the Trump administration. Those at the top of the pyramid—major shareholders and CEOs—are gaining more wealth, while employees and workers are increasingly struggling. "For decades large corporations have sought to ensure that the majority of economic gains are absorbed by executives and shareholders—not employees, who are the backbone of the American economy," according to research released by the Center for American Progress in August 2019.[101] Our economic system is unfair. This chapter looks at how we got here, how bad the situation really is, and Donald Trump's contributions to more economic inequality. If we are to be moral people who practice the values we preach, we can, and we must, demand change.

What's enough? How much income and wealth does any one person need? It is estimated that nearly one third of the total U.S. population, 100 million Americans, live at or near the poverty level. Since 1979 income gains at the top dwarf those of low- and middle-income households. Income gains were 226 percent for the top one percent between 1979 and 2016. Wealth is even more concentrated than income. The Federal Reserve Board's Survey of Consumer Finance (SCF) is conducted every three

---

[101] Saharra Griffin and Malkie Wall, "President Trump's Anti-Worker Agenda," Center for American Progress, August 28, 2019, https://www.americanprogressaction.org/issues/economy/reports/2019/08/28/174893/president-trumps-anti-worker-agenda/.

years. According to the SCF, in 2016 the top one percent owned 39 percent of total wealth in the United States and the next nine percent owned an additional 39 percent of the total wealth. In other words, the wealthiest 10 percent of the population held 78 percent of the wealth. The remaining 90 percent of the population was left with a total of 22 percent of the wealth.[102] Concentration at the top has risen since the 1980s and the gap will be even more dramatic when the 2019 SCF survey is published later this year and reveals the effects of the 2017 tax cuts. This ever-widening income and wealth disparity certainly raises questions about fairness and about whether we truly are a free market capitalistic economy driven by the consumer.

OUR INCOMES ARE LIKE OUR SHOES

> Our incomes are like our shoes; if too small, they gall and pinch us; but if too large, they cause us to stumble and trip.
>
> —attributed to John Locke, political philosopher, Seventeenth Century

The popular aphorism that our incomes will burden us if either too large or too small has been attributed to Enlightenment philosopher John Locke. It refers to the different sets of problems people face with either not enough or excessive income. It suggests that those at the top of the income pyramid are liable to stumble and fall, morally and as leaders, when their wealth is so great that they are out of step with everyone else, not to mention losing perspective on their own actual needs.[103] Those who lack sufficient income feel the pain of it in every step they take—and it is hard

---

102 "Survey of Consumer Finances", Board of Governors of the Federal Reserve System, July 23, 2018, http://www.federalreserve.gov/econres/scfindex.htm.
103 This quote is commonly attributed to John Locke (1632-1704) English philosopher and physician, and a leading figure of the Enlightenment. However,

to go very far. Income inequality is an extreme concentration of income in the hands of a small percentage of the population; it is the size of the gap between the richest and the rest.

This gap has been growing markedly in the United States for forty years. In the past two decades the bulk of economic gains have gone to those who already have the most. The United States consistently exhibits much higher rates of income inequality than most developed nations. In fact, according to the Organization for Economic Cooperation and Development, the United States has the sixth-largest income inequality in the world behind only South Africa, Costa Rica, Chile and Mexico (tied), and Turkey, according to data gathered from 2015–2018.[104] In short, the American worker has been drawing the short end of the stick for decades and it is getting worse. Joseph Stiglitz, a Nobel-prize-winning economist, argues that Americans generally underestimate the magnitude of inequality that exists in the United States, the rate at which it has occurred, the economic effects on society, and the ability of government to affect it; these claims are also supported by other research.[105]

Plato in his Republic distinguished "… three classes of men—lovers of wisdom, lovers of honor, lovers of gain," each of which has a role to play in a society. However, Plato goes on to argue, "… the pleasure of the intelligent part of the soul is the pleasantest of the three … the wise man speaks with authority

---

it has also been attributed to Charles Caleb Colon, a nineteenth century English clergyman and gambler who traveled throughout the United States.

104   Income Inequality Indicator, Organization for Economic Cooperation and Development (OECD), accessed February 4, 2020, doi: 10.1787/459aa7f1-en.

105   See Stiglitz's book, *The Price of Inequality* (W.W. Norton, 2012). An article by Jordan Weissman for *Slate* points to additional research: "Americans Have No Idea How Bad Inequality Really Is," Slate.com, September 2014, http://www.slate.com/articles/business/moneybox/2014/09/americans_have_no_idea_how_bad_inequality_is_new_harvar d_business_school.html.

when he approves of his own life." Next is "the soldier and lover of honor," and then last in having a pleasant and honest life is "the lover of gain." There is a long-held belief that all Americans have great opportunity to earn enough for a comfortable life. If we work hard enough, we all have the chance to move up to a more privileged class. Unfortunately, this belief best serves the ultra-wealthy, since it assumes anyone not holding great wealth must either not be working hard enough or not using their opportunities.

The wish to acquire more and provide for ourselves is a natural and common thing, and when men and women succeed in garnering enormous wealth, they are generally praised for intelligence or work rather than condemned for greed. This is due to our belief in the framers of our nation's free-market capitalist economy. However, the structure has become increasingly unfair as the super-rich have continued to rig the system in their favor and at the expense of the rest of America. The super-rich have made the barriers too tall for most of us to scale, barring a catapult into winning the lottery (and even that would be a matter of luck, not skill or hard work). As the rich have accumulated more and more wealth they have purchased, through their political contributions, more and more favorable legislation to further increase their wealth and power. Cristina Kirchner was the leftist president of Argentina from 2007 to 2015. Her regime in Argentina was built on two foundations: concentration of power and accumulation of wealth, but only for herself.[106] The Trump administration is expediting that process in the United States. Kirchner also served as

---

106   See: Rory Carroll, "Argentina's first couple deliver prosperity – for themselves", *The Guardian*, July 26, 2009, https://www.theguardian.com/world/2009/jul/26/argentina-kirchner-wealth; and Sabrina Martin, "Kirchner's Fortune Grew 800 Percent While She Ruled Argentina", *PanAm Post*. March 16, 2016, https://panampost.com/sabrina-martin/2016/03/01/kirchners-fortune-grew-800-percent-while-she-ruled-argentina/?cn-reloaded=1.

Argentina's first lady from 2003–2007; her wealth increased during her husband's presidency and went up 800 percent while she was president. She was charged with treason, secretly conducting foreign and economic policy counter to national interests, and indicted for corruption and bribery. She is now vice president of Argentina. Is there any similarity with our current situation and Donald Trump's plans for himself? We think so.

According to Bankrate's Financial Security Index Survey, as of January 18, 2018, only 39 percent of Americans had enough savings to cover a $1,000 emergency. Young people attending college (and their families) must take on such huge amounts of debt that even if they are able to complete college and graduate, many will lack the financial means to support themselves, much less support a family or contribute to economic growth. With low wages and little accumulated wealth common now, the focus for most families is keeping a roof over their heads and food on the table. If the family is hit with a breadwinner losing a job, a serious medical diagnosis or some other unforeseen crisis, it can be ruinous. As a result of the pandemic millions of families are experiencing that now.

Persuading the Sheep

> The shepherd always tries to persuade the sheep that their interest and his are the same.
>
> —Stendhal, author and novelist, circa 1818

Marie-Henri Beyle, the nineteenth-century French writer who wrote under the name Stendhal, is one of the earliest and foremost practitioners of realism, literature that tries to illustrate the value of everyday life using real-life experiences. His adage about shepherd and sheep was written in a letter to explain how people in power will use false or misleading information to sway public opinion in their favor.[107] The reality is that most of our politicians depend on the financial contributions of the super-wealthy to be elected and re-elected. The floodgates were opened by the Supreme Court's 2010 *Citizens United* decision allowing unlimited election spending by corporations and PACS. Untold amounts of political contributions have been made since and it is certainly in politicians' perceived self-interest to maintain the status quo. You cannot change how people vote without first changing the way they think. The super-wealthy are able to invest massive amounts of money on advertising (propaganda) campaigns in print, broadcast and social media to try to control and shape the way people think. One of the Trump administration's most frequently utilized strategies is to divide and conquer popular opinion by finding or manufacturing an enemy to point a finger at, and redirecting the focus away from what is really going on and truly important to our nation. And we're sorry to say, this strategy seems to be working quite effectively.

Over the past several decades there have been significant tax cuts aimed at stimulating the economy based on the theory of "trickle-down economics." However, instead of growing savings or investment to expand the economy and create more jobs, these targeted tax cuts for the rich have only generated increased consolidation of income at the top. The Economic Policy Institute's (EPI) July 2019 Productivity–Pay Gap report found that, "The income, wages and wealth generated over the last four decades have failed to trickle down to the vast majority largely because policy choices made on behalf of those with the most income, wealth, and power have exacerbated inequality."[108] Trickle-down economic

---

107 Matthew Josephson, *Stendhal, or the Pursuit of Happiness* (Jorge Pinto, 1946).
108 "The Productivity-Pay Gap," Economic Policy Institute, July 2019, accessed

theory advocates tax cuts to corporations, capital gains and savings. It doesn't promote across-the-board tax cuts, instead the tax cuts go to the wealthiest.

The Laffer Curve, developed by supply-side economist Arthur Laffer, illustrates the theoretical relationship between rates of taxation and resulting government revenue. Supply-side economics assumes that all tax cuts, regardless of income level or economic status, spur economic growth. Laffer in an interview with Fox News on March 23, 2020 proclaimed that he hoped that the stimulus package to respond to the novel coronavirus would die. He contended that a "helicopter money proposal of handouts never works it just causes the problem to get worse and worse." Laffer proposed cutting payroll taxes for the next seven or eight months "to make sure it's more attractive for people to work and for companies to hire" and that we needed to end the coronavirus mitigation measures and get back to work quickly. Apparently, he believes that tens of thousands of American lives are expendable, the cost of doing business. Or that people are choosing to stay home, they are lazy, in order to receive free money from the government rather than work.[109] Last year Laffer co-authored a tribute to Trump and his agenda. On March 23, 2019 Trump bestowed the Presidential Medal of Freedom on Laffer. We hope Trump also bought Laffer a large supply of Chapstick—we hear spewing "BS." and excessive ass kissing can really dry the lips.[110]

Trickle-down proponents turn to the Laffer Curve to

December 3, 2019, https://www.epi.org/productivity-pay-gap/.

109   "Reagan's economist Art Laffer 'Stimulus' will make things worse – Instead cut the payroll tax for the next 8 months", *Climate Depot*, March 24, 2020, https://www.climatedepot.com/2020/03/24/reagan-economist-artt-laffer-stimulus-will-make-things-worse-instead-cut -the-payroll-tax-for-the-next-8-months/.

110   Jonathan Chait, "Trump Awards Kook Art Laffer for Inventing Fake Curve", New York Magazine Intelligencer, June 19, 2019, https://nymag.com/intelligencer/2019/06/art-laffer-curve- medal-freedom-tax-cuts.html.

illustrate how, theoretically, tax cuts would produce a powerful multiplier effect creating enough growth to replace government revenue lost from the cuts. In theory, the resulting prosperous economy provides a larger tax base. According to trickle-down economics, corporations and other employers would make capital investments such as plant expansion and new equipment purchases, and they would increase employee training and create more jobs. The employees would then spend the additional income and expand the economy. Sounds good, a win-win situation. However, employers generally haven't made significant investments as a result of these tax cuts, instead pocketing most of the tax savings as a windfall to the business, and distributing the profits among the executives and major shareholders.

Trickle-down economics has yet to prove effective in stimulating the economy enough to offset the lost revenue from reduced taxes on corporations and the rich. Instead of trickling down, the prosperity finds itself moving to a higher plane inhabited exclusively by the rich. The decades-long economic experiment attempting to prove the validity of trickle-down economics has obviously failed. It is difficult to escape the fact that these practices and policies haven't materially increased business investment or economic growth; nor have they benefited the working class whose earnings have actually declined since the theory's inception.

Another problem of trickle-down economics is that with nearly full employment, potential job creation would be extremely limited. If employers did actually create new and better jobs (higher wages, more security), who would, or could, fill them? If the workers who are underemployed or in lower-paying jobs were to fill these newly created positions, who will be available to backfill the jobs they are leaving? Are we assuming that these lower-paying jobs will automatically be filled by recent immigrants, as we have seen happen repeatedly in America's history and come to rely on? How could that happen with such an anti-immigrant administration?

Historically and in the present, a great number of immigrants come to the United States and work jobs that many Americans won't fill for a variety of reasons including pay, difficulty, hazardousness, physicality, location, or seasonal nature such as temporary or migrant farm labor and landscaping. Without hard-working immigrants to harvest crops for relatively low wages, what do you think happens to food prices? The proposed deportation of 11 million immigrants, many of whom had been performing valuable daily work, would leave a giant vacuum sucking the life out of the service industry, housing markets, food processing, farming and agriculture, child care, and the list goes on. The economic impact would be felt across the entire country, all because the president and many in his base are uncomfortable or feel threatened by what they view as "desperate, asylum-seeking immigrants" they feel are invading the United States. We think this might be a good place for a little Sunday school lesson, familiar to those of you of the Christian faith who might fall into this category. **Exodus 22:21: You shall not wrong a stranger or oppress him, for you were strangers in the land of Egypt.** These are people who are seeking a better life while contributing to our economy and culture. Christian theology teaches that the stranger who resides with you should be treated as one of your citizens. You should love him as yourself. Of course, that assumes that you believe the teachings of your faith and strive to do what's right. We all fall short of the glory of God, however following the demagoguery and accepting policies of hatred and contempt for refugees is not falling short. It's more like jumping off a cliff.

The Only American Principle

> Here is my principle: taxes shall be levied according to ability to pay. That is the only American principle.
>
> —Franklin Delano Roosevelt, U.S. president, 1936

America's thirty-second president, Franklin Roosevelt was a member of America's elite class, yet he saw the need not to overburden people who lacked great wealth and resources with excessive taxation. Addressing a campaign rally in 1936, Roosevelt said the only way to align taxation with our founding principles was to levy them "according to ability to pay."[111] The Trump administration seems to follow another set of principles in this area. An overwhelming percentage of the benefits from the 2017 Trump/GOP tax cuts went to large corporations and the top one percent of income earners. The income gains for the wealthy through 2019, once calculated, will undoubtedly reveal a significant increase over 2016. From 1979–2016, middle-income households had a 47 percent increase in their income. Comparatively, the wealthiest one percent of the United States population gained approximately 235 percent—five times more than the middle class—over the same period. And, due in large part to the 2017 tax cuts for the rich, income inequality will continue to increase. The nonpartisan Congressional Budget Office (CBO) predicts earnings to grow even faster for high income earners in the next decade.[112]

The people of our democratic nation should not have to depend on the good graces of the rich to trickle money down to everyone else. In the first place, experience shows that as a rule they

---

[111] Franklin Delano Roosevelt, "Speech Given at Campaign Rally October 21, 1936", in Gordonskene, "FDR Has Words About Taxes," *Crooks and Liars*, July 15, 2011, https://crooksandliars.com/gordonskene/fdr-has-word-or-two-about-taxes-1936.

[112] Data from Inequality.org, accessed April 15, 2020, https://inequality.org/.

simply don't do it. The richest Americans continue to accumulate greater and greater wealth and donate more and more to politicians who will serve their interests and perpetuate the status quo. Tom Steyer, the billionaire hedge-fund manager and philanthropist who had put his hat in the Democratic presidential ring, explained this in simple terms: "The more we allow Republicans to concentrate the lion's share of the wealth in the hands of a few, the more power these wealthy few will have. And they will use this power to continue rewriting the rules of both our economy and our political system in their favor."[113] For America to stick with its core values, at some point the rich need to pay a fair share. Perhaps then the middle class can actually have taxes reduced, as the president and congressional Republicans promised. Putting money directly into the hands of the middle-class through reduced taxes will stimulate the economy because the middle-class will spend the additional income on things they need and want for their families—the goods and services that actually drive economic growth.

Democracy is rule by the people, what Abraham Lincoln called "government of the people, by the people, for the people." The key to ensuring the continuation of our democracy is providing a level playing field for our workers and insisting on the accountability of elected officials to voters. Democracy should be consumer-driven. Ensuring an equitable distribution of income through a progressive tax policy is democratic, not socialist as some groups claim. Our politicians, both Republicans and Democrats, have insufficiently stood up for us, as evidenced by forty years of essentially stagnant wages.

We have relied on the benevolence of politicians to protect us, and witnessed that most of them have failed us. We have to

---

113   Tom Steyer, "I'm a Billionaire. Please Raise My Taxes.", *Los Angeles Times*, October 5, 2017, https://enewspaper.latimes.com/infinity/article_popover_share.aspx?guid=a11bd15a-81c7-4ebc-9a41-6fe82ee53b9e.

make it in their best interest to act on our behalf. The best way we do that? Just un-elect the bastards when they act in their own best interest instead of ours. Why? Their policy enactments are in the best interest of their big donors instead of the constituency. The reason for the rapid growth of income at the very top level is due to factors including globalization, technology, and government policy, notably the 2017 tax cuts—all of which can be addressed if we have leaders committed to increasing wealth and opportunity for all Americans and not just paying attention to the ones who are powerful and rich.

Globalization: America Last?

The growth of multinational corporations with no allegiance to the United States or any other government continues to worsen the problem. There is no reliable data to determine how many Americans have lost their jobs to workers in lower-cost countries, but in 2009 Alan Blinder, co-director of Princeton University's Center for Economic Policy Studies and former Vice Chairman of the Federal Reserve Board, estimated that up to 30 million U.S. jobs were potentially "offshorable" in the coming decades.[114] A decade later that number may be much larger. Trump's tax policy is set to worsen this problem. A March 2018 article by Justin Miller in *The American Prospect* stated; "Trump's Tax Cuts Incentivized Corporate Offshoring. The Dems Want to Reverse that." He points out that while Trump campaigned on his "America First" message, the 2017 tax reform, "established a 10.5 percent tax rate—half of the domestic corporate tax—on the income American corporations earn abroad. The tax law provides a real incentive to set up shop

---

114   Alan S. Blinder, "How Many U.S. Jobs Might Be Offshorable? CEPS Working Paper 142", Center for Economic and Policy Studies, March 2007, http://www.princeton.edu/ceps/publications.shtml.

and stash profits abroad."[115] This is an "America last" mentality. It is certainly not making America great.

A Lesson Learned from Coronavirus

From our experience fighting the novel coronavirus it seems we will need to reduce the degree of globalization and become more self-sufficient as a nation. When COVID-19 hit the United States, we were woefully lacking the equipment and supplies needed to combat it. And since this is a worldwide pandemic the demand for the requisite supplies and equipment made it virtually impossible to shop the global markets. An increase in U.S. manufacturing to ensure a ready supply of these items should begin immediately—the novel coronavirus is expected to return in the fall. And an adequate stockpile and the capability to mass produce whenever needed is essential. New global health crises are possible.

Technology and Job Opportunities

There was a time when business enterprises (factories, corporations, etc.) required vast amounts of labor. However, since as early as the 1940s, many jobs in industries which Americans have historically relied upon for employment have been steadily eliminated by automation. According to Darrell West, founding director of the Center for Technology Innovation at the Brookings Institute, "Firms have discovered that robotics, machine learning and artificial intelligence can replace humans and improve accuracy, productivity, and efficiency of operations."[116] Union

---

115   Justin Miller, "Trump's Tax Cuts Incentivized Corporate Offshoring. These Dems Want to Reverse That.", *American Prospect,* March 1, 2018, https://prospect.org/power/trump-s-tax-cuts-incentivized-corporate-offshoring.-dems-want-reverse-that./.

116   Darrell M. West, "What Happens if Robots Take the Jobs? The Impact of

membership has been under relentless attack by employers seeking to reduce employee protections, eliminate benefits and restrict workers' wages. More and more people are making less and less money. The younger generations fail to understand the historical correlation between increases in union negotiated wages and benefits and those in nonunion jobs; and often resist organizing efforts. The higher-paying blue-collar jobs are being replaced with retail and home health care and similar low-paying service positions. Not everyone has access to the tech training needed (and frequently negotiated for by unions in the past) to become sufficiently skilled for the new jobs. And as far as we know, robots don't demand equal pay or health benefits, nor need to leave early to pick up a sick child, or report harassment—and haven't yet joined forces to negotiate for better working conditions.

Tax Cuts

The 2017 Republican tax cut significantly heightened the problem. The corporate tax rate was reduced from 35 percent to 21 percent, a 40 percent reduction. This led to a $40 billion decline in corporate tax revenues coming into the U.S. Treasury. The theory behind the 2017 tax cuts was the cuts would boost economic growth and more than pay for themselves. However, the facts are unassailable. Continued wage stagnation is visible in monthly data compiled by the Bureau of Labor Statistics (BLS). In order for the cuts to pay for themselves, the gross domestic product would need to have increased by nearly 7 percent in 2018. It increased 3 percent, less than half of what was needed to accomplish what

---

Emerging Technologies on Employment and Public Policy", Brookings Center for Technology Innovation, October 26, 2015, http://www.brookings.edu/research/what-happens-if-robots-take-the-jobs-the-impact-of-emerging-technologies-on-employment-and-public-policy/.

was promised. They are falling far short of paying for themselves. Wonder who is going to pay for that shortfall?

Lower income and middle-class individuals did not fare well. In 2018 their real wages, after adjustments for inflation, increased by only 1.2 percent. The 2017 tax cut did increase the standard deduction and child care credit; but what the Trump administration and the GOP don't tell you is that these were mostly offset by reducing or eliminating personal exemptions, such as those for state and local taxes, that families benefited from before. It was a shell game. Few were really surprised that the tax cut was largely directed at benefiting executive-level business owners and extremely wealthy individuals; "trickle-down economics" has always yielded the same results. Albert Einstein defined insanity "as doing the same thing over and over again and expecting different results." What the Republican-led Congress and Trump did was not insane, just dishonest. The results of their tax cuts were just as they expected.

The Trump administration and congressional Republicans may not have called the 2017 tax cuts "trickle-down economics" but that is exactly what they were. Supporters of these cuts publicly predicted that the December 2017 cuts would result in dramatically higher wages for workers and increased corporate investments, and the tax cuts would pay for themselves. That didn't happen. Analysis of the economic impact of the tax cuts in the first year conducted by the nonpartisan Congressional Research Service, an arm of the Library of Congress, found that the cuts have had virtually no effect on wages and have not contributed to a surge in investment.[117] The

---

117 Brendan Duke, "CRS: 2017 Tax Law Proponents' Trickle-Down Claims Haven't Materialized", Center on Budget and Policy Priorities, June 5, 2019, https://www.cbpp.org/blog/crs-2017-tax-law-proponents-trickle-down-claims-havent-materialized.

cuts also have not come close to paying for themselves and did not result in a reduction in taxes for average taxpayers.

THE STOCK MARKET

The stock market is Trump's prime rationale for his claim that the U.S. economy before the pandemic was the best it has ever been. He is taking credit for the strong economic growth shepherded by President Obama after he bailed us out of the deep recession handed to him by President George W. Bush, himself an advocate of trickle-down economics. Using his usual fear mongering tactics to increase wealth for the few paid for by the middle class, Trump professes that a redistribution of income through changes in the tax laws would negatively impact the retirement accounts of U.S. workers. Again, "Pinocchio" Trump is misleading the public.

It is both common sense and a matter of fairness that if workers are better compensated for their work; they will be far more able to participate in the stock market gains and other wealth-increasing investments. In the September 2014 issue of the *Harvard Business Review*, William Lazonick blamed the record corporate stock buybacks for reduced investments in the economy and the corresponding impact on prosperity and income equality. Lazonick is professor of economics and director of the University of Massachusetts Center for Industrial Competitiveness, and co-founder and president of the Academic–Industry Research Network. In Citing Lazonick's empirical research, Harold Meyerson, an editor-at-large for *The American Prospect*, asserted in a *Washington Post* article: "The purpose of the modern U.S. Corporation is to reward large investors and top executives with income that once was spent on expansion, research, training and employees."[118] Journalist Timothy Noah in his 2012 book, *The Great Divergence: America's Growing Inequality Crisis and What We Can Do About It*, explained how this is happening and argues that those at the economic top of the scale are well aware of the costs to the rest of us:

> ... stockholders appropriated what once belonged to middle-class wage earners. As a percentage of national income, corporate profits have (on an after-tax basis) mostly been rising since the early 1990s even as the non-wealthy's income share has dwindled, and in recent years corporate income share has reached historic levels. Is this coincidental? *Washington Post* columnist Harold Meyerson argued that it was not. Meyerson is a political liberal strongly sympathetic to the labor movement, but his source was impeccably pro-capital: Michael Cembalest, chief investment officer at JP Morgan Chase. In a 2011 newsletter for Morgan clients, Cembalest stated, "U.S. labor compensation is now at a 50-year low relative to both company sales and GDP. ... Reductions in wages and benefits explain the majority of the net improvement." That "majority" was more like 75 percent.[119]

And "wages" in this case, "does not include compensation for those at the top of the income scale," Noah pointed out.[120]

Why have we allowed the Republicans and the ultra-rich to define what constitutes a healthy economy for all of us? The health of the economy should not be defined solely on how the stock market is faring; the stock market does not directly benefit

---

118   Harold Meyerson, "In Corporations, It's Owner-Take-All", *Washington Post*, August 26, 2014, https://www.washingtonpost.com/opinions/harold-meyerson-in-corporations-its-owner-take-all/2014/08/26/.
119   Timothy Noah, *The Great Divergence: America's Growing Inequality Crisis and What We Can Do About It* (Bloomsbury, 2012).
120   Noah, *The Great Divergence*.

the majority of our population. An essential element of assessing America's economic health must include determining the health of all economic classes. Since current prosperity is not being shared with lower-income Americans or much of the middle class in any significant way, the economy does not seem particularly healthy for a majority of Americans.

The Tax Burden

The marginal tax rate is the percentage taken from your next dollar of taxable income above a predetermined income threshold. A person's effective tax rate is derived by taking the total taxes paid by the individual and dividing it by the person's taxable income. In other words, this is the rate you are actually paying on your total income, not your marginal or bracket rate. It has become abundantly clear that corporations are enjoying unprecedented profits and paying an average of 7 percent of the profits in their federal taxes. CEO salaries are on average 361 times higher than that of their workers' salaries, and CEO's tax rates have been reduced while workers' wages have been stagnant for 40 years. The richest 400 families in America are paying a lower effective tax rate than the lowest 50 percent of our taxpayers. That is more than a little bit unfair.

In the 1950s under Republican President Eisenhower there was a period of substantial economic growth with shared prosperity, along with a 91 percent top marginal tax on individual income for the ultra-rich. In addition, corporate tax revenues were a markedly higher share of total federal revenue than they are today. Eisenhower denounced attempts to reduce tax rates as fiscally irresponsible. He was correct in general, although 91 percent may be a bit excessive today. Top marginal rates stayed near 90 percent until 1964 when the top marginal rate was lowered to 70 percent. The top marginal rate has continued downward over the years. In 2017 it was decreased to 37 percent from 39.6 percent. For 2019, the marginal federal tax rate of 37 percent for individuals means that people with taxable income of $510,300 and higher for a single taxpayer, and $612,350 and higher for married couples filing jointly, will pay 37 percent in federal taxes on every dollar above those thresholds. Based on the average of $17.6 million in compensation for the top 200 CEOs in the United States, they will each pay 37 percent on an average of approximately $17 million above the threshold. This equates to $6.3 million in taxes, leaving them $10.7 million. The highest-paid CEO in 2017 made $103 million (total compensation); in 2019 the second-highest made $246 million (Elon Musk was highest at $2.3 billion). Even without seeing these executives' tax returns, it is obvious to us that by taking advantage of all legal deductions and loopholes available, their actual tax burden will be even less than before.[121]

As we stated earlier, the corporate rate was reduced from 35 percent to 21 percent. A corporate tax rate is a levy placed on a firm's profit by the government. The money collected from corporate taxes goes to the treasury and is a source of the nation's income. A firm's operating earnings are calculated by deducting expenses, including the cost of goods sold, salaries and depreciation from revenue. Corporations, like individuals, understandably use every means possible to reduce their taxes. A new report, based on an in-depth analysis of Fortune 500 companies' financial filings, from the Institute of Taxation and Public Policy, reveals some interesting findings. Because of Trump's 2017 Tax Cuts and Jobs Act, 60 of the nation's biggest companies didn't pay a dime in federal taxes in 2018 on a collective $79 billion in profits. Did

---

[121] Karl Russell and Josh Williams, "The Highest-Paid C.E.O.s of 2018: A Year So Lucrative, We Had to Redraw Our Chart", *New York Times,* May 24, 2019, https://www.nytimes.com/interactive/2019/business/highest-paid-ceos-2018.html.

you get that? Sixty companies, $79 BILLION in profits, and **NO** taxes. (And where did that money go?) Overall, the largest 500 U.S. corporations paid just 7 percent of their profits as federal taxes. According to the data provided to Yahoo Financial by research firm Oxford Economics, that's the lowest effective tax rate since 1947. The loss to the treasury was $40 billion in 2018 alone.[122] It's starting to amount to real money!

Worker Productivity and Compensation

CEO pay has exploded since the 1970s. The CEO–worker pay gap is now nine times larger than in 1980 according to a May 2018 report in *Forbes* magazine.[123] In 1980 the average big company CEO earned 42 times as much as the average U.S. worker. According to the AFL-CIO, executive pay watch report, in 2017 CEO's annual pay (in cash terms) averaged $13.94 million compared to the average annual pay for a worker of $38,613. On average, CEOs made 361 times as much as one of their workers. Thirty-three of these firms reported pay gaps between CEOs and workers of larger than 1000 to 1. The *New York Times* published its ranking of the 200 highest-paid CEOs for 2018 showing the median pay for these top 200 executives was $17.6 million.[124]

Productivity is real output per hour of labor worked. Economic equity requires that employee compensation rise with

---

122   Kristin Myers, "Corporations paid $91 billion less in taxes in 2018 under Trump's tax law", *Yahoo Financial,* May 30, 2019, https://finance.yahoo.com/news/corporations-paid-91-billion-less-in-taxes-in-2018-under-trumps-tax-law-160745447.html.
123   Diana Hembree, "CEO Pay Skyrockets To 361 Times That of The Average Worker", *Forbes,* May 22, 2018. http://www.forbes.com/sites/dianahembree/2018/05/22/ceo-pay-skyrockets-to-361-times-that-of-the-average-worker/#396b39a7776d.
124   Russell and Williams, "Highest Paid CEOs."

productivity. In other words, the greater employees' production, the more they should be paid. Inequality grows if pay lags behind productivity. The Economic Policy Institute's July 2019 report found that from 1948–1979 as the economy expanded everyone reaped the benefits; during that period, productivity rose 108.1 percent and hourly compensation rose 93.2 percent.[125] In the 1970s, corporate productivity rose in tandem with employee compensation (wages plus benefits such as health insurance). Since then productivity has vastly outpaced employee compensation. From 1979–2018 productivity rose 69.6 percent but hourly compensation only rose 11.6 percent. After adjusting for inflation, productivity has grown six times more than pay since 1979. To put these numbers in perspective: if a worker's pay for a similar job in 1979 had risen in line with the increase in productivity, that job would be paying approximately 50 percent more than it is today. The workforce represented by unions has declined to less than 11 percent from their peak of about 40 percent in the 1950s, as those at the top of the income scale have increased their power and influence on economic rules and regulations in their favor, further increasing income inequality. There is a direct correlation between the decline in union jobs and the decline in employee wages and benefits in all sectors of employment. What was once the mantra of the manufacturing industry, "What's good for General Motors is good for America" was due in large part to GM's organized labor force negotiating wages and benefits for its workers that set the standard for employees across America and around the world, both union and nonunion members alike.

There are other variables that must be considered in determining the equity of employees' compensation, but this glaring gap in productivity gains versus employee pay is telling. Equity

---

125 "The Productivity Pay Gap."

cannot be achieved overnight, but we sure as hell need to change government policies to address this huge disparity and to adjust the American tax structure expeditiously. Many big employers offered bonuses to workers last year. Some attributed these bonuses to the tax cuts. Others, however, claim the corporations actually offered bonuses because there was a tightening of the labor market and they wanted to retain experienced employees. It is, in any case, fruitless to debate the rationale for the bonuses since they were minuscule. The Congressional Research Service estimates that the bonuses amounted to an average of $28 per employee; so, $40 billion to corporations and the ultra-rich and $28 per worker.[126] That appears to be a little imbalanced. Did you really expect something different? As long as Trump is president and the Senate is under McConnell and Republican control, don't.

The National Debt

According to the Congressional Budget Office (CBO) the United States will be spending more on interest on the national debt than on agriculture, veterans' programs and Medicaid combined. The United States has to pay interest primarily to foreign lenders in order to cover the cost of decisions made a long time ago. The rise in the debt will cause heavy burdens for future generations. The national debt jumped from $10.6 trillion to $19.9 trillion under the eight years of the Obama administration as he led the nation out of a very dangerous deep economic recession caused in part by the Republican-led Congress and the 2001 and 2003 tax cuts. Since then, in 2017 the GOP-led Congress passed a $1.5 trillion tax cut bill and the two-year spending bill. Together these are expected to drive the deficit significantly upward. The Committee for a

---

126   Duke, "Trickle-Down Claims."

Responsible Budget (CRB) estimates that the annual deficits could top $2.1 trillion per year for the next 10 years.

Many Senators, both Democrat and Republican, cite the national debt as the greatest threat to our nation. According to the U.S. Treasury Department website, as of April 15, 2019, the national debt was over $24 trillion, up $2.1 trillion in a year and continuing to rise rapidly, as predicted by the CRB. The national debt is the highest level since World War II. The only countries with a higher debt load are Portugal, Italy, Greece and Japan.

There is strong disagreement among economists whether the U.S. debt level is problematic. Some believe that the U.S. can borrow as much money as it wants at low rates because of the dollar's role in the global finance system. No problem. Others believe that today's huge debt could threaten the U.S. economy during future downturns. They contend therefore, the current economic expansion is the time to get it under control by spending less and paying down the debt. Moreover, the debt disrupts spending priorities because in the next few years interest payments are expected to rise rapidly. For most of us this could create a huge economic problem. The effects of the coronavirus pandemic will significantly increase our national debt; due to COVID-19 it will soar much faster over the next few years.

Mitch McConnell's Legislative Graveyard
(aka, His Desk)

Making matters even worse, Senate Majority Leader Mitch McConnell has turned the Senate into a legislative graveyard. Proposals sitting on McConnell's desk languish because he refuses to bring them to the Senate floor for debate and a vote, including many proposals that would alleviate income and wealth inequality. Congressional Republicans and the White House ballyhooed the pre-COVID-19 "great economy" to exclaim they were doing a fantastic job as leaders, but the saying that "a rising tide lifts all boats" does not apply in this situation. The only boats that are dramatically rising are yachts owned by the wealthiest one percent of the electorate. The top one percent fared overwhelmingly better than the rest of America, which is trying to tread water in order not to drown in the "rising tide" of the rich getting richer. Congressional Republicans and President Trump have bragged about the number of jobs that had been created and the extremely low unemployment rate the U.S. was enjoying. As of late 2019 the rate was at a 50-year low of 3.5 percent. However, the truth is that the vast majority of the jobs that were created were low-paying service-related jobs. These were not the high-paying manufacturing jobs that were promised. And now the unemployment rate stands at approximately 17 percent in large part due to Trump's sluggish response to the pandemic.

The Republicans devised the "trickle-down" plan. It failed to produce the promised results. They reintroduced it. It failed to meet their promises again. In 2017 they trotted it out once more. Same results: corporations and the ultra-rich received huge benefits, next to nothing for the rest of us although they continue to claim it was a middle-class tax cut despite all evidence to the contrary. Plato said that, "Truth is the beginning of every good to the gods, and every good to man",[127] but from congressional Republicans and the administration we get the more sinister, deceitful, "alternative facts," as Trump "BFF" Kelly Ann Conway labeled the misinformation wafting out of the Trump cesspool. Let's call it what it really is: pure "BS" and just plain lies.

McConnell's attempts to injure the Obama presidency were at the expense of obstructing and killing legislation, earning him his

---

127 Plato, *The Republic of Plato* [1888], *Project Gutenberg*, last updated 2017, https://www.gutenberg.org/files/55201/55201-h/55201-h.htm.

nickname of "Grim Reaper." It appears that Trump and McConnell have had one focused mission: to undo absolutely anything and everything that Barack Obama had anything to do with, to destroy Obama's legacy. We're convinced their obsessive hatred and disdain for our former president has affected their judgment and decisions including the reorganization and elimination of policies, treaties and environmental safeguards even to the point of elimination of medical benefits for millions of Americans. That obsession includes the elimination of pre-existing conditions under the Affordable Care Act. President Trump was claiming that his healthcare bill to replace "Obamacare," as ACA measures are known, would ensure coverage for pre-existing conditions. But anyone who believes in the benevolence of Mitch McConnell and/or President Trump may be unaware that Trump Attorney General Barr, with a lot of Republican support, was in court challenging the entire Affordable Care Act including coverage of pre-existing conditions. If Trump is successful then your healthcare coverage will be turned inside out and upside down, and likely not include coverage of pre-existing conditions. Hey, don't worry. Health insurers will become even more profitable and "The Chosen One" and his "Grim Reaper" will still be covered for any medical condition—and at taxpayer expense.

A Judicious Hand

> ... it is impossible to devise any specific tax that will operate equally on the whole community. It must be the province of the legislature to hold the scales with a judicious hand and balance one by another. The rich must be made to pay for their luxuries; which is the only proper way of taxing their superior wealth.

—Alexander Hamilton, founding father and Secretary of the Treasury, 1782

Alexander Hamilton, our nation's first Secretary of the Treasury, wrote these words recommending balance and consideration when determining the taxes that people must pay in order for our nation to function. Since complete equality in taxation is virtually impossible, he explained that, with our separation of powers, it would be Congress' responsibility to legislate tax systems that accounted for national needs alongside individuals' ability to pay—or else there might be trouble. He also suggested that special attention be paid to taxing the "superior wealth" of the rich and the luxuries that this wealth allows.[128]

The GOP prefers to obscure its true economic policy goals by serving up platitudes about their economic growth agenda of creating good jobs and getting the government off America's back. So as the old TV commercial said in promising quality and substance over junk and filler, "where's the beef?" While the commercial was about the quality, quantity and source of meat in a fast-food burger (in contrast to competitors' burgers), "Where's the beef?" has become a rallying cry when something seems to lack any real substance. The "beef" here would be policies that put actual dollars in the pockets and bank balances of middle-class and low-wage workers; and in the longer term, decreasing the great (and growing greater) disparities in wealth we are seeing. To meet basic needs, low-wage workers have to spend nearly every dollar they earn on essentials. There is little left for luxuries much less to save for the future. The super-wealthy by contrast can afford whatever they desire, whenever they desire it, and still have plenty left to invest and further increase their fortunes. For anyone but the super-wealthy it is a downward spiral that is picking up speed.

We believe it is time to rethink some common assumptions

---

128   Alexander Hamilton, "The Continentalist No VI, 4 July 1782", *Founders Online,* National Archives, accessed March 20, 2020, http://founders.archives.gov/documents/Hamilton/01-03-02-0031.

about the tax burden and to more actively explore new ideas since the old ones just aren't working for most of us. Economists Emmanuel Saez and Gabriel Zucman have a compelling approach to estimating tax rates, detailed in their 2019 book, *The Triumph of Injustice: How the Rich Dodge Taxes and How to Make Them Pay*. The book opens with this finding: "In 2018, for the first time in history, America's richest billionaires paid a lower effective tax rate than the working class."[129] Saez and Zucman employed an analysis different from other published estimates: their estimates of tax burdens encompass not just federal taxes but also corporate taxes, state and local taxes, and "indirect taxes" such as payments for licenses for businesses and motor vehicles. Based on the totality of taxes that Americans pay, the study concluded that the average effective tax rate paid by the richest 400 families in the United States was 23 percent in 2018 compared to 24.2 percent paid by the bottom half of households. The effective tax rate paid by the bottom 50 percent has remained relatively the same from the mid-1950s to present. In contrast, in 1980 the 400 richest families had an effective tax rate of 47 percent; it has appreciatively declined with every tax bill since.

While their findings are new and subject to debate, we commend their arguments and urge our elected officials to read the book themselves and assess the merits of the many policy and legislative ideas posed to alleviate the growing income and wealth inequality in our country. Some of the more obvious initiatives discussed by Saez and Zucman include: increase taxes on the ultra-rich to make the tax code progressive again; enact comprehensive immigration reform and provide work authorization to undocumented workers, enabling them to earn higher wages and thus increasing wages for U.S. workers employed in the same fields;

---

129   Emmanuel Saez and Gabriel Zucman, *The Triumph of Injustice: How the Rich Dodge Taxes and How to Make The Pay* (W.W. Norton, 2019).

reverse the spread of right-to-work laws in order to give workers more bargaining power; raise the federal minimum wage; undertake public investments in infrastructure to create jobs; update overtime rules to make those earning over $23,600 a year eligible under the Fair Labor Standards Act; and end discrimination that contributes to race and gender inequalities. While additional policy changes may be needed to get to a more equitable society, this is a good start. Unbridled capitalism leads to greed.

Hard Work, Fair Pay

As corporations and the ultra-rich have increased their power union membership has been substantially depressed. "Our labor unions are not narrow, self-serving groups. They have raised wages, shortened hours, and provided supplemental benefits. Through collective bargaining and grievance procedures, they have brought justice and democracy to the shop floor," said John F. Kennedy.[130] According to the Bureau of Labor Statistics in 1983 the union membership rate was 20.1 percent before it began its steady decline. Right to work laws must be changed. We need collective bargaining: "The only effective answer to organized greed is organized labor."[131]

Sharon Block is the Executive Director of the Labor and Work Life Program at Harvard Law School and was a member of the National Labor Relations Board under President Obama.

---

130   Kennedy said this in a speech in Detroit, Michigan, on September 5, 1960. For full text of the speech see: John F. Kennedy, "Speech of Senator John F. Kennedy, Cadillac Square, Detroit, MI," online by Gerhard Peters and John T. Woolley, The American Presidency Project, https://www.presidency.ucsb.edu/node/274359.

131   The American Labor Studies Center attributes this quote to Thomas Donahue, former head of the AFL-CIO and of our most influential labor leaders. See: "Labor Quotes," American Labor Studies Center, posted October 15, 2010, https://www.labor-studies.org/by-education-level/elementary/labor-quotes/.

In an article published in *Newsweek*, "We Need Strong Labor Unions to Protect the Middle Class"[132], Block made several astute observations: Before the passage of the National Labor Relations Act in 1935 that protects the right of employees to join a union "Workers were more likely to be union members (13.2 percent) when they had no right to do so than they are now (10.3 percent)"; and, "This decline is having a dramatic effect on all American workers because the decline in union density suppresses wages for all workers, it accounts for about one-third of income inequality over the past several decades."

The more people are focused on basic needs and mere survival of their families, the less time they have to focus on the big picture and planning for the future. Trump and his minions spent the first three years of his presidency tearing down the institutions of our nation's foundation. If his behavior and complete lack of respect for the balance of power is reinforced by his reelection, Trump will see it as a confirmation that he is, in fact, the monarch or more likely, the anointed dictator. The sycophancy and subservience displayed by Republican elected officials is confirmation that people will generally act in their perceived self-interest. We live in a global economy now, not an economy focused on community or even nation. The ultra-rich have little interest in national boundaries. Energy companies and other multi-nationals are about maximizing their profits. Like Pinocchio Trump, many of the ultra-rich wrap themselves in an American flag when it serves their personal interests. Under a second Trump term, income inequality would continue to worsen, and the increasing consolidation of income and wealth at the top of our economic pyramid is a condition that can hasten the onset of tyranny.

---

132   Sharon Block, "We Need Strong Labor Unions to Protect the Middle Class," *Newsweek*, September 4, 2017, https://www.newsweek.com/we-need-stronger-labor-unions-protect-middle-class-658614.

Putting People Back To Work

In the midst of the COVID-19 pandemic an estimated 33 million Americans are out of work due in large part to the shutdown as a result of the virus. The United States needs to work expeditiously to get people back to work and our economy up and running. We cannot do this in a way to just return to what we had, and we believe that has become very, very evident as a result of the strange social conditions caused by this crisis. We must create jobs that meet America's needs and that provide dignity and fair wages to workers. This is possible if we consider other needs. Massive investments in infrastructure improvements can help keep the United States competitive with the rest of the world. Transitioning to a green economy would help ensure that our descendants will have a planet to live on and fewer disastrous disruptions in our lives, and would help mitigate our health concerns. These initiatives will greatly assist in creating and maintaining higher-paying new jobs. We hope that these new jobs will be unionized to ensure employee protections and benefits. This alone would provide a good foundation for reducing the inequalities in our current economy.

After decades of massive income inequality, it is time for us to demand a change. We have had the experiment of lowering taxes for the rich since the 1980s (remember Regan's trickle-down economics?) and income disparity has soared ever since. The bottom half of our population has seen no gains whatsoever while the next 40 percent have seen only modest gains. Yet, money is gushing up to the wealthiest Americans. The vast majority of us are poorer and less equal. The president keeps telling us the economy before the pandemic, was better than it had ever been and wages had risen significantly. Alternate universe, alternate facts?

CHAPTER 5

BEWARE: THE REBIRTH OF FASCISM

> The art of leadership… consists in consolidating the attention of the people against a single adversary and taking care that nothing will split up that attention.
>
> —Adolph Hitler, politician and leader of Germany's Nazi Party, 1925

> Nazis. I hate these guys!
>
> —Indiana Jones, archeologist and adventurer, 1938, from the movie *Indiana Jones and the Last Crusade*, 1989

"Nazis. I hate these guys!" declares hero Indiana Jones in disgust when he realizes who he's up against, yet again. This line from the movie *Indiana Jones and the Last Crusade* is obviously done for comedic affect; the movie is set in 1938 but it came out in 1989, and of course by then American audiences would well know that Nazis are bad guys—and anyone who had seen the previous movies aware that Nazis always cause problems for Indy's archeological adventures. In the twenty-first century now, you would think that Americans would be just as wary of anything that smells of fascism, and unthinkable to express as a political or social view. Sadly, not.

In America today the deepening and excessive income inequality is fueling a rise in populism. The long-term worsening economic inequity is placing a big squeeze on the American middle class. People are angry. This is how President Trump won many of the swing states in the 2016 election. People were desperate for a new approach and believed Trump's promises and rhetoric that he could deliver the goods. Then and now, Trump promotes bigotry and hatred. He targets the press as enemies of the people and immigrants as invaders. It is very apparent that the president of the United States will not say anything against neo-Nazis. Saul Levine, Professor Emeritus in Psychiatry at the University of California at San Diego, has written:

> Authoritarian leaders and rabid followers have emerged in many countries, and have encouraged anger and hate-filled rhetoric. Expressions of dislike and rancor are now commonplace with heightened conflict and proclamations of nationalism, chauvinism and nativism: hallmarks of nascent and even burgeoning Fascism.[133]

Connect the dots. Trump's stated admiration for totalitarian dictators as well as his absence of criticism of neo-Nazis leaves questions as to where his loyalty really lies.

Adolph Hitler understood that the power of controlling public opinion could be achieved by turning a group of people against a single enemy, even if the charges against that enemy are false. Hitler used the fear and despair of the German people resulting from the Great Depression to his advantage. He convinced them that he was the only solution to Germany's economic problems, and then used ultra-nationalism to identify an "adversary." Hitler's "studies" had taught him that great men who were destined to lead were above the law and morals of ordinary men. William L Shirer in his book "The Rise and Fall of the Third Reich" argues that Hitler's maniacal feeling that he was destined to lead the German people to glory, was bolstered by a culture that did two crucial things simultaneously: it glorified great men who could

---

[133] Saul Levine, "Dislike and Anger: A Slippery Slope to Fascism", *Psychology Today*, October 1, 2018, http://psychologytoday.com/intl/blog/ouremotionalfootprint.

demonstrate willfulness and power, and it glorified the contented servitude of the masses who would gladly accept that power.

Hitler knew that mayhem in the streets could benefit the cause of an authoritarian takeover. John Vliet Lindsay was a member of Congress, mayor of New York City, and a presidential candidate who stated, "Those who suppress freedom always do so in the name of law and order." Trump threatened that if the House of Representatives impeached him there would be civil unrest with rioting in the streets. He even made a comparative reference to the Civil War. Had he been convicted by the Senate and removed from office, who knows what Trump would have tried to instigate. But we all knew that the Senate voting to remove him from office wasn't going to happen and it didn't.

Confusion of Principles

"One of the great secrets of the day is to know how to take possession of popular prejudices and passions in such a way to introduce a confusion of principles which make impossible all understanding between those who speak the same language and have the same interest."

—Niccolo Machiavelli, Renaissance philosopher and writer,
as imagined by writer and satirist Maurice Joly in 1864

Niccolo Machiavelli (1469-1527) was a writer, politician and a philosopher. His most famous book, "The Prince," brought him a reputation as an immoral cynic, in large part because his work had become synonymous with the idea that "the ends justify the means" no matter how cruel or immoral those might be. While Machiavelli never comes out and says those words exactly, the advice in "The Prince" does seem like a "how to" manual for autocrats, and includes some moves that are definitely non-democratic.

It appears "The Donald" and some of his evangelical Christian supporters have taken a page out of Machiavelli's playbook. As interpreted by Maurice Joly in 1864, Machiavelli would argue that to be an authoritative leader, do whatever you think is necessary to sway your subjects, including creating confusion and discord if that's what it takes.[134] Our democracy is in danger; we expect our politicians to be ethical. How would you rank President Trump? How about Senate Majority Leader McConnell? We are beginning to have more than a little bit of a problem with their honesty and integrity. It doesn't appear they have any when it comes to fulfilling their obligations under the Constitution rather than protecting their self-interest.

Trump's particular style of political leadership is to employ a divide-and-conquer approach, seasoned with falsehoods, inconsistencies, and statements about people that range from incoherent to cruel. Rather than engaging in a serious fact-based discussion, Trump resorts to appealing to fears and name-calling. He relies on people being content with sound bites and catchy labels. Consider what has happened with Senator Bernie Sanders announcing he is a Democratic Socialist. Republicans and other critics seized on the word "socialist" to claim that all Democrats have become so left-wing that they want our country to be a communist state. Obviously, that is false, but it is a key component of the GOP strategy to win in 2020 (along with getting China, Ukraine and Russia to help smear Trump's political opponents). The GOP playbook dictates that when someone demands fair wages for workers or a better safety net for our elderly and other needy citizens, they respond by calling them a communist or a socialist (which is code for saying they are totalitarians who want to take

---

134 Maurice Joly, "Dialogue in Hell Between Machiavelli and Montesquieu (1864)", trans. 2008, Internet Archive, last updated April 4, 2011, https://archive.org/details/DialogueInHellBetweenMachiavelliAndMontesquieu/page/n2/mode/2up.

your property and don't believe in freedom or democracy). It is undoubtedly an insult when used this way; but in reality, they are criticizing a person for their adherence to our nation's values and their viability as a political leader.

Let's examine the facts, though, and put Bernie's declaration in proper context. The first step is to back up and remind ourselves of what it means to be a democratic system and the role of economics in different systems of government.

There is a democratic system of government in capitalism that assumes individual freedom is of utmost importance, and the state's power is limited and defined by a social contract, such as the Constitution of the United States. In this system, individuals can own property and have the right to gain wealth through work as well as investment, and to hold this wealth as their own, with the exception of some amount that is ceded to the government for its operation, national infrastructure, and, if we are humane and caring, to provide for those people who are unable to provide for themselves. In our case, that is done through taxes levied on our income, earnings, assets, and purchases. There have been some reasonable criticisms of capitalism for encouraging exploitive practices in the service of individuals striving for wealth that leads to inequality between social classes, monopolies (in which the state allows corporations some control of authority over national resources and policies), oligarchies (government by a few select elites), or even fascism (strict and regimented control of government, resources, and labor by an autocrat, often a dictator).

In a totalitarian system, the state's power is, no surprise, total: the state owns everything and there's no limit to state control over individuals "The state" is usually a dictator or a small or elite group of self-appointed leaders. Under communism it is assumed that resources (natural resources, infrastructure, land, buildings, government money, etc.) are communally owned by all citizens but managed by a small group, and that some individual freedoms exist but are subordinate to the good of the state. The idea is that everyone has equal status and equal ownership: no classes, no excessive profits for any one person or group, all profits cycle into the running of the state and are distributed by the state to workers based on individual abilities and needs as determined by the state. However, history shows that communist economies eventually develop classes with differences in wealth and access to power, with government officials (as the power-brokers) at the top, a fringe-like middle, and a large lower-class composed of workers who have limited say in government decisions or resource distribution. In practice, communist regimes have been tyrannical, authoritarian, and oppressive. The same thing has been seen in socialist systems as well. However, while capitalism and socialism are somewhat opposing schools of thought as economic systems, the argument is more about the role of government than about the ideals. Socialists believe economic inequality is bad for society overall, so the state is responsible for maintaining some level of equality through state-administered and state-funded programs for education, healthcare, social security for the elderly and the poor, and in order to do all of this, higher taxes on individuals' income and other assets.

Under free markets, capitalism purports to grant free choice. Individuals make decisions for themselves with the assumption that people will make good economic decisions because they have to live directly with the consequences of their choices. Freedom of choice is supposed to allow consumers of all economic levels to participate in driving the economy. At the same time, to make sure that all people have equal access to opportunities to gain wealth and participate in the economy, our government is entrusted with insuring against discrimination based on race, color, gender, sexual orientation or other arbitrary classifications. If classifications create a system in which one gender, racial group, religious group, or professional class, has more opportunities and control than all others, self-interest means the group in power benefits from keeping all others out of the resource pool. Our democracy is threatened when the income gap grows so large that the ultra-rich have control over our economy and the rest of America cannot exercise the full range of freedoms granted by our democratic system. Our democracy is threatened when basic needs are no longer being met. State capitalism differs from free-market capitalism in that the state owns or co-owns business enterprises, can earn profits, and more or less runs like a large corporation; under this system, the government may have policies that, intentionally or not, favor some workers or industries over others.

Going back to Bernie, his critics are essentially calling him a socialist (or communist) as an insult because he has proposed increased government funding for something those critics don't particularly care for and they use a label that intentionally scares a lot of people. Consider this: the U.S. government already provides subsidies for farmers, oil companies, and other industries, claiming it is justified for the common good. At least for the farmers, we agree. Their lives, their communities, and their very position in our economic system, is under threat because of Trump's tariff wars. Many have lost farms that have been in their families for generations. The supply chains on which they have relied through foreign trade are broken and foreign customers have had to find suppliers in other countries. People have to eat; governments that are moral have to ensure their people have food, and even those governments that don't seem to adhere to a moral code risk rebellion if the people are starving. U.S. farmers may never get back these global customers.

As farmers struggle economically, food prices in the U.S. will rise, creating more recession pressure. Farm subsidies are a way to say, "Because you provide food for our country and contribute to the economy through foreign trade, we have your back." Do these subsidies mean we want State Capitalism and not Free-Market Capitalism? Does it mean we want to see the U.S. move toward socialism? The answer is "No!" on both counts. We believe that the farm subsidies are, when needed, a necessary tweaking of our capitalist system, because if our farming industry is not sustained, the effect on our economy would be devastating. If you don't agree and would rather see more government support for some other industry in times of economic distress, such as the automotive industry, shipbuilders, textiles, or recently the bailouts for cruise ship owners, airlines and other large corporations contained in the CARES Act is that enough reason to label you a socialist and say you are unfit for our democracy? Bernie's "democratic socialist" platform is his effort to weave health care, education and a living wage into America's existing social programs, the ones already in place. This is his view of what our people and economy need. The problem is "socialism" is a boogeyman label used to scare the hell out of people and Trump is already gearing up to use his arsenal of dirty tricks to label the entire Democratic Party "socialist." Even the Russians saw the advantage of trying to propel Bernie to the front of the line in their efforts to get Trump re-elected.

As a society we have determined that we must provide safety nets for our most needy citizens through programs such as Medicaid, free public education (K-12) and Social Security. For most of us this is consistent with our religious and moral values, and with the ideals of our nation's founders. If we ceased to do this, the people among us who are most vulnerable—the infirmed, disabled, children, and the elderly—would suffer. If providing for our neediest citizens is by some assessment "socialist," then the United States has long been a democratic-socialist system in some ways, and it would be morally wrong to do otherwise. What's in a name? In this case, for Trump and Republicans, just another chance to divert attention away from what really matters so they can win elections at any cost.

On March 19, 2020, the president invoked the Defense Production Act (DPA) to require companies to prioritize any federal orders for products—including masks, respirators and other critical items needed to fight the novel coronavirus—over other orders. This was a crisis and immediate action was needed to protect those on the front lines of this effort, yet as of March 23, administration officials admitted that the federal government had not yet made a single order under the DPA.[135] Healthcare workers across the country were desperate and had been pleading for the president to use the DPA. Trump offered two excuses to explain the lack of orders. He said that companies were stepping up to make these products on their own, and also that using the mechanism would be tantamount to socialism. Neither excuse is valid.

First, companies are motivated by maximizing profits not altruism. They will compare the profits they can get from these products against other manufactured products they can make. And, they will sell the products they make for COVID-19 response to the highest bidder meaning they will not necessarily go to the state with the greatest immediate need, but to the state that bids the highest. The ensuing bidding war wastes critical time and costs taxpayers significantly more. As a result, the N95 masks that had cost $.85 each now sell for $6.00. Some, but not enough, companies have stepped up to the plate. The federal government is needed to coordinate the manufacturing and distribution process. Absent life-saving equipment and PPE many people will not be afforded a fighting chance to live.

Second, use of the DPA is not socialism. The DPA is a law

---

[135] Alex Ward, "Trump's Excuses for Not Using the Defense Production Act are Wrong — and Dangerous", *Vox*, March 23, 2020, https://www.vox.com/2020/3/21191003/coronavirus-trump-defense-production-act.

that has its origins in the War Powers Act of World War II which granted the executive branch powers to direct industrial production for the war effort. Under the DPA the federal government does not take over and run private businesses. The United States government would, out of necessity, be ensuring that essential products are available to fight the pandemic. Businesses would still get paid for what they produce. Protecting the safety and health of its citizens is the primary goal of government in a democracy. if ignorance is bliss, Donald Trump must live in a state of ecstasy. Or perhaps our president does not believe in American democracy.

On March 27, Trump announced that he had finally implemented the DPA by ordering General Motors to expedite production of ventilators. However, as of mid-April there was no evidence that the order—or any orders—had been put in under the DPA. Trump coined the phrase, "In Trump time" saying it meant to, "do it now" but it appears "Trump time" really means "maybe later, we'll see, not important."

What does all of this have to do with modern-day fascism? A great deal, we think. An article in *Rolling Stone* called "The End of Facts" clearly shows how Trump has proven that, "If you connect with America's anger and paranoia, you can steamroll our most sacred institutions without ever having to tell the truth" (that's the article's subtitle). The author, journalist Matt Taibbi, warns: "Amid all the howling about Trump's deceptions, the far more upsetting story is the mandate behind them—not so much the death of truth in politics, but the irrelevance of it."[136] We add to that: our politics are out of whack and it is putting the future of democracy in danger.

---

136   Matt Taibbi, "The End of Facts", *Rolling Stone*, September 19, 2017, http://www.rollingstone.com/politics-features/the-end-of-facts- in-the-trump-era.

The Secret of Tyranny

> The secret of freedom lies in educating people, whereas the secret of tyranny is in helping to keep them ignorant.
>
> —Maximilien Robespierre, politician and lawyer, 1792

Maximilien Robespierre was a French lawyer and politician and one of the most influential figures associated with the French Revolution, so he knew what he was talking about when he publicly warned that tyranny thrives in ignorance.[137] The more we know, the better armed we are to fight social wrongs. A free press to inform the people is part of the core values of the United States. A free press also is often the first thing to go under authoritarian rule. Famous authoritarian and French Emperor Napoleon Bonaparte is alleged to have said: "If I were to give liberty to the press, my power could not last three days." At the beginning of Nazi control of Germany, the Nazis controlled less than three percent of the German press. Adolph Hitler quickly took control of the media, holding total control of every press after only a few weeks and eliminating all public opposition voices that might impair or question the Nazi agenda.

Representative authoritarianism is the same sentiment that in the 1930s-1940s fueled European fascism. In 1933 Nazi Germany ceased being a society based on laws. The Nazis removed from the judiciary those whose commitment to the party wasn't complete and packed the courts with officials sympathetic to the Nazi regime. Hermann Goering, Hitler's right-hand man, explained this logic of manipulation during the course of the Nuremberg trials, according to private interviews with American intelligence officer

---

137   Maximilien de Robespierre, "Public Statement, November 1792", *Oevres*, Vol. 2. 1840, WikiQuotes, accessed December 7, 2019, http://en.wikiquote.org/wiki/Maximilien_Robespierre.

and psychologist Gustave Gilbert. In an exchange that is chilling to us in the current crisis, Gilbert asked Goering why a people would back a leader who brought war and destruction to their society. Goering explained:

> Naturally, the common people don't want war; neither in Russia nor in England nor in America, nor for that matter in Germany. That is understood. But, after all, it is the *leaders* of the country who determine the policy and it is always a simple matter to drag the people along, whether it is a democracy or a fascist dictatorship or a Parliament or a Communist dictatorship.

Gilbert responded that America was different because, "In a democracy the people have some say in the matter through their elected representatives, and in the United States only Congress can declare wars." Goering replied: ""Oh, that is all well and good, but, voice or no voice, the people can always be brought to the bidding of the leaders. That is easy. All you have to do is tell them they are being attacked and denounce the pacifists for lack of patriotism and exposing the country to danger. It works the same way in any country."[138]

It seems clear to us that something beyond economics or foreign policy motivate Trump's minions and backers. To them, it appears that Trump hates the right people. Trump's response to any fact-based criticism by the press, or even just facts that don't promote his agenda, is to cry, "fake news." Trump says of news reports with which he disagrees—or just doesn't like: "Hoax! Fake News!" He regularly, virtually daily, calls the free press "the enemy of the people." He has challenged the independence of our judiciary and Congress. He has put himself above the law and then questioned the patriotism of his critics. The reality is that the vast

---

138   G.M. Gilbert, *Nuremberg Diary* (Farrar Strauss, 1961 [1947)]).

majority of any "fake news" out there flows from Trump's lips and tweeting fingers, and those of his minions. America is now in danger of being more swayed by fear than inspired by high ideals. Fear mongering to create discord is a favorite tactic of our current president. He is relentless in this, and there are thousands of examples of fear-inducing and incendiary statements: "If the Democrats capture the White House they will destroy the economy, the stock market will crash, people will be fighting in the streets", "This impeachment is a coup to remove your elected president from office", "They want to make us a socialist country", "Pelosi and Schiff hate America." He does not stop.

Trump believes he can do anything he wants without fear of reprisal. He has bragged that he could shoot someone on Fifth Avenue in Manhattan in broad daylight and not lose a vote. In our view he is figuratively using assault weapons carelessly and with an endless supply of ammunition, and mowing down millions without anyone stopping him. We have opined (and assumed) that no one is above the law. However, in totalitarian regimes certain people are, and we believe that this is precisely where Trump wants to take America.

In a government that seems rife with officials looking away and pretending this is all not happening, we are relieved when we see courageous men and women in the administration sounding alarms and stepping forward in the face of threats and character assassinations, and we are grateful to the Democrats on the Hill who continue to press the administration on its bad actions and false statements. Aside from Mitt Romney criticizing Trump about his call with President of Ukraine Volodymyr Zelensky, and voting for witnesses at the trial, where are the Republicans with a sense of real decency? Other than Romney, are there any left with even a shred of morality or ethics? If so, they have remained silent and in the shadows. Others colluded with the White House by disseminating propaganda and already-debunked conspiracy theories, such as the one from Trump's personal lawyer, Rudy Giuliani, and Trump himself that "it wasn't Russia that interfered in the 2016 election, it was Ukraine—and Joe Biden and his son Hunter Biden were part of the corruption in Ukraine." Not a scintilla of evidence exists to back up those innuendos. Not one! However, there is plenty of evidence that a host of Republican lawmakers including Devin Nunes were up to their eyebrows in the cesspool conspiring with Rudy Giuliani, Lev Parnas and others to go after Hunter and Joe Biden and create a false narrative for Trump to use in his re-election bid.

Not From Power or Riches, Grandeur or Glory

> The existence of such a government as ours for any length of time is a full proof of a general dissemination of knowledge and virtue throughout the whole body of the people. And what object or consideration more pleasing than this can be presented to the human mind? If national pride is ever justifiable or excusable it will spring, not from power or riches, grandeur or glory, but from conviction of national innocence, information, and benevolence.
>
> -John Adams, U.S. President and founding father, 1797

Even in the first years of our nation's formation, John Adams understood the benefits of an informed, engaged public over a society that places more value on wealth or glory, because "knowledge and virtue" require truth and integrity. We know because he said as much in his 1797 inaugural address – and his actions as our nation's leader showed that he meant.[139] Trump

---

139 John Adams, "Inaugural Address, 4 March 1797", *Founders Online*, National Archives, accessed February 2, 2020, https://founders.archives.gov/documents/Adams/99-02-02-1878.

seems to be taking Adams' wise words and point-by-point doing the opposite. Trump has established a cult of personality. He has convinced many of his followers that he and he alone is chosen by God to deal with the challenges America faces, whether real or created by him through his strategy of deception and distraction. After approximately two and a half centuries of a government of the people, our liberty and our country are facing a clear and present danger from the man who now leads our nation.

Trump figuratively wraps himself in the American flag and then targets those who criticize him as un-American. He spouts the belief that as president he should be immune from criticism and by virtue of holding the office, he can do no wrong. In stark contrast, one of America's most highly respected presidents, Theodore Roosevelt, once stated:

> To announce that there must be no criticism of the President, or that we are to stand by the President, right or wrong, is not only unpatriotic and servile, but is morally treasonable to the American public. Nothing but the truth should be spoken about him or anyone else. But it is even more important to tell the truth, pleasant or unpleasant, about him than about anyone else.[140]

Out of these two men, Trump or TR, we know whose advice we would follow. Teddy Roosevelt is known to have had great pride of self, as Trump also displays, but that is where any possible likeness ends. We are not naïve about politics and politicians, and our view of human nature echoes that of Adam Smith: People are inclined to act in their perceived self-interest. Best not to

---

140 Theodore Roosevelt, "Editorial in the Kansas City Star, May 7, 1918", *Quotations from the Speeches and Other Works of Theodore Roosevelt*, Theodore Roosevelt Association, https://theodoreroosevelt.org/content.aspx?page_id=22&club_id=991271&module_id=339333.

appeal to a person's better nature, as she or he may not have one; instead, appeal to an individual's self-interest since that's usually more effective. However, Trump takes self-interest to a new low. Maybe he does not understand the difference between political disagreement in a civil society and maliciously criticizing a person for their views. To us it seems more likely that he perversely thinks his behavior shows he is a tough, strong leader.

There are several quotes from the fascists of Nazi Germany and the Third Reich that describe Hitler's political strategy and that seem disturbingly similar to the political strategies of our current president and his minions. While some attributions are unverified, but we are more interested in the sentiments and how they are popularly known to originate. We are concerned with the fact that the sentiments and tactics directly reflect what we see going on now as a direct contrast with our understanding of the ideals of some of our nation's great leaders of the past.

That Elitist Approach to Government

> The American citizen must be made aware that today a relatively small group of people is proclaiming its purposes to be the will of the People. That elitist approach to government must be repudiated.
>
> –William E. Simon, Treasury Secretary and free-market capitalist, 1978

William E. Simon was Secretary of the Treasury from 1974-1977 under Presidents Nixon and Ford, and a strong believer in free-market capitalism He believed business should largely be left without government interference (within legal limits), which also meant not getting special treatment or bailouts for losses. Simon was an ultra-conservative and a leader in forming the New Right. His statements about elitism point to the dangers of a small minority claiming to represent all interests and "the will of the People," while in truth serving their own interests and wealth.[141] Simon's words are true today, maybe even more than when he wrote them. What happens when this elite is based mostly on wealth and is hand in hand with big business? A 2014 study jointly conducted by Princeton and Northwestern universities concluded:

> America is no longer a democracy—never mind the democratic republic envisioned by our founding fathers. Rather it has taken a turn down elitist lane and become a country led by a small dominant class comprised of powerful members who exert total control over the general population, an oligarchy so to speak.[142]

Elitism is the idea that while political democracy may be fair, it can result in mediocrity; cultural egalitarianism produces social mediocrity and we should not entrust the perpetuation of our culture to those deemed just average by the elites. Elitists believe that culture is best served through a meritocracy, not a democracy, and assume that the evolution of their system has entrusted to them the perpetuation of the system's highest standards. Elitists strongly believe that in a country without actual aristocracy, in order to have acceptably high standards and be able to meet them, exclusive organizations are one of the few cultural anchors available. Pluralists argue that there cannot be class domination in the United States because the wealthy upper-class is too fragmented to be able to organize for power. This argument is very wrong. The power-brokering is just out of most Americans' field of vision. It

---

141   William E. Simon, *A Time For Truth* (Readers Digest Press, 1978).
142   Martin Gilens and Benjamin I. Page, "Testing Theories of American Politics: Elites, Interest Groups, and Average Citizens", *Perspectives on Politics*, Cambridge University/American Political Science Association, September 2014, accessed January 20, 2020, https://doi.org/10.1017/S1537592714001595.

is occurring in socially elite gatherings and other exclusive group meetings most Americans have no knowledge of, let alone access to. At the same time, gross violation of the separation of powers is occurring. We believe this is directly related to the rise of elitism and politicians assuming that their "in group" of like-minded believers knows best.

Private clubs that heavily restrict membership, or whose membership and purpose are shrouded in secrecy, smack of elitism. There is literature on social philosophy (small group dynamics) which shows people who meet as a group in relaxed or informal settings that feel exclusive, will become even tighter with one another than people who meet in more open groups. People in exclusive groups are more likely to listen to others in their group and come to compromise: this social cohesion aids the formation of policy consensus. While often this may be the same old "smoke filled back rooms" as politics of yore, there are also more insidious forces lurking behind the scenes.

The Evangelical Elite: Hiding in Plain Sight

Religion is one area in which exclusion makes some sense; members of a church or religious group generally are expected to follow the beliefs and practices of that faith when meeting for strictly religious reasons. Places that are sacred to a religion might be limited to followers of that religion, or at least to request adherence to specific dress or practices out of respect to that religion. Politicians in the United States are free to practice any religion or none at all, and religious groups may support a political or social agenda and advocate for that agenda. However, the separation of church and state in America means that no specific religion may conspire with government to promote a religious agenda or belief, nor may the state impose any set of religious beliefs on the people.

In August 2019 Netflix released *The Family*, a documentary series based on the work of writer Jeff Sharlet, who has done impressive research and written books about the fundamentalist Christian association. The Family is an intensely secretive and influential organization known also as The Fellowship and The International Foundation. Sharlet had gone undercover within The Family in the early 2000s as one of its "interns," young men who join The Family as crusaders-for-God in training.[143] We found the series thought-provoking and also frightening. It sheds light on the deep ties between religion and politics that this group has been fostering for decades. The Family should not be dismissed as part of a lunatic fringe. Prominent evangelical Christians have described The Family as perhaps the most politically well-connected ministry in the world. Michael Lindsey, a sociologist who studies evangelical movements' intersection with politics, said: "There is no other organization like the Fellowship, especially among religious groups, in terms of its access or clout among the country's leadership."[144]

To consider elitism's undermining effect on a moral democracy, a discussion of the information reported in *The Family* is helpful to understand its importance to America's current situation. In 1935 a Norwegian immigrant named Abraham Vereide, a Methodist clergyman, started The Fellowship Foundation in the United States with the specific goal of creating a religion intended for an elite group. Sharlet states that Vereide created this group in response to a labor union effort which he considered evil, and in a report on NPR in 2009 that featured

---

[143] Jesse Moss (dir.), *The Family*, Netflix, 2019, https://www.netflix.com/title/80063867
[144] Michael D. Lindsey, *Faith in the Halls of Power: How Evangelicals Joined the American Elite* (Oxford University Press, 2007).

some of Sharlet's work, he explained that Vereide's purpose was to oppose Franklin Roosevelt's New Deal.[145]

Vereide believed that Christianity had achieved little in its 2,000 years because it directed its energies to the poor, the sick, and the starving. Harkening back to English theocracy with divinely appointed kings and their subjects divinely commanded to obey, The Family chose to embrace the construct by recruiting a ruling class of Christ-committed men. In this "trickle-down faith" theology the world would be run by "key men" chosen by God to rule over the rest of us. The Family's view of Christ seemed to portray Jesus as a muscular leader interested primarily in power. The Family puts forward an elitist, totalitarian view of politics with a direct line to fascism: the elites have special access to truth and the power that comes with it, giving them the right to rule over others. The Family proposes subjugation of the people for what they claim will be the greater good, and do so under Jesus' name. Is this really about Jesus? Is this the Jesus you know? We hope not!

Douglas Coe took over leadership of The Family upon Vereide's death in 1969. Coe was named one of the most influential evangelists in the world by *Time* magazine in 2005. Coe died in 2017, but during his leadership he built a worldwide network of allegiances, including with Russia and many totalitarian leaders. In the United States these allegiances with The Family are intended to function as a shadow alternative to our democratic government.

The interns for The Family are told they are being trained to rule the world. From his time undercover, Sharlet reported that interns: "… were taught the leadership lessons of Hitler, Lenin, and Marx and that Hitler's genocide wasn't an issue for [The Family]. It was the strength that he, Coe, emulated."[146] Coe compared the

---

145 "'Family': Fundamentalism, Friends in High Places", *Fresh Air*, National Public Radio, broadcast July 1, 2009, https://www.npr.org/transcripts/106115324.
146 Moss, *The Family*.

leadership of Jesus to leaders such as Ho Chi Minh and Osama bin Laden. A 1989 videotape that was part of a lecture series led by Coe provides irrefutable evidence of the dangers presented by The Family and adds credence to Sharlet's reports. In the tape, Coe expresses admiration for Hitler, Goebbels and Himmler, and compares Jesus' teachings to the Red Guard during China's Cultural Revolution. Of the Red Guard members' willingness to execute their own mothers in the name of their cause, Coe said: "That was covenant; a pledge. That is what Jesus said." To us this doesn't sound like it's about Jesus at all. It seems to be about power. Josephine Livingston explained of Coe's teachings in *The New Republic*: "Coe's admiration for Hitler cannot be forgotten once learned. Meetings can be secret and diplomacy can be covert, but videotape is forever." The point is that the truth about Coe and The Family is there for all to see and hear, but what is being done about it?

Despite our constitutional prohibition on church management of government, Coe did not act solely as a spiritual leader in his engagement with other nations and foreign leaders, and he was directly involved in U.S. diplomatic matters. Sharlet describes several examples of Coe's direct government involvement and influence, including President Carter's recollection of how helpful Coe was during the Camp David Accords to negotiate the peace deal between Egypt and Israel, behind closed doors. Coe travelled the world to build diplomatic back-channels with leaders like Muammar Gaddafi. He was a man every key politician seemed to know. Coe himself even said of his affiliation with some of the world's most tyrannical and cruel leaders, "Most of my friends are bad people. … They all broke the Ten Commandments, as far as I can tell," adding his own justification that, "Jesus even met with the Devil."[147]

Despite The Family's warped interpretation of Christian Scripture, members of the Washington elite, Democrat and Republican alike, lined up to get close to Coe. A large percentage of the House and Senate attend The Family's Annual Prayer Breakfast, one of the biggest events on the U.S. religious—and congressional—calendar. The Prayer Breakfast has been held every February for 55 years, and every sitting president since Eisenhower has participated in at least one Prayer Breakfast. President Carter called Coe "a fine Christian;" Hillary Clinton is said to be a member of The Family and after meeting privately with Coe at the White House in December 1997, she wrote: "Coe is...a unique presence in Washington: a loving spiritual mentor and guide to anyone regardless of party or faith, who wants to deepen his or her relationship with God." Former Vice President Gore also referred to Coe as a friend. There are innumerable prominent Republican Senators and Representatives who have also been intimately involved with The Family. In 2009 Rachel Maddow reported that politicians including Mark Sanford, Tom Coburn, John Ensign and Mike Pence were also members of The Family.

Donald Trump has expressed pride in his close personal relationship with Coe. Trump's childhood pastor, Norman Vincent Peale, was a friend of Vereide. Fascist rhetoric has entered into fundamentalist conversational politics. The Family has cultivated an intimate relationship between the evangelical movement and President Trump, leading some Christians to accept Trump as the

---

147 Original text in Peter J. Boyer, "Frat Houses for Jesus", *The New Yorker*. September 6, 2010, referenced in Coe's obituary: Zach Montague, "Doug Coe, Influential Evangelical Leader, Dies at 88", *The New York Times*, February 22, 2017, http://www.nytimes.com/2017/02/22/us/obituary-doug-coe-fellowship-foundation.html.

"imperfect vessel" for Jesus' will. Connect the dots: it seems unlikely that Trump sounds like a dictator by accident. Livingston said that Trump, "… speaks that way because men like Douglas Coe idolized fascist rulers of the mid-twentieth century and spread their appeal. The covenant offered by Christian fundamentalists is popular because of, not in spite of, its similarity to the Nazi brotherhood, and it was engineered on purpose to be its equivalent."[148]

We've mentioned Trump's impromptu press briefing on the White House lawn on August 21, 2019, when he looked up at the sky and proclaimed: "I am the chosen one!" These are strange, frightening words from this man, and it was a disturbing scene. Does he truly believe he is the Messiah? Although he later claimed he was only joking, he repeatedly implies his "chosen," status by, "tweeting some quotes from conservatives that he is the 'second coming of God'," as reported by the *Washington Post*'s Eugene Scott.[149] Some food for thought: we believe Trump may have been confirming his role in The Family that he is, in fact, their "Chosen One."

Coe died with no successor named to lead The Family, but it hasn't disbanded and there are hundreds if not thousands of cells throughout the world. Coe's sons are key leaders, and Coe's son-in-law, Doug Burleigh, is also a key leader and has assumed Coe's role organizing the National Prayer Breakfast. Burleigh was said to be one of the people questioned by the FBI for his interactions with a convicted Russian agent. What's going on? This is not a wild conspiracy theory: The Family has been in business in the United States since 1935, and there's a 1989 videotape of its leader, Coe, revealing his crazed theology. Yet, The Family continues to work in the shadows, unknown to most Americans and on behalf of some of our government officials. The Family and others in the

---

148 Moss, *The Family*.
149 Scott, "Comparing Trump to Jesus."

evangelical movement provide political support under a false cloak of righteousness that perpetuates elitism and secrecy. If there is some truthful, reasonable explanation for Coe's recorded statements, why haven't our politicians told us? There seems to be a severe lack of transparency, along with apparent evidence that several of our politicians, past and present, may have violated the separation of church and state prohibition. The Family is allowed to run the Prayer Breakfast each year and our elected officials are scrambling over one another to get next to them. Is there some credible explanation for this? If Sharlet's substantial work includes fabrications, why hasn't Sharlet been sued? We are raising questions here to which we can't provide verifiable answers ourselves. But wouldn't you like to know? Why not start questioning Republicans and Democrats alike about their relationships with The Family, and what they think about Coe's views and the videotape?

Social Elite Leadership: By Invitation Only

According to the Princeton/Northwestern study that found rising elitism in American politics and government, the U.S. government now represents the rich and powerful over average citizens: "the central point that emerges from our research is that economic elitism and organized groups representing business interests have established independent impacts on the United States government's policy, while mass-based interest groups and average citizens have little or no independent influence at all."[150] We believe this is getting worse by the day under Trump's presidency, despite the anti-elitist rhetoric made to supporters during his presidential campaign. The reality is Trump grew up an elitist, continues to live that lifestyle and surrounds himself with the trappings of wealth. He has appointed and placed some of the wealthiest Americans to

---

150   Gilens and Page, "Elites, Interest Groups, and Average Citizens."

powerful and influential government positions, even when their credentials were no match to the positions assigned. Why would he do this when there are plenty of conservatives with policy credentials and decades of relevant experience? The other question we ask ourselves is, "where does he find these people?"

There are venues for the wealthy and powerful to connect with one another socially and off-the-record, to make deals, alliances and compromises out of the public eye and under the radar. For these elites, their faith is in money and its attendant power is their God. But a country club or a benefit gala might not be private enough. There are several private clubs for the ultra-rich and powerful that are hidden from public purview, and there have been rumors that these are where the secret rulers of the world gather. They meet privately to determine America's policies and develop their own vision for the proper direction of the world. Exploring these clubs helps illuminate what is evolving as our society becomes more unapologetically divided and elitist. We will look at two of the most influential: The Bohemian Club and The Bilderberg Group.

The Bohemian Club

The Bohemian Club, a private, men-only "gentleman's club" in San Francisco. It owns Bohemian Grove which is a restricted 2,700-acre campground located in Monte Rio, California 75 miles north of San Francisco. Bohemian Grove serves as a camp for those who consider themselves the masters of the universe, and its name is synonymous with elitism. In the 1984 movie *Secret Honor*, director Robert Altman shows a powerful group manipulating Richard Nixon throughout his political career. This group has all the attributes of the Bohemian Club and Altman's movie calls the group "The Committee of 100." A May 2009 *Vanity Fair* article,

"Bohemian Tragedy," shed more light on these powerful elitists.[151] "Bohemians," as members are called, are drawn in large measure from the corporate leadership of the United States and from every sector of the economy. The Grove has served as an ideal setting for the wealthy powerbrokers to size up politicians. Members of the Bohemian Club have reportedly been a significant factor in deciding who will be nominated to become the president of the United States.

There is an annual retreat at the Grove featuring serious recreation and socializing. The Bohemian Club represents itself as a social club not a secret meeting place to plot, or plan and conjure. No recording devices or cell phones are allowed in. The members are sworn to secrecy. The patron saint of the club is St. John of Nepomuk, martyred for his devotion to the sanctity and secrecy of the confessional. It makes sense that he would become the patron of the businessmen, politicians and powerbrokers of the Bohemian Club. Despite the emphasis on secrecy, quite a bit is known about members and guests of the club.

Dr. Edward Teller, father of the hydrogen bomb, was a club member; he reserved the grounds in September 1942 and the groundwork for the Manhattan project was laid there. Herbert Hoover appeared at the Grove. In 1948, Dwight D. Eisenhower was there. In 1971 Ronald Reagan allegedly promised Richard Nixon at the Grove that he would only enter the Republican primaries if Nixon faltered. President George H.W. Bush was a long time Bohemian. Bush was nastily attacked in a 1994 speech by the ultra-conservative William Simon, who castigated Bush for his abandonment of the Reagan agenda. Members of the Kennedy, Johnson and Carter administrations were also prominent guests, but for almost three decades now the membership has been

---

151   Alex Shoumatoff, "Bohemian Tragedy," *Vanity Fair*, April 1, 2009, https://www.vanityfair.com/culture/2009/05/bohemian-grove200905.

solidly Republican. In the 1990s there was a complete absence of representatives of the Clinton administration. There were no representatives of the Obama administration either. It appears that now only Republican business gets done at the Bohemian Club.

The Bilderberg Group

The Bilderberg Group was established in 1954 by two men, one a former member of the German Nazi party, and the other a spy for the Vatican. Prince Bernhard of the Netherlands was a Nazi Party member in Germany. In 1934 Bernhard left school to work for the German chemical company IG Farben, maker of poisonous gas used to kill people in the Nazi death camps. Josef Ritinger was a political advisor and a spy for the Vatican.

Jim Tucker of *The American Free Press* describes the Bilderberg Group as an organization of political leaders and international financiers that meet secretly every year to make global policy.[152] The compound where meetings are held is guarded by 400 heavily armed guards. Members of the Bilderberg Group are some of the richest, most powerful and famous people in the world. According to information from the official website for Bilderberg Meetings, the annual meeting is attended by 120-150 political leaders, government officials and experts from industry, finance, media and academia. The 2019 meeting took place in Montreux, Switzerland, from May 30-June 2. There were approximately 130 participants, about two-thirds from Europe and a third from North America. There is no detailed agenda, no votes taken, and no policy statements issued. The participants are free to use the information received, but neither the identity nor the affiliation of the speaker or

---

152 James B. Tucker, "What Is Bilderberg?", *American Free Press*, June 2, 2012, https://americanfreepress.net/what-is-bilderberg/.

any other participants may be revealed. The conference is a forum for informal discussions about megatrends and major issues facing the world. The agenda that the Bilderberg Group sends out prior to each year's meeting is absent specificity and since all participants are sworn to secrecy, it cannot be determined if it is an accurate list of their discussions.

The Bilderberg Group is a conspiracy theorist's dream come true. Since no one except attendees of the meetings knows what is said or done there, anything imaginable might be going on. One theory is that the Bilderberg Group's goal is one world government. Research journalist Daniel Estulin has made it his life's work to study the Bilderberg Group. Estulin claims to have penetrated the layers of the Bilderberg Group with the help of "conscientious objectors" from the inside. In his book, *The True Story of the Bilderberg Group*, he declares that the group's agenda includes:

- one international identity (observing) one set of universal values
- centralized control of world populations by "propaganda"; in other words, controlling world public opinion
- a new world order with no middle-class, only "rulers and servants (serfs)", and, of course, no democracy
- "a zero-growth society" without prosperity or progress, but greater wealth and power for rulers
- manufactured crises and perpetual wars
- absolute control of education in order to program the public and train those chosen for various roles
- centralized control of all foreign and domestic policies, one size fits all globally
- using the U.N as a de facto world government imposing a tax on all "world citizens"
- expanding NAFTA and WTO globally

- making NATO into a world military
- imposing a universal legal system
- a global welfare state in which obedient slaves are rewarded and non-conformists targeted for extermination

While we cannot attest to the accuracy of Estulin's list, based on the information available we find it plausible. If some of these seem far-fetched, remember that no one would have believed Hitler was going to exterminate six million Jews either. Henry Kissinger was Secretary of State under Richard Nixon from 1973-1977. A *Wall Street Journal* opinion piece by Kissinger, "Henry Kissinger on the Assembly of a New World Order," shows him as a key front man for a powerful movement aimed to impose what he and other globalists refer to as a "New World Order."[153] Estulin cites a speech made by Kissinger in 1992 at the Bilderberg meeting:

> Today, Americans would be outraged if UN troops entered Los Angeles to restore order; tomorrow they will be grateful. This is especially true if they were told there was an outside threat from beyond, whether real or promulgated, that threatened our very existence. It is then that all people of the world will plead with world leaders to deliver them from this evil… individual rights will be willingly relinquished for the guarantee of their well-being granted them by their world government.[154]

The Bilderberg meeting website lists the people invited to attend each year (attendance is by invitation only), and the lists include some of the most powerful, influential individuals in the world. President Bill Clinton has attended and Hillary Clinton is

---

153   Henry Kissinger, "Henry Kissinger on the Assembly of a New World Order", *Wall Street Journal,* August 29, 2014, https://www.wsj.com/articles/henry-kissinger-on-the-assembly-of-a-new-world-order-1409328075.
154   Daniel Estulin, *The True Story of the Bilderberg Group* (Trine Day, 2009).

said to attend every year. Nearly all presidential candidates have attended the Bilderberg meetings. A year after Bill Clinton attended as governor of Arkansas in 1991; he was elected president of the United States. Hillary Clinton has reportedly received millions of dollars in speaker fees through her relationships with other attendees over the years. Tony Blair attended the Bilderberg meeting; four years later he was prime minister of Great Britain. Kissinger attends the meeting every year. Stacy Abrams, James Baker, Robert Altman, David Petraeus, Robert Rubin, Lindsey Graham, and many, many other prominent Americans and Europeans have attended as well. In 2019, both Jared Kushner and Secretary of State Mike Pompeo attended.

The Bilderberg meetings may simply be a chance for the elite to meet for some back-channel deal-making and professional networking to solidify power and opportunities for wealth. However, the absolute secrecy adhered to is discomforting. What is really being discussed or planned? If it's just a little rubbing of elbows, why isn't anyone allowed to talk about it?

From Stability to Chaos in a Few Short Moves

Control by a few self-appointed leaders is tyranny. Does anyone see the similarities between the current playbook and the rhetoric and manipulations of demagogues not so very far in the past? Just asking. We want to avoid hyperbole. We are not calling for a revolution. We don't want to tear down and replace our democracy. We want to take it back, within the rules, and make it work as intended. We are extremely concerned by the way Trump is portraying America. We are alarmed that our leaders are ignoring their duties under Article One of the Constitution. We are alarmed by the deafening silence generated by the party of Lincoln. The people we have elected to ensure our freedoms and protect the rule of law appear more interested in grasping Trump's coattails in the next election than in upholding their oath of office. We expect better from our leaders and should be able to look to them as role models for ourselves and our children. But that feels like asking for the impossible and we want to throw up our hands and say, "let's not even bother to go there!" These days, it is difficult to find politicians who embody any of these qualities, but we must do our best and begin working to truly clean up the Washington cesspool. President Trump has decided to captain the cesspool swim team, and so for the future of our democracy we must mobilize against the invasive species that have taken up residency in the cesspool, the ones who are dividing and damaging America.

The definition of Utopia in Wikipedia is an imagined community that possesses highly desirable or nearly perfect qualities for all citizens. It focuses on equality in economics, government and justice with the method and structure of proposed implementation varying based on ideology. Unlike socialism, in our democracy we seek fair economic opportunity—a level playing field on which we can all compete for financial success—not economic equality. The opposite or antonym of Utopia is Dystopia which is a community or society in which people lead wretched, dehumanized, fearful lives. It is characterized by human misery, squalor, oppression, disease and overcrowding. Utopia may not be a realistic goal for our society but we contend that under President Trump we are moving further and further away. The coronavirus gives us a glimpse of dystopia and what our leadership is made of.

In the spring of 2020 amid the coronavirus pandemic, as primaries were canceled or states tried to move them to distance/absentee or online voting, Trump tweeted that absentee voting has, "tremendous potential for voter fraud and, for whatever reason, doesn't work out well for Republicans." If there is insufficient funding for this initiative, Trump would see this as being to his advantage. First, Republican voters in general have shown far less concern about the dangers of contracting the virus and would therefore be more likely to vote in person than Democrats. Second, if Trump loses the election and the insufficient election funding raises questions about the individual states vote counts, he might manage to have the results declared invalid and ask the Supreme Court to intervene. If the court does not rule as Trump would like, he may refuse to vacate the White House or turn over power to the president deemed elected. He may also declare it a temporary emergency, call in the military to impose martial law over the civilian population. Don't put it past him—he believes he is above the law and so far, Barr has supported him. That would not mean that our military leaders would accede to his demands, but it would certainly rank as the most serious Constitutional crisis in our history, result in massive civil unrest and place our democracy in dire consequences. However, if the election is not close—we crush him at the polls—we can virtually eliminate this potential nightmare.

CHAPTER 6

THIS IS OUR DEMOCRACY

> Indeed it has been said that democracy is the worst form of government except all those other forms that have been tried from time to time.
> —Winston Churchill, prime minister of the United Kingdom, 1947

> Where law ends tyranny begins.
> —John Locke, philosopher, 1690

WE AGREE WITH WINSTON CHURCHILL'S STATEMENT to the British House of Commons in 1947 that while a democracy may have its problems, it is a better and fairer system than any other that humans have tried so far.[155] English philosopher John Locke's theories of government heavily influenced our founders' writing of our Constitution. In his *Second Treatise of Government* (1690), Locke warned:

> Where-ever law ends, tyranny begins, if the law be transgressed to another's harm; and whosoever in authority exceeds the power given him by the law, and makes use of the force he has under his command, to compass that upon the subject, which the law allows not, ceases in that to be a magistrate; and, acting without authority, may be opposed, as any other man, who by force invades the right of another.[156]

---

155 Winston S. Churchill, "Democracy is the Worst Form of Government (Speech to the House of Commons 11 November 1947)", *RichardLangworth.com*, June 26, 2009, http://richardlangworth.com/worst-form-of-government.

156 John Locke, "Second Treatise of Government (1690)", *Project Gutenberg*,

Locke's work contributed one of our founding principles: that legitimate government requires the people's consent in a "social contract" in which the people can decide on a smaller group to represent society's best interest, but must maintain checks on this group in case of power grabs. For us that means if our elected officials act outside what our Constitution allows, or misuses the power granted by their office, they are no longer legitimate leaders and can and should be removed from office. Our system relies on the rule of law and our politicians and elected officials are not above the law. President Trump's actions are a perfect illustration of how to move toward tyranny, according to Locke's principles and those of our founders. Make no mistake, our legislative branch has been successfully undermined, if Trump is reelected the Supreme Court will be next, resulting in an overpowering executive branch that acts with complete indifference to the laws of our nation.

In establishing our democracy, America's founding fathers had an extraordinary understanding of human nature that led them to establish three equal branches of government with a system of checks and balances that serve as guardrails to ensure against excesses and power grabs by any one branch. Our Legislative Branch is listed first in the Constitution, in Article 1: Congress, comprising the House of Representatives and the Senate. The Executive Branch is listed under Article 2 of the Constitution, and consists of the president of the United States and the cabinet members with control over the various departments of government. The Judicial Branch is under Article 3: the federal courts and the United States Supreme Court. This balance was intended to prevent the control of government by any one branch or a takeover by any one group or individual. Our founders put this in place specifically to prevent a monarchy from arising in the new nation because the

---

September 5, 2017, accessed December 20, 2019, http://www.gutenberg.org/files/7370/7370-h.htm.

whole purpose of our nation was to create something different and better than before.

The Trump presidency is reading like a frightening page out of a world history book: undermine confidence in the press; set up your own propaganda state; run news outlets; sow discord among the population and find a bogeyman to blame everybody's troubles on; undermine the rule of law and use your position of authority to scare and intimidate anyone who doesn't go along with your agenda; target anyone standing in your way, impugning their reputation and questioning their patriotism; and cause everyone who opposes you to be in fear of losing their jobs and livelihoods, or being attacked by the crazies. We have read this chapter of history before and it does not end well. Why would anyone be surprised? This has been going on since the start of Trump's presidential campaign. Trump's presidency is a large repository of conflicts of interest. It is more and more apparent that the main beneficiary of President Trump's actions is Donald Trump. People are more disillusioned now than before the 2016 election. This president has had a corrupting influence on virtually everything he has touched. Welcome to Trump's America, a safe haven for corruption and greed.

The Very Definition of Tyranny

> "The accumulation of all powers, legislative, executive and judiciary, in the same hands, whether of one, a few or many, and whether hereditary, self-appointed, or elective, may justly be pronounced the very definition of tyranny."
>
> —James Madison, founding father, statesman, and U.S. President, 1788

James Madison, founding father and our nation's fourth president, held strong to the principle of separation of powers for our three branches of government, especially between the judicial and executive branches because of the opportunity for corruption and abuse of power.[157] The Trump administration and Republicans in Congress have breached this separation, and it's like the cesspool has a leak. There are many examples, but two of the most egregious are the actions (or lack of) of the Republican Senate led by Mitch McConnell of Kentucky, and Attorney General William Barr. George Conway and a few fellow Republicans have attributed our nation's problems to the "craven acquiescence" of congressional Republicans, who in their support (or silence), "have done no less than abdicate their Article I responsibilities."[158] Conway, along with Steve Schmidt, John Weaver, and Rick Wilson, stated this in a *New York Times* editorial announcing their formation of the Lincoln Project which is intended to encourage Republicans to move away from Trump and ensure he is not re-elected in 2020. Their article was subtitled, "The president and his enablers have replaced conservatism with an empty faith led by a bogus prophet." We heartily agree, and here we discuss two reasons why: McConnell and Barr.

    The role of the U.S. attorney general is to serve as the head of our federal Department of Justice. However, Barr as attorney general has been behaving like a private attorney for Donald Trump rather than fulfilling his official role of chief law enforcement officer of the United States. McConnell as Senate Majority Leader has, in turn, abdicated his responsibilities to the

---

157   James Madison, "The Particular Structure of the New Government and the Distribution of Power Among Its Different Parts. The Federalist Papers: No. 47, February 1, 1788", *The Avalon Project,* Yale Law School Lillian Goldman Law Library, http://avalon.law.yale.edu/18th_century/fed47.asp.

158   George T. Conway III, Steve Schmidt, John Weaver and Rick Wilson, "We Are Republicans, and We Want Trump Defeated", *The New York Times,* December 17, 2019, http://www.nytimes.com/2019/12/17/opinion/lincoln-project.html.

will of the executive branch. Senate Republicans have responded with "craven acquiescence," doing nothing without the approval of Trump because, as politicians and members of the Republican Party, they fear incurring this president's wrath. They fear that Trump's loyal core will turn away from them and they'll lose their seats. In other words, these elected representatives are more interested in protecting their own beloved jobs and positions in the power structure than in holding an out of control president to account or upholding their sworn oath to protect and defend the Constitution of the United States.

Mitch's Magic: Keep Expectations Very, Very Low

As Senate Majority Leader, McConnell's responsibility is to bring legislative proposals to the floor of the Senate for open debate and votes. In addition to the economic and tax proposals that Mitch has left to rot in the legislative graveyard of his desk (we discuss these in our chapter on economics), some of the measures wasting away under Mitch's intentional neglect are proposals to improve background checks for firearm sales, addressing voter registration issues, election security, lowering prescription drug prices, climate change measures, minimum wage increases and domestic violence prevention. We wonder why McConnell won't let these see the light of day. After all, if something is not what the people want and not supported in Congress, then it would just be voted down, right? Maybe that is Mitch's magic act: watch progress disappear right before our very eyes.

Under the separation of powers edict of the Constitution, if Congress sends a bill to the president but the president decides to veto that proposed piece of legislation, the majority leader (yes, that's Mitch) has the responsibility to put that legislation back on the Senate floor for a determination of whether or not to override the veto. Since Democrats took control of the House of Representatives in 2016, the House has passed over 400 pieces of legislation and forwarded them to the Senate for consideration. McConnell has let the House-passed legislation languish on his desk, going nowhere. As only one example, McConnell has been unwilling to bring to the floor any bill addressing gun control until Trump tells him what, if any, legislation he will agree to sign into law, despite the fact that over 90 percent of Americans reportedly support tighter background checks prior to gun purchases, a claim validated by *PolitiFact* in 2017.[159]

Moreover, Congress is the only body with constitutional authority to address any potential wrongdoing by the president of the United States. While the House of Representatives has the exclusive authority to impeach the president for high crimes and misdemeanors, and did so, it was an effort in futility when the body in charge of conducting the trial was the GOP-led Senate. Before the matter even got to the Senate, McConnell publicly announced that he was coordinating with the White House and Trump himself, on efforts in the Senate concerning the trial. McConnell further announced that he had already made up his mind, along with several other senators including Lindsey Graham of South Carolina, that there was no need for further evidence or to hear witness testimony. In light of comments made by McConnell and several other Republican senators, it was always doubtful that McConnell would uphold his oath of office to the Constitution in this matter. While McConnell chooses to "see no evil and hear no evil" we wish he would also "speak no evil." We've never heard of

---

159   This figure is supported by a Quinnipiac poll per PolitiFact: "Chris Abele stated on October 2, 2017 in a tweet: 90 percent of Americans 'support universal background checks' for gun purchases", *PolitiFact*, October 3, 2017, http://www.politifact.com/factchecks/2017/oct/03/chris-abele/do-90-americans-support-background-checks-all-gun-/.

a case in the United States where the accused got to set the rules of his own trial. It must be pretty nice to be a defendant in a trial and be able to coordinate with the judge and the jury to ensure a not guilty verdict and acquittal. We are proud to say that we have no knowledge of any similar experience in any court or Congressional forum in our nation's history.

We wonder if the fact that Senate Majority Leader McConnell's wife, Elaine Chao, was appointed by Trump as his Secretary of Transportation, might have any influence in McConnell's decision. Is there, perhaps, a potential conflict of interest? House Democrats have initiated an ethics probe into whether Chao, as head of the U.S. Department of Transportation (DOT), has used her position to provide financial and other benefits to members of her family and herself. In May 2019, the *Wall Street Journal* reported that Chao, "retained shares in a construction-materials company more than a year after the date she promised to relinquish them, federal disclosure forms show."[160] The *Wall Street Journal* followed up in September 2019 to report that Chao still had not divested her shares in a crushed stone, sand and gravel company which supplies construction materials for the transportation sector.[161] In June 2019, the *New York Times* reported that Chao did not recuse herself from DOT decisions affecting the shipping industry, and at the same time DOT had proposed budget cuts that would hurt competitors of the Chao family's shipping business.[162] Later in June, both *Politico* and *Yahoo* reported on

---

160   Ted Mann and Brody Mullins, "Transportation Secretary Still Owns Stock She Pledged to Divest", *The Wall Street Journal*, May 28, 2019, https://www.wsj.com/articles/transportation-secretary-still-owns-stock-she-pledged-to-divest-11559035921.
161   Natalie Andrews, "House Panel to Probe Possible Conflicts of Interest by Transportation Secretary Chao", *The Wall Street Journal*, September 1, 2019, https://www.wsj.com/articles/house-panel-to-probe-possible-conflicts-of-interest-by-transportation-secretary-elaine-chao-11568677954.
162   Michael Forsythe and Eric Lipton, "For the Chao Family, Deep Ties to

actions taken by the Federal Maritime Administration, Federal Highway Administration and Federal Aviation Administration, all within DOT, that would benefit Senator McConnell (Chao's husband, in case you forgot), in Kentucky.[163] It appears that what's good for the goose is good for the gander and vice-verse—so long as all the geese involved are backing Trump and there's no reason to expect the DOJ will be looking into any of it.

We did not expect a lot from this Senate majority leader regarding this administration's wrongdoing, and it turns out we were right. It was apparent from the beginning even with a smoking gun, a picture of the gun in the president's hand, his own written declaration of guilt and a proclamation from Jesus himself, the Senate would still fail to convict Trump in an impeachment trial. The Republicans refused to call any witnesses and the only Republican to vote for an article of impeachment was Mitt Romney. Come on Kentucky, it is time for Mitch to become a private citizen again. Note from the authors to Senator Collins, you don't get a pass on this one. We sincerely hope your time in the cesspool will soon be over.

William Barr, Attorney at Law: What Laws?

The stated mission of the U.S. Department of Justice, according to the DOJ website, is:

> To enforce the law and defend the interests of the United States according to the law; to ensure public safety against threats foreign and domestic; to provide federal

---

the World's 2 Largest Economies", *The New York Times,* June 2, 2019, https://www.nytimes.com/2019/06/02/us/politics/transportation-secretary-elaine-chao.html.
163   Tucker Doherty and Tanya Snyder, "Chao Created Special Path for McConnell's Favored Projects", *Politico,* June 10, 2019, https://www.politico.com/story/2019/06/10/mcconnell-elaine-chao-1358068.

leadership in preventing and controlling crime; to seek just punishment for those guilty of unlawful behavior; and to ensure fair and impartial administration of justice for all Americans.

For us to say Mr. Barr lacks understanding of some of the laws that he has taken an oath to uphold would be extremely disingenuous. It is more likely that he has simply chosen to ignore established law and follow the president's personal doctrine that facts, rules and laws are what the president says they are. To start, Barr opined that the president should not be required to release his tax returns. While there is no law that requires our president to release his tax information to the public, there is a law that requires any person, including the president of the United States, to provide the House Committee on the Judiciary with a copy of his/her taxes on request and without question or interference with the House's legally constituted right to request such documents. The committee's request would be for reasons of inquiry if, for no other reason, to ensure that the president or any other person from whom tax returns are requested, is not accepting improper or illegal gratuities or emoluments, or compromising their position or our nation's security.

Barr and the president's actual personal attorney, Rudy Giuliani, have been linked to possible involvement in the bribery plot involving Ukraine. Tax returns would reveal the financial relationship of Russia and Ukraine to the president and whether or not the decisions being made by the president are being influenced by an improper financial relationship. This is statutory law. For the president of the United States to interfere or hinder the release of his taxes constitutes a violation of his oath of office to protect and defend the laws and the Constitution of the United States. And for Barr to go along with it to us seems to constitute a breach of his fiduciary duty to the American people as the Attorney General of the United States. Perhaps the House of Representatives should be looking into his impeachment as well.

From our perspective, Barr misrepresented the findings of the Mueller report simply to control the narrative for the president. By putting out false and misleading information he gave the Trump administration cover to claim that there was absolutely no wrongdoing or anything improper relative to Russian interference in the 2016 election. Nothing could be further from the truth. Everyone knows or should know that Paul Manafort admitted, and the Mueller report verified, that a representative of the White House (Manafort) passed polling information on the 2016 election to Russian oligarchs tied to Putin. We know through intelligence sources that the Russians clearly interfered in the election with a favorable eye to helping Trump get elected. Every member of the American public has a right to know that his/her vote counts.

There was no determination reached in the Mueller Report on Trump's specific involvement with the Russians for two reasons. The first was because Trump was never interviewed by Mueller, which made it nearly impossible for Mueller to determine intent. Second, even if there was intent, Mueller could not indict a sitting president in accordance with existing Department of Justice policy. That policy is not a binding law, but rather an internal DOJ policy. But clearly its enforceability would be determined by Barr, who made his feelings publicly known.

Simply put, a lot of people doubt everything Barr does or says as attorney general. For all the deflection, lies, and misdirection being offered by the president we found it curious when it was recently revealed that the president knew about the Russian interference all along. The motto of the Federal Bureau of Investigation (FBI) is, "Fidelity, Bravery and Integrity." As an institution the FBI has long adhered to that motto and has deservedly garnered the respect of the American public as have the dedicated, patriotic members of our intelligence community. Those who work in the FBI all deserve our appreciation for their unselfish public service. Instead, this president constantly denigrates these pillars of our democracy. Calling them deep-state operatives is Trump's way to deflect attention away from his actions which represent a serious threat to our democracy. To us Barr was obviously lying, while denigrating honest patriots who were doing their job for their country and protecting our Constitution. He maligned Mueller, our intelligence community, the FBI and others trying to investigate potential wrongdoing. Talk about bearing false witness! Our president's modus operandi was obviously learned at a very early age from his mentor Roy Cohn. Attack! Attack! Attack! Cast doubt on anyone and everyone who is perceived as potentially injurious to your position, personal interests or finances.

The Pestilence of Foreign Influence

> Propagating knowledge, virtue, and religion among all classes of the people, not only for their benign influence on the happiness of life in all its stages and classes, and of society in all its forms, but as the only means of preserving our Constitution from its natural enemies, the spirit of sophistry, the spirit of party, the spirit of intrigue, the profligacy of corruption, and the pestilence of foreign influence, which is the angel of destruction to elective governments.
>
> —John Adams, founding father, statesman and U.S. president, 1797

President John Adams said these words in his inaugural address to the Congress of our young nation. It was a clear and heartfelt message to elected leaders to stay true to our national values, not give in to our worst impulses of deception and corruption, and be confident that as a nation we would thrive without ceding power to foreign entities, even our allies or trade partners, or foreign interests promising to support our young nation in some way.[164] There's no such thing as a free lunch, especially in global politics. The reality of our current situation is that we don't know if Putin has some kind of leverage over Trump, however, our president certainly seems to be pandering to Putin and allowing Russia more and more influence around the globe at the cost of U.S. interests. That is a very costly "free" lunch! Trump seems fearful and desperate in his reactions to all things Russia.[165] At the same time, Trump seems hell-bent on emulating Putin—not a good thing for American democracy. It seems clear to us that Russia under Putin is an enemy of the United States and should be treated accordingly. As Putin himself said, "There is no such thing as a former KGB man."[166] Yet Putin is being courted by our president, who seems to be intently watching Putin's undemocratic tactics and reworking them for his own use.

As a practical matter, Putin holds the reins of power in Russia. He is, in essence, omnipotent. In reality he acts more like a monarch or dictator. Putin maintains the pretext of a democracy while governing as a tyrannical strongman dictator. A totalitarian dictatorship usually refers to a country in which the central government has total control over all aspects of people's lives under the rule of a strong authoritarian leader. Officially,

---

164   Adams, "Inaugural Address."
165   The substance of this information on Russia and Vladimir Putin is from the editors of *Encyclopedia Britannica* (EB) and EB's Manager of Geography and History, Jeff Wallenfeldt, as of December 19, 2019. See: https://www.britannica.com/biography/Vladimir-Putin.
166   Putin has reportedly said this more than once, for example see: Anna Nemtsova, "A Chill in the Moscow Air", *Newsweek*, February 5, 2006, http://www.newsweek.com/chill-moscow-air-113415. This has been stated about Putin by both critics and supporters.

however, the government of Russia is a federal semi-presidential republic. Under this structure the president and prime minister share governing responsibilities as head of state and head of government, respectively. As in the United States, there are three branches of government: executive, legislative, and judicial, but the greatest power resides with the president. The president is elected by the general population for a six-year term and can serve two consecutive terms. The president is commander-and-chief of the military, can veto any laws set forth by the legislative branch, can establish laws without review or approval by other governmental bodies, and signs international agreements and treaties. The president nominates the parliament and the prime minister.

Putin served fifteen years as a foreign intelligence officer for the KGB (Committee for State Security), the all-in-one state security, intelligence, and secret police agency, when Russia was the controlling authority of the Union of Soviet Socialist Republics (USSR, or Soviet Union), until the USSR dissolved in 1991. Andrei Soldatov, Russian investigative reporter and critic of Russian surveillance operations, said of the KGB: "Its primary task was protecting the regime. Its activities included hunting down spies and dissidents and supervising media, sports and even the church. It ran operations both inside and outside the country but, in both spheres, the main task was always to protect the interests of whoever resided in the Kremlin." The Soviet Union was vast and comprised fifteen countries: Armenia, Azerbaijan, Belarus, Estonia, Georgia, Kazakhstan, Kyrgyzstan, Latvia, Lithuania, Moldova, Tajikistan, Turkmenistan, Ukraine, Uzbekistan, and Russia. In December 1991 the USSR was effectively dissolved when Russia, Ukraine and Belarus seceded. In addition, the Eastern European countries that had not been officially within the USSR but had been under Soviet domination were freed from direct control at that time: Poland, East Germany, Czechoslovakia, Romania, Bulgaria,

Hungary, Albania, and Yugoslavia as well as Croatia, Bosnia and Herzegovina, Serbia, Montenegro, and the disputed territory of Bosnia. The KGB's power extended at least as far as Soviet influence, if not further.

Putin has filled every state agency and institution with former KBG officers and agents, and has ensured former KGB agents and officers are well-placed in the Russian business sector. In an article in *Politico* in September 2016, "Vladimir Putin Resurrects the KGB," journalist Owen Matthews wrote: "Over Putin's years in power, not just the Kremlin but almost every branch of the Russian state has been taken over by KGB men like himself."[167] In 2016 Putin established a new "super agency," in Matthews' words: the Ministry of State Security, designed specifically as a guarantee of Putin's rule. As the true head of both the Russian state and its security organizations, Putin garnered the power to prosecute and eliminate independent voices and to silence those who would question him. On February 27, 2015 opposition leader Boris Nemtsov was gunned down just days after he had spoken out against Russian intervention in Ukraine.

In the months prior to the 2016 U.S. presidential election a series of high-profile hacking attacks targeted the Democratic Party and its presidential nominee, Hillary Clinton. The FBI began an investigation. Trump joked that Russia released hacked emails because, he said, "Putin likes me," and later in a televised appearance invited Russia to, "find [Clinton's] 30,000 emails that are missing." On July 16, 2018, Putin held a summit meeting with Trump in Helsinki, Finland. The two met alone with only translators present for two hours. After the meeting Trump ordered the translators' notes to be destroyed. In a press conference

---

167   Owen Matthews, "Vladimir Putin Resurrects the KGB", *Politico*, September 28, 2016, https://www.politico.eu/article/vladimir-putin-resurrects-the-kgb-moscow-security/.

following the meeting, Putin denied any Russian interference in the 2016 U.S. elections. Trump then said he trusted Putin's denial more than the conclusions of his own intelligence agencies and cast blame on the United States for its strained relationship with Russia. Days earlier the U.S. Department of Justice had indicted 12 Russian intelligence agents for their meddling in the election. If you still don't think there's something to this relationship, take a look through the *CNN Interactive* timeline of "80 Times Trump Talked about Putin" from 2013 through 2017.[168]

Economics, Russia Style

Russia is a totalitarian state. Putin is a dictator. Russian elections are a sham. Putin and his oligarch cronies have allegedly stripped Russia's wealth and pocketed it. Putin is said to be the wealthiest person in the world while the Russian economy is in shambles. In case you need a reminder: Trump believes that Putin is a really good guy, a strong leader and somebody to admire.

So, how is the Russian government ensuring economic equality for its people? The Russian economy is not diversified; it is largely dependent on oil and gas exports. Loss of oil revenue dropped as much is 60 percent from 2014 to 2015, according to a 2017 Congressional Research Service report.[169] This helped spark the collapse of the Russian currency which in turn significantly raised the price of Russian consumer goods. Russia has been the world's top oil producer and largest exporter of natural gas.

---

168   Andrew Kaczynski, Chris Massie, and Nathan McDermott, "80 Times Trump Talked About Putin", *CNN Interactive*, March 2017, accessed April 1, 2020, https://www.cnn.com/interactive/2017/03/politics/trump-putin-russia-timeline/.
169   Congressional Research Service, *U.S. Sanctions and Russia's Economy*, by Rebecca M. Nelson, February 17, 2017 (R43895 Version-6), Congressional Research Service, accessed May 1, 2020, https://crsreports.congress.gov/product/details?prodcode=R43895.

Russia has large reserves of shale and significant deposits of heavy oil in the Arctic Sea and elsewhere. However, they need foreign investment, equipment and expenditure to harvest it. Because of their ties to Putin and the Russian oligarchs, Rosneft, a Russia's state-controlled oil company and Gazprom, a multinational energy corporation headquartered in Russia, are now subject to ongoing sanctions. The international consortium Nord Stream AG is a major shareholder in the Russian state company; the consortium includes Gazprom, Germany's Wintershall, PEG Infrastrukture based in Germany but linked to Finland and Russia, Gasunie of the Netherlands, and France's ENGIE, but Gazprom holds 51 percent of the shares. Gazprom intends to complete a pipeline under the Baltic Sea to pump Russian natural gas through Germany for the European Union cutting Ukraine, Poland and the Baltic States out of the loop. The United States sanctions have delayed the building of the Nord Stream 2 pipeline. However, Putin has made it clear he will complete it no matter what, and the pipeline is slated for completion in 2020. Even if it could be delayed longer, it may only be a matter of time before Russia develops the needed technology on its own.

A May 13, 2019 article in *Foreign Policy* by Amy McKinnon and Robbie Gramer states there is broad bipartisan opposition to Nord Stream 2. Critics say the pipeline "makes little commercial sense" labeling the building of the pipeline a "geopolitical power play by Moscow to exert energy leverage over Western Europe." McKinnon and Gramer warn that, "it could destabilize Ukraine as it wages war against Russian-backed separatists in the eastern part of the country."[170] That actually sounds like a plan.

---

170 Amy McKinnon and Robbie Gramer, "U.S. Senate Threatens Sanctions Over Russian Pipeline", *Foreign Policy*, May 13, 2019, https://foreignpolicy.com/2019/05/13/us-senate-threatens-sanctions-over-russian-pipeline-nord-stream-two-geopolitics-energy-germany-europe-gazprom/.

A ten-year transit contract between Ukraine and Russia which earned Ukraine between $2 billion and $3 billion annually was due to expire at the end of 2019. If not renewed, the loss of transit revenues could tip Ukraine's fragile economy into a recession, according to Yuri Vitrenko, Chief Operating Officer for the Ukrainian state energy company. It seriously affects the Ukrainian economy and allows the Russian government to essentially blackmail Ukrainians into capitulation to whatever it is they want. On December 19, 2019 Russia and Ukraine reached an "agreement in principle" on the future transit of Russian gas through Ukrainian territory. Putin said "we will preserve transit through Ukraine." He also said "We will search for a solution acceptable to all, including Ukraine."[171] The details must be agreed upon before the agreement is finalized. Russia appears to have great leverage in these negotiations. It will take some time to uncover what concessions Russia extracted from Ukraine before finalizing the agreement.

The Nord Stream 2 pipeline has been vehemently defended by many countries including Germany and Russia as a purely economic venture. Agnia Grigas, author of the book *The New Geopolitics of Natural Gas*, said that the pipeline, "… was part of the Russian effort to solidify its hold on European gas markets." At a time when there is increasing competition globally, the Kremlin claims the opposition to Nord Stream 2 results from an American campaign to sell its natural gas to Europe. Denmark has opposed the pipeline by threatening to refuse Russia access to Danish waters under the Baltic Sea. A *National Review* article on July 16, 2018, claimed that Trump has softened his stance on the Nord Stream 2

---

171   Vladimir Soldatkin and Katya Golubkova, "Russia, Ukraine, EU Agree 'In Principle' on New Gas Deal: EU Official", Reuters, December 20, 2019, https://www.reuters.com/article/us-ukraine-russia-gas/russia-ukraine-eu-agree-in-principle-on-new-gas-deal-eu-official-idUSKBN1YN1LH.

project, citing Trump's press conference following the US/Russian Summit in Helsinki. Senator John McCain called Trump's summit with Putin in Helsinki a "tragic mistake" and said Trump "was doing what the Russian strongman wanted." After his private sit-down with Putin, Trump was more amenable to Russia's and Germany's position and said he knows, "where they're all coming from." Trump also framed America's dispute with Russia over energy issues "as one between good natured competitors." That's the same meeting where the interpreter's notes were confiscated and no formal written record of the conversation has been seen or heard.

On May 25, 2019 Trump was filmed while walking with the NATO leaders in Brussels by a CNN video. We viewed the video. Trump moved from the back of the pack of world leaders by getting physical and stepping in front of Dusko Markovic, the prime minister of Montenegro, and pushing Markovic aside with one hand. Trump then planted his feet and straightened his jacket without any appearance of regard for Markovic. Montenegro is the newest member of the NATO alliance. Russia was opposed to Montenegro joining NATO. Journalist Matt Yglesias opined on Twitter: "It's weird that Donald Trump had a long private meeting with Vladimir Putin and suddenly emerged with a new-found interest in undermining U.S. security guarantees to Montenegro." Moscow has been accused of meddling in Montenegro's elections and a coup was allegedly planned by pro-Russian militants. Trump later called the people of Montenegro "very aggressive" and suggested that Montenegro could cause World War III.[172] All

---

172   Guardian Staff and Agencies, "'Very Aggressive': Trump Suggests Montenegro Could Cause World War Three", *The Guardian,* July 19, 2018, https://www.theguardian.com/us-news/2018/jul/19/very-aggressive-trump-suggests-montenegro-could-cause-world-war-three.

of this, including Trump's silly macho routine, appeared to be yet another gift to Putin.

The exact relationship between Trump and Putin remains a mystery. Not only does Trump lack a modicum of transparency to the public, he apparently often refuses to inform anyone in his own administration about his communications with foreign leaders, preferring to conduct a shadow foreign policy. The tide of public opinion in the United States has begun to shift and many are beginning to believe what Trump would like from Putin is what he may have done for him in the last election: interfere in the United States (and likely elsewhere) on Trump's behalf. In August 2019 it was revealed that at a 2017 meeting in the White House, Trump allegedly told the Russian ambassador he was not concerned with Russian interference in the 2016 election because the United States interferes in elections in other countries. It appears that Trump was not concerned with the fallout of the investigation. Was that a tacit signal that future interference might not be of concern? Trump's behavior has been characterized across party lines as reminiscent of *The Godfather* character Vito Corleone, a dictatorial crime lord. But that seems like an oversimplified explanation of what we know. We believe there is much more to the Trump/Putin relationship, and that some people are going to great lengths to hide it.

Trump asked China and Ukraine to get involved in his reelection campaign, so why wouldn't he get Russia to do it again? While that may be a looming concern for many Americans, for us the more pressing question is: what does Putin want from Trump? That begs other questions: Exactly what was in those now super-secret transcripts of his conversations with Putin and the Saudi Crown Prince? What is being hidden? Such lack of transparency easily leads to speculation. Trump said about his conversations with the Crown Prince of Saudi Arabia Mohammed bin Salman ("MBS") and Ukrainian President Zelensky: "they were perfect." If they were so "perfect" and there is nothing nefarious about them, why does he hide them? Why not let everybody in the country see just how perfect they were? Just some food for thought. The president may just want Putin to let him build a hotel in Moscow. Not that it would be legal (it would constitute a violation of his oath of office) but we suppose it could be as simple as that. If you believe that, someone has a bridge to sell you.

Money and More Money, Power and More Power

> There is only one thing in this world that is to keep acquiring money and more money and power and more power all the rest is meaningless.
>
> —Napoleon Bonaparte, emperor and military leader, 1795

The opportunity to feed on post-Soviet spoils was a godsend to needy borrowers like the Trump Organization. Napoleon Bonaparte, French emperor and military leader driven to conquer Europe, if not the world, saw power as an end in itself, and the need for money to achieve that power—and if those around him were going to get rich out of it, he should as well.[173] It is conjectured that there was a need for Putin and his friends to launder ill-gotten spoils pilfered from the Russian people. Consequently, it has been suggested that, post-2000, criminal oligarchs and investors funded Trump's high-risk real estate and casino ventures, most of which failed financially. Due to Trump's dismal track record and several bankruptcies, he was unable to secure loans from more credible sources to continue financing his turbulent business career. Many believe that the primary reason "The Donald" refuses to release his tax returns is that they would reveal that Russian bankers did, in fact, bail Trump out of a dire financial situation.

---

173   Frank McLynn, *Napoleon: A Biography* (Random House, 2019).

The speculation about the Russians bailing out The Trump Organization when it couldn't get loans from U.S. banks or anybody else has been characterized by Trump as hearsay. Review of Deutsche Bank financial records related to the Trump Organization and/or the yearly tax audit by the IRS required of all presidents could put all of that to rest. Our question: why is the White House apparently fighting tooth and nail to keep those records from coming to light or allowing a legally required audit to take place? In case you missed it, a new whistleblower came forward with information that Trump-appointed officials in the IRS have been blocking the legally required audit of the president's and the vice president's taxes. At some point, even someone of limited mental capacity will smell a rotten fish. BS does not require a spectral analysis; a smell test is usually sufficient. The latest court ruling concerning President Trump's taxes is that Congress had the legal right to demand the president's tax returns. That court order was being appealed to the Supreme Court. I guess we will have to wait and see what the Supreme Court does.

The first round of sanctions coincided with a crash in global oil prices that cut deeply into Russian revenues from their primary exports: heavy oil and natural gas. Russia's economy was already struggling under the weight of low oil prices and high inflation. The battered economy resulted in capital fleeing the country. Putin and his oligarchs were desperate to convert their devalued Russian currency (rubles) to U.S. dollars and euros to protect their wealth. That monetary flow slowed appreciably as the U.S. and European sanctions took hold. No doubt, tying up their personal assets has had direct and significant impact on Putin and his oligarchs.

It has been postulated that the reason Russia interfered in the 2016 U.S. presidential election was a commitment from candidate Trump that, if elected, he would work to rescind the Magnitsky Act sanctions to free up Putin's (and his oligarchs') money. This has gone from being a postulation to a plausible concern. Sergei Magnitsky was a Russian tax accountant and whistleblower who was killed in a Moscow prison. In 2012 the United States enacted the Magnitsky Act with widespread support from both Republicans and Democrats. The Magnitsky Act punishes Russia for human rights abuses. The Obama administration imposed additional sanctions on Russia from 2013-2016. However, recall that Trump's campaign manager Paul Manafort was involved in changing the 2016 GOP platform with regard to the U.S. attitude towards Russia. Despite the Putin/Trump relationship, during the Trump administration the U.S. Congress decided to increase the number and severity of the sanctions. It has been speculated that part of the quid pro quo between Trump and the Russians seems to be a Putin promise that if Trump did get the sanctions withdrawn, then Russia would allow Donald to build a Trump Tower complex in Moscow. Personally, we think it may have more to do with oil than real estate.

The U.S. has been a lifeline to Ukraine. The threatened withdrawal of United States' support and assistance severely weakens Ukraine's bargaining power with Russia. The war has been going on with Russia for five years. Russia seized Crimea and Russian backed separatists are now occupying parts of Eastern Ukraine. The German intelligence service estimates that 50,000 deaths (civilian and servicemen), including Ukrainians and Russians have occurred so far. The U.S. and much of Europe have imposed severe sanctions on Russia as a result. Over the past six years, the United States has imposed, in cooperation with the European Union, 60 sanctions spanning nine issue areas, including the 2017 sanctions for the Russian 2016 interference in the United States election. In addition, the measures freeze assets and prohibit specific transactions with Russian companies and individuals, including any exports that are used in oil and gas exploration, or have military use. Ukraine-related sanctions were related to Russia's annexation of Crimea and the resulting conflict for which no end seems to be in sight, and aimed at deterring further Russian aggression against Ukraine.

In May 2017, Congress gave the White House until October 1 of that year to begin implementing the sanctions against Russia that Congress had demanded as direct punishment for Russia's meddling in the 2016 U.S. election. Congress passed the bill with overwhelming bipartisan support. In fact, it was a veto-proof majority. This was a message to the president that Congress was enforcing its authority under the separations of power edict in the United States Constitution. Trump expressed his displeasure. In an October 25, 2017 *Vox* magazine article, "The Trump Administration is Delaying Russian Sanctions That Congress Demanded," Tara Golshan reported that Trump "…has emphasized wanting a warmer relationship with Russia [and] did not want to sign the bill into law—and did so grudgingly" and noted that Trump "…released a statement claiming he is much better at deal making than Congress is and angrily tweeted that Republican lawmakers were ruining his relationship with Russia."[174]

Trump missed the October 1, 2017 congressional deadline and did not start implementing the sanctions until mid-March, 2018. Since Trump has gained increased political control over Republicans in Congress, May 2017 may be the last time the current United States Senate attempts to assert its congressional authority.

The House initiated an impeachment investigation. This call for action came on the heels of Trump's, Attorney General Barr's and, the president's personal attorney Rudy Giuliani's involvement in a scheme to pressure Ukraine into interfering

---

174   Tara Golshan, "The Trump Administration is Delaying Russian Sanctions That Congress Demanded", *Vox*, October 25, 2017, https://www.vox.com/policy-and-politics/2017/10/25/16548688/trump-administration-delaying-russia-sanctions.

with the 2020 presidential election on behalf of Trump. Trump's Secretary of State Mike Pompeo now admits he was on the phone call between Zelensky and Trump. Pompeo became a person of interest to Democratic House investigators, but Pompeo, like the president continued to stonewall the inquiry and threatened State Department employees not to testify before Congress or supply any documents in response to congressional subpoenas. Unlike with the Mueller Report that was mired in a tyranny of facts designed to instill confusion in the minds of many Americans due to Trump's and his minions' obfuscation; "Teflon Don" is having a rougher time deflecting criticism following the whistleblower report and his own public statements.

A plethora of witnesses came forward bringing this story to light, including testimony from a witness that overheard the president's phone conversation with Ambassador Gordon Sondland, who was in Ukraine. The witness reported that during that conversation Trump asked Sondland about the status of his request for Zelensky to announce an investigation of the Bidens. Perhaps if we had access to the testimony and documents from Roger Stone's trial, in which he was found guilty of obstructing an official proceeding and making false statements to Congress, we could corroborate that Mr. Trump did indeed collaborate through Stone on the interference by the Russians in the 2016 election. Once again, thanks to Barr and congressional Republicans, the American electorate may never know the facts.

Apparently, there is compelling evidence to suggest that Trump has pressured Zelensky to reach a compromise with Putin to end the war under Putin's terms. In turn, if the war does cease much of the rationale for the sanctions against Russia would end with it. Trump could then cancel the sanctions—which are exactly what Putin wants. This would be a great favor from his admirer, the president of the United States. What reciprocity will the Donald expect? No one truly believes that the "Great Negotiator" would do something for nothing? Surely, he would want Putin to do something for us though, with "us" meaning him, Trump. Would the quid pro quo further America's interests in any way above and beyond Trump's? Or has Trump already received this "something" in advance? Let's just say we are extremely skeptical. Color us "cautiously pessimistic." "The Donald" seems to be quite the deal maker, as he frequently claims, but these deals don't seem aimed at benefitting the citizens of the United States.

Let us also not forget Trump recently went to the White House lawn and asked China and Ukraine to investigate a political rival. This is exactly what the whistleblower exposed. Obviously, he can't justify asking a foreign government to help him get dirt on an opponent so after hiding and lying about it for weeks he has now admitted it, and is employing an alternative strategy of hiding in plain sight. He admitted that he did it and said he would do it again, that his goal is to root out corruption and he now uses that as an excuse for withholding $391 million in military aid to Ukraine. He is trying to normalize this blatant violation of the law. He also provided written talking points to his Republican enablers in an effort to give them cover to continue to violate their own oath of office and constitutional duties of oversight because of their fear of Trump voter's wrath. Trump's sudden admission and new justification is a specious argument and casuistry at its best. It is a transparent ruse to justify his unconscionable behavior. Moreover, he continues to call those who have exposed him liars and traitors. There is every indication that his new strategy is not working.

The interference by Russia in our 2016 presidential election has been verified by every United States intelligence agency, yet Trump continues to dispute it. In fact, Rudy Giuliani has reportedly visited Paul Manafort in prison to try to get his help in challenging the findings. It should be noted that the lack of a quorum on the

Federal Election Commission (FEC) removes a key check and balance to enforce any electoral wrongdoing. Insolently, they're doing it again. Yet, the Republicans in the senate are still sitting on bills designed to stop it and Trump still fails to nominate anyone to the FEC. It's beginning to look as though the Republicans in congress, except Romney, may not want to stop the interference because they're hoping it will help them.

For the last few months we watched Republicans in Congress scrambling for excuses and claiming there was no quid pro quo involved in Trump's request for Zelensky's assistance in the 2020 U.S. presidential election. "The president did not promise the Ukrainians anything in return therefore, there was no crime." So maybe the president did withhold military aid to Ukraine already approved by Congress, but he can do that. They then trotted out even more specious reasons to try to explain that seeking reelection assistance and holding back the aid were unrelated.

However, all that was irrelevant—there did not need to be a quid pro quo! Whether there was one or not, withholding and refusing to comply with the subpoenas was a direct violation of the president's constitutional duty to uphold the laws of the United States. Moreover, requesting a foreign government to interfere in an American election is abhorrent and seriously jeopardizes our national security. In addition, the request makes him complicit in their actions and guilty of breaching his oath of office. He was guilty and the Republican Senate gave him a get out of jail free card and a license to kill along with it.

Sell Not Virtue To Purchase Wealth

Sell not virtue to purchase wealth, nor Liberty to purchase power.

—Benjamin Franklin, statesman and founding father, 1738

Benjamin Franklin, statesman, diplomat, and philosopher, was one of the most influential founders of the United States. He had a way with words that combined common sense about the present with advice (warnings perhaps) about the future. He often warned about the hazards of pushing aside personal ideals and the national good in order to focus more on money and the drive to gain wealth.[175] We are certain that Franklin would have a few words for Donald Trump.

In 2008, the Trump Organization signed a multimillion-dollar branding deal with the Dogan Group, which is run by one of the most politically influential families in Turkey, to build a two-tower apartment, office, and shopping complex in Istanbul. Turkish President Recep Tayyip Erdogan presided over the opening ceremonies for the complex in 2012. In 2013 the Trump Organization partnered with Dorya International to produce luxury furniture under the Trump house brand. The furniture has been distributed throughout Turkey, and Dorya claims on its website to have furnished Erdogan offices, the Turkish prime minister's office, the Turkish armed forces, and embassies around the world. These deals give Erdogan leverage over Trump. He could cut off millions flowing to the Trump Organization and Trump's children if the president of the United States is not accommodating to his demands. In an *Atlantic* magazine article in 2017, Jeremy Venook explained what this revealed about Trump:

> That he chose to discuss the towers with Erdogan, albeit obliquely, through his references to his business partners when he has already acknowledged the impropriety of doing so simply reinforces the perception that he may be

---

[175] Benjamin Franklin "Poor Richard, 1738", *Founders Online*, National Archives, accessed December 10, 2019, https://founders.archives.gov/documents/Franklin/01-02-02-0035.

unable to separate his businesses from his official duties while in office.[176]

Turkey has the largest number (119 by last count) of foreign ventures connected with the Trump Organization, and the Turks are reportedly the largest foreign users of Trump properties. Erdogan fears Kurdish separatists in Turkey, but despite Erdogan's objections, the United States worked with the Kurdish militia in Syria to reclaim the ISIS stronghold of Ragga. After ISIS had lost its caliphate in Syria, on October 8, 2019 Trump announced the withdrawal of U.S. military forces stationed on the border between Syria and Turkey. U.S. troops have served as a buffer to protect the Kurds. Trump abandoned the Syrian Kurds after telling them to trust us. He did this after the United States had promised the Kurds if they helped defeat ISIS, we would provide them with military protection. Turkey began bombing the Kurds on October 9, 2019. We believe that Trump's unilateral withdrawal of U.S. troops will result in an ethnic cleansing of the Kurds and prove disadvantageous to American foreign policy. The apparent beneficiaries of this move are the governments of Turkey and Russia, ISIS, and Syrian President Bashar al-Assad.

Simply put, the Kurds found themselves in a position to either guard the 12,000 ISIS prisoners they had detained or abandon them and concentrate on the formation of their own defense against impending slaughter by the Turks. Trump's response: he hoped the ISIS fighters would, "go to Europe and not come here." In addition, the Kurds have reportedly seen it necessary to strike a deal with Assad, long their enemy, in order to try to ensure their own survival. Trump then outrageously called the Kurds traitors

---

176   Jeremy Venook, "Trump's Interests vs. America's, Dubai Edition", *The Atlantic*, August 9, 2017, https://www.theatlantic.com/business/archive/2017/08/donald-trump-conflicts-of-interests/508382/.

to the United States. Unmitigated gall! Israel was outraged by Trump's move. As a result of Trump's decision to unilaterally remove U.S. troops from Syria without consulting Congress, the State Department, the intelligence community, or U.S. European allies and Israel, many Republicans were for the first time publicly critical of Trump. It seems senseless for the president to strengthen the hand of Putin and other dictators to the detriment of the United States, Israel and America's other allies. We know one possible way to explain this: follow the money, follow the oil.

Like Self-Preservation, A Duty to God

> We are all qualified, entitled and morally obligated to evaluate the conduct of rulers (leaders). This potential judgment, moreover, is not simply or primarily a right, but like self-preservation, a duty to God.
>
> —attributed to John Locke, philosopher, circa 1660

John Locke was philosophically and practically opposed to a divinely ordained, hereditary, absolute leader; as these words show, he believed the people should have some authority over those who ruled them. He saw this authority as a human right, a "duty to God," and on par with the right to food, shelter, and other basic needs of "self-preservation."[177] In our democratic system of government, we elect our leaders with the understanding that anyone they appoint or hire to serve the government are bound to act legally, morally, and ethically. The words of John Locke remind us that citizenship is a responsibility, and a large part of that is to check our leaders periodically and be aware of what they are doing. If we don't like

---

177   Attribution unconfirmed. For context see: "Locke's Political Philosophy", *The Stanford Encyclopedia of Philosophy*, last updated January 11, 2016, https://plato.stanford.edu/entries/locke-political/.

what they're doing, we have the opportunity to vote them out of office. With regard to Trump, that's been difficult because of all the misdirection and hiding of information. We can't just know what he's doing, we really need to know why. From everything now being revealed, along with Trump's own actions and/or inactions, his fierce attacks and incoherent rants on everyone from his own intelligence agencies to the press and whistleblowers, it is becoming abundantly clear. He is coming unhinged with anger and fear. Based on what we know to date, there is now more than sufficient reason to raise suspicions that the president of the United States may have something to hide, and we need to find out what it is and/or defeat him in the November election and get him out of the White House before we find ourselves in a hole we can't climb out of.

We fear that Trump has confused "self-preservation" with self-interest and personal wealth; and "duty to God," as a duty to himself. We now consider putting forth our own conspiracy theory and we could start off with one of Trump's often-used favorite phrases, "People are saying…" Perhaps Trump has been closely coordinating with Putin since before his nomination and throughout his presidency. People are saying that Putin, former head of the KGB in the Soviet era, is hell-bent on restoring Russia to its former glory and putting the Soviet Union back together. Russia was a driving force behind Brexit with the goal of dismantling the European Union. With Putin's energy initiatives, he is increasing Moscow's economic leverage over Europe and will soon be poised to annex Ukraine and have a stranglehold over Poland and the Baltic States with further annexation in mind. Is it Trump who believes NATO is obsolete and a waste of time, or is this part of Putin's plan?

The opportunity to feed on post-Soviet Union spoils was a godsend to needy borrowers like the Trump Organization. It is conjectured that there was a need for Putin and his friends to launder ill-gotten spoils pilfered from the Russian people. Consequently, it has been suggested that post-2000, criminal oligarchs and investors funded Trump's high-risk real estate and casino ventures, most of which failed financially. Due to Trump's dismal track record of failed projects and several bankruptcies, he was unable to secure loans from other, more conventional sources, to continue financing his turbulent business career. Many believe that the primary reason "The Donald" refuses to release his tax returns is that the returns would reveal that Russian bankers did, in fact, bail Trump out of a dire financial situation.

Russia is positioning itself to soon be the primary powerbroker in the Middle East. Central America is in chaos. Trump's tariff wars with China seem to be designed to weaken the economy of both China and the United States. Fascism is on the rise worldwide. And, American allies no longer feel they can trust and rely on the United States. Much of this has been facilitated by Trump and his seemingly nonsensical policies which directly benefit Russia and its allies, and appear to have us playing for the wrong side. Has all of this been carefully planned to create a shift in power and control over energy resources and economies around the world? Does this seemingly outrageous conspiracy theory actually have merit? If so, what is the common thread at the core of this conspiracy theory? Fossil fuel!

While we don't excuse any Democrats who partake of these vast pools of campaign money, there is a clear link between donations to Republican campaigns and GOP support for the fossil fuel industry over responsible attention to the climate crisis. Just six weeks before the 2016 election, the independent nonpartisan and Pulitzer Prize-winning *InsideClimate News* published an analysis of campaign contributions from fossil fuel interests, using CRP and other data:

> Political polarization on climate change has become so stark this election cycle that researchers say the gulf between Republicans and Democrats is wider than they have seen in more than 20 years of polling. The polarization has an equally startling financial corollary: an overwhelming 91 percent of fossil fuel industry campaign donations now flow to Republican candidates and 9 percent to Democrats. … From the beginning of this election cycle in 2015 through the first six months of [2016], fossil fuel industry political action committees and employees donated $37.2 million to Republicans running for federal office. In contrast, industry giving to Democrats totaled just $3.8 million.[178]

InsideClimate News reporter Marianne Lavelle contrasted these numbers against the 2000 race between George W. Bush and Al Gore, in which, "the pot of fossil fuel spending was split almost evenly, with 60 percent going to Republicans, 40 percent to Democrats."[179]

Rex Tillerson was selected as the Secretary of State for a reason. After all, he was the CEO of Exxon and worked closely with Putin. Energy companies have long been major drivers in the U.S. economy and they hold enormous political power. In 2013 Tillerson, as Exxon's CEO, received the Russian Order of Friendship from Putin after signing deals with the state-owned Russian oil company Rosneft. Rosneft's chief, Igor Sechin, is seen as Putin's loyal lieutenant. The partnership had begun as a drilling program in the Arctic's Kara Sea. Exxon had agreed to explore shale oil areas of West Siberia and the deep waters of the Baltic

---

178   Marianne Lavelle, "Fossil Fuel Money to GOP Grows, and So Does Climate Divide", *InsideClimate News*, September 15, 2016, http://insideclimatenews.org/news/15092016/fossil-fuel-funding-gop-grows-climate-divide-republican-donald-trump-hillary-clinton.
179   Lavelle, "Fossil Fuel Money."

Sea. But then the U.S. sanctions against Russia over the Russian annexation of the Crimea kicked in, the partnership to extract the vast oil reserves in Russia were put on hold. Perhaps in appointing Tillerson, the president's goal was to make Putin feel more confident that sanctions would soon be lifted and the plan would resume. Or possibly, Tillerson was put in place to work with both Putin and Trump to devise a plan to get the sanctions lifted. That hasn't happened yet. One thing for sure, it won't be with Tillerson.

Trump and others with financial interest in the fossil fuel industry refuse to recognize the scientific evidence of the damage being directly caused by the industry. This despite the evidence clearly before us: increases in the severity of storms, flooding, tornadoes and a multitude of other natural disasters. If we continue to ignore this escalating crisis, we are putting our children and future generations at serious risk of a radically changed planet where life, as we have known it, may very well become unsustainable.

Energy companies are global corporations and their loyalties and allegiances are not bound by national borders. They are not patriots, but rather power elites with boundless levels of corruption and greed. They are zealots worshiping the gods of OIL and MONEY with demonic vengeance. Assuming that Trump is not, in fact, stupid, then why would he deny climate change? Fossil fuel interests! Money! A deal like that could make someone a "Real Billionaire" a hundred times over. Under this theory, the new order that Putin and Trump have been formulating is built on the world's economies remaining dependent on oil and natural gas. The development of alternative fuel sources and reducing dependence on fossil fuels would destroy those well-laid plans.

While you're at it, you may want to consider getting rid of some of Trump's servile dependents in Congress. For instance, Devin Nunes, Ranking Minority Member of the House Intelligence

Committee, who was reportedly feeding information to the White House when he chaired that committee. Lev Parnas and Igor Fruman were arrested on October 23, 2019 and indicted on charges of campaign finance violations. They had worked closely with Rudy Giuliani, aiding him with his search for dirt on Trump's political opponents. Joseph A. Bondy, an attorney who represents Parnas, revealed multiple phone conversations between his client and Devin Nunes. According to Sanjana Karanth of *HuffPost Politics*, Bondy told *PBS NewsHour* that Nunes, "…was definitely part of an attempt to gather information about the Bidens. He was definitely involved in the Ukraine [sic]. He definitely has involvement in the shadow diplomacy efforts in Ukraine, contrary to his claim."[180] A report by Sean Colaressi on November 25, 2019 in *PoliticusUSA* was headlined: "Devin Nunes is about to get smacked with an ethics investigation."[181] Nunes, like anyone, is innocent until proven guilty, but perhaps he is a candidate for the Trump cesspool swim team.

Some people say Jim Jordan of Ohio is another collaborator who appears to be complicit in deflecting the truth without regard to facts on behalf of the president. Jordan appears to have no shame, honor or integrity about what he is willing to say and do to hide the truth. Jordan and Nunes are not the only ones in Congress who have turned a blind eye to the Constitution and gone along with this administration to hoodwink the American people. Men such as these seemingly without honor or integrity should not represent the people of the United States in the halls of Congress. Each of us

---

180 Sanjana Karanth, "House Intelligence Report: Devin Nunes Was in Contact with Rudy Giuliani, Lev Parnas", *HuffPost*, last updated December 4, 2019, https://www.huffpost.com/entry/house-intelligence-report-phone-calls-devin-nunes-rudy-giuliani-lev-parnas_n_5de6e1f9e4b00149f737870a.
181 Seth Colarossi, "Devin Nunes is about to Get Smacked with an Ethics Investigation", *PoliticusUSA*, November 25, 2019. https://www.politicususa.com/2019/11/25/devin-nunes-smacked-with-ethics-investigation.html.

must give serious consideration as to who deserves our votes and our support in the next election.

It is our sincerest hope that with the events now unfolding, some of the elected representatives in Congress will finally gather some intestinal fortitude and put their nation before their political careers and potential to line their pockets in the future. We need to vote for men and women who are willing to put our country and Constitution over their self-interest. It is insufficient to concentrate solely on the elimination of national shame. We must restore national pride. That is our duty to God and our country. And by "we," we don't just mean the two of us. This should be a national citizen effort. If you think the president has done something wrong, or that he hasn't kept his promises or has not acted in the best interest of the nation, you can no longer rely on the United States Senate to make a fair and impartial decision. You're going to have to get off your backsides and vote him out or put up with four more years of this insanity.

CHAPTER 7

CRISIS

> Extreme weather change is here.
> —headline, front page of *The Washington Post*, 2019

> Climate change is a hoax.
> —Donald Trump, businessman, television personality, and U.S. President

CLIMATE CHANGE IS REAL. MOST OF us just need to go outside on a regular basis or watch The Weather Channel to know this, but if it helps, the information was a front-page headline in *The Washington Post*. There are no credible arguments to refute it—and that especially includes Donald Trump's random and inconsistent comments about our environment.[182] The climate change occurring in our world is affecting everyone. It is the paramount issue facing the world today. Part of the problem that we have is the deliberate misinformation we are constantly being bombarded with by the driving forces behind the global warming itself. The main cause

---

182   Trump has said repeatedly that he thinks climate change is false or "a hoax," sometimes with that term and at other times using different phrasing with essentially the same message. In January 2020 he contradicted himself when he said, "Nothing's a hoax about that," on the same day he announced major rollbacks in environmental protections. See: Rachel Frazen, "Trump Says 'Nothing's a Hoax' about Climate Change," *The Hill*, January 9, 2020, http://thehill.com/policy/energy-environment/477548-trump-says-nothings-a- hoax-about-climate-change. For a longer list of Trump's variable comments on the environment, see the *Mother Jones* timeline, "Every Insane Thing Donald Trump Has Said about Global Warming," http://www.motherjones.com/environment/2016/12/trump-climate-timeline/.

of climate change is emissions of heat trapping greenhouse gases. Most scientists worldwide continue to warn that human activity is heating up the planet at a dangerous rate and high temperatures pose a more lethal threat than any other extreme weather event. They have an abundance of facts to prove it. The truth is, once again, we are being misled, misdirected and confused by a tyranny of data generated by those with ties to the oil industry. There was a reason why the Russians didn't sign the Paris Agreement, which makes us wonder if Russia is the reason why Trump, the president of the United States, decided to withdraw from it. The misdirection, confusion, and deliberate lies are enough to cause anyone to question the reality.

Moreover, the global warming cycle in and of itself creates a confusing contradiction in weather conditions. Greenhouse gases trap heat in the atmosphere. The additional heat is absorbed by the oceans. The oceans give off more heat and water vapor. More water vapor intensifies storms and changes the flow of the wind and the rain. The warmer temperatures melt the ice at the poles which are fresh water. The melted ice dilutes the salt in the ocean. The desalinization slows down the Gulfstream preventing warmer water to flow north. The North Atlantic then begins to cool, which leads to disruptions in rain and snowfall.

With all the misinformation and contradictory information, it's no wonder people don't know what to believe. From our perspective, simple mathematics should put the gravity of this situation into proper perspective. A gallon of gasoline weighs 6.3 pounds. When gasoline is burned it uses oxygen in the combustion process. One gallon of gas, produces 20 pounds of carbon dioxide (CO_2).[183] There are 42 liquid gallons of oil in a barrel. Worldwide

---

183   "How Can a Gallon of Gasoline Produce 20 Pounds of Carbon Dioxide?", FuelEconomy.gov, U.S. Department of Energy, accessed May 1, 2020, https://www.fueleconomy.gov/feg/contentIncludes/co2_inc.htm.

use is 93 million barrels per day. Every barrel of oil produces 20 gallons of gasoline, 12 gallons of diesel, four gallons of jet fuel and other products like liquefied petroleum gas and asphalt. Just accounting for the gasoline portion alone, this amounts to 1.86 trillion gallons of gasoline being burned per day which produces 20 times as much carbon dioxide. That equates to 37.2 trillion pounds (18.6 million tons) per day of CO2 going into the atmosphere. That's approximately 6.8 trillion tons per year.

No one needs to be a rocket scientist to figure out those numbers and to understand that they are staggering. A tree can absorb about 48 pounds of carbon dioxide (CO2) a year at peak, about 28 percent is absorbed by plant life (1.9 trillion tons) and approximately 26 percent of all carbon dioxide released is absorbed by the oceans (1.77 trillion tons) That means that roughly 46 percent, or 3.13 trillion tons, of carbon dioxide enters the atmosphere each year.[184] Consider the deforestation occurring globally and the result of fewer trees able to absorb the increasing amounts of released carbon dioxide. Consider the ocean pollution killing off catastrophic amounts of phytoplankton which creates 80 percent of the world's oxygen supply. It isn't hard to see that there's a real problem. If we don't make it our number one issue globally, we can expect a radically different future than we'd hoped for. It's possible that before our children or grandchildren have the opportunity to live a full life, global warming will mark the end of our way of life. According to the *Washington Post*, NASA Photos from Antarctica between February 4, 2020 and February 13, 2020, showed a 20 percent melt of snow cover on one of the islands. On February 9, 2020, the weather research station on Seymour Island recorded a temperature of 69.3 degrees Fahrenheit. That is the hottest temperature on record for an ice covered Continent.

---

184   For more information and forecasts see: "The Keeling Curve," Scripps Institution of Oceanography, http://doi.org/10.6075/J08W3BHW.

Antarctica's Trinity Peninsula reached 65 degrees just a few days earlier.

No Time to Lose

> "We see the consequences of the climate crisis… We have no time to lose."
>
> —Katrin Jakobsdottir, prime minister of Iceland, 2019

The warning by Prime Minister of Iceland Katrin Jakobsdottir that the crisis is now, not in the future, was spoken at the mock funeral for the first glacier lost to climate change in Iceland, in August 2019.[185] The event was attended by several world leaders as well as scientists and others who were mourning the loss of the glacier from excessive warming—and who see that we need to act now because there may not be a later. July 2019 was the hottest month ever recorded on earth since record-keeping began 140 years ago. The average global temperature was 1.71 degrees Fahrenheit above the twentieth-century average and followed the hottest June ever recorded. This was announced by the National Oceanic and Atmospheric Administration (NOAA). NOAA has also reported that 2019 was tied with 2017 as the second-warmest year on record. Despite all evidence (and there is a lot of it, and it is fact-based, proven, and visible), many people continue to refuse to believe the science, and conjecture that it is not greenhouse gases causing the increase in global temperatures. However, global warming has not occurred overnight. The last five July's have been the five hottest ever recorded, and the end of Trump's third year in office marked 420 consecutive months (35 years) with temperatures at least nominally above the twentieth-century average. Climate

---

185 Zoya Teirstein, "Here's Why Iceland Is Mourning A Dead Glacier", *National Observer*, August 21, 2019, https://www.nationalobserver.com/2019/08/21/news/heres-why-iceland-mourning-dead-glacier

change deniers (and ignorers) are threatening basic human rights including the right to life, health, and a place to live.

In an *InsideClimate News* article, "Donald Trump's Record on Climate Change," Lavelle and Stacy Feldman describe how the Trump administration, "… has undone or delayed—or tried to—most regulatory or executive actions related to climate change while proposing new ones to accelerate fossil fuel development." The article noted that since Trump has been president, there have been no less than 131 federal actions toward federal climate deregulation.[186] Trump and his minion of loyal servants of the fossil fuel industry, as well as most Republicans and even some Democrats in Congress, balk at doing anything that could interfere with the campaign contributions they receive from this industry. Our elected representatives are putting our lives and property at risk for the sake of their own profit. Their counter arguments reflect their greed and/or willful ignorance by which they continue to allow the extraction of fossil fuels, for at least as long as their own natural lives—future generations be damned.

According to Wobble.com, Europe experienced life-threatening heat conditions in July 2019. France, Germany, Belgian, the Netherlands and Britain all hit record temperatures. It hit 100 degrees Fahrenheit in London and 109 degrees in Paris, the highest temperature ever recorded there. In southern France they recorded a temperature of 113 degrees. In India, on June 17, 2019, temperatures reached 124 degrees Fahrenheit, causing millions of people to abandon their homes in search of water. Northern Kuwait recorded the second hottest temperature in world history in 2019, at 126 degrees. The only higher recorded temperature on earth

---

[186] Stacy Feldman and Marianne Lavelle, "Donald Trump's Record on Climate Change", InsideClimate News, January 2, 2020, https://insideclimatenews.org/news/19122019/trump-climate-policy-record-rollback-fossil-energy-history-candidate-profile.

was in Death Valley, California, on June 20, 2013 and in Mitribah, Kuwait on July 21, 2016: 129.2 degrees Fahrenheit, according to Wikipedia.[187]

According to "Live Science," on July 31, 2019, "11 billion tons of ice melted across the country of Greenland in just one day, roughly 197 billion tons of ice melted into the Atlantic Ocean in July" as the heat wave moved from Europe to Greenland and melted its ice at a dramatic rate, explained Ruth Mottram, climate scientist and glaciologist for the Danish Meteorological Institute. That equates to about 36 percent more than scientists expected in an average year. Heat waves on four continents are causing wildfires, electric grids to crash, and wreaking havoc on the harvest of staple grains.

The president of the United States continues to make claims in repudiation of almost all the world's scientists, but cites no credible evidence to contradict reams of documented proof. His energy industry constituents and their lobbyists are far more interested in self-enrichment than admitting the inevitable truth about global warming and the greenhouse gases the fuel industry is creating. Make no mistake, the fate of the human race as we know it is clearly at serious risk.

The Biggest Threat

> I was asked what is the major national security issue we face, and people thought I'd say ISIS or al Qaeda... The answer that I gave in terms of national security is climate change.
>
> —Bernie Sanders, U.S. senator and presidential contender, 2015

---

[187] "Highest Temperatures Recorded on Earth", Wikipedia, accessed February 4, 2020, https://en.wikipedia.org/wiki/Highest_temperature_recorded_on_Earth.

It is no overstatement to say that climate change is more than an environmental problem, but also a threat to our national security, as Bernie Sanders has argued. When Sanders made this statement at a campaign rally in 2015, he was mocked by conservatives and others for being alarmist and misguided.[188] However, what has been ignored is Sanders' explanation: "If we are going to see an increase in drought, flood and extreme weather disturbances as a result of climate change, what that means is that people all over the world are going to be fighting over limited natural resources," Sanders said in a television interview a few days later. "If there is not enough water, if there is not enough land to grow your crops, then you're going to see migrations of people fighting over land that will sustain them, and that will lead to international conflicts."[189] The United Nations Security Council has warned that poor countries are the most vulnerable to conflict and fragility. Global warfare is now a real potential hazard of the global warming issue, explained Joe Bryan of The Atlantic Council.[190] If you're still not convinced, read the U.S. Department of Defense 2014 Quadrennial Defense Review (QDR) cited by Bryan, which states:

> Climate change poses another significant challenge for the United States and the world at large. As greenhouse gas emissions increase, sea levels are rising, average global temperatures are increasing, and severe weather

---

188   In August 2019, Fox News reported that Sanders said this on November 15, 2015, at a campaign rally in Des Moines, Iowa: https://www.foxnews.com/politics/bernie-sanders-climate-change-isis-2020.

189   Rebecca Kaplan, "Bernie Sanders Doubles Down on Climate Change-Terrorism Link", *CBS News*, November 15, 2015, https://www.cbsnews.com/news/bernie-sanders-doubles-down-climate-change-terrorism-link/.

190   Joe Bryan, "Climate Change as a Threat Multiplier", The Atlantic Council. November 16, 2017, https://www.atlanticcouncil.org/blogs/new-atlanticist/climate-change-as-a-threat-multiplier/.

patterns are accelerating. These changes, coupled with other global dynamics, including growing, urbanizing, more affluent populations, and substantial economic growth in India, China, Brazil, and other nations, will devastate homes, land, and infrastructure. Climate change may exacerbate water scarcity and lead to sharp increases in food costs. The pressures caused by climate change will influence resource competition while placing additional burdens on economies, societies, and governance institutions around the world. **These effects are threat multipliers that will aggravate stressors abroad such as poverty, environmental degradation, political instability, and social tensions—conditions that can enable terrorist activity and other forms of violence.**[191] [*our emphasis*]

Like Bernie said. The Trump administration replaced the QDR with a new National Defense Strategy (NDS) report for 2018, which is classified so most of us are not allowed to see it beyond the unclassified summary released by then-Secretary of Defense Jim Mattis. Climate and environmental issues aren't mentioned in the summary and we wonder if they were even considered in the NDS report.

The fight against global warming requires the participation of the United States; without us, it will be nearly impossible to stem. By 2025 it will be too late to begin the process to meaningfully reduce carbon emissions worldwide. The rest of our lives will be spent fighting the massive ill effects of rising temperatures; and knowing that we have failed in providing a sustainable planet for our children and future generations. Effective changes can be made if the countries of the world work together cooperatively, but time is running out. All credible evidence supports that decreasing

---

191 U.S. Department of Defense, "Quadrennial Defense Review 2014", accessed May 1, 2020, http://dod.defense.gov/News/Special-Reports/QDR/.

reliance on fossil fuels is effective in stemming climate change, and it will be nearly impossible for international cooperation on this if the nations of the world are mired in chaos and strife and wars over resources.

There is a genuine fear that the proposed Russian pipeline will increase Europe's dependence on Russian gas. The pipeline would also mean billions of dollars of revenue flowing out of European countries into Russia. We view Putin and his oligarchs as ever-thirsty opportunists looking to secure control of more territory with more natural resources. Oil prices are low and the cumulative EU and U.S. sanctions' "bear traps" are financially painful. The Russian economy is in shambles. It is clear that Putin has to find a solution to his economic dilemma. Obviously, like all totalitarian dictators, he is not likely to give up power and allow a regime change for his nation's good. He will use any and all powers at his disposal in this fight. Ultimately, this pipeline will exacerbate global warming and make it more difficult for the world to respond to climate change because it further promotes reliance on fossil fuel. Who would want that?

If Donald Trump is reelected in 2020, he will be emboldened to double-down on his deleterious policies and further serve his own interests, possibly preparing to line his own pockets once he's out of office and no longer beholden to the American people. Trump will continue to destabilize our nation's long-standing alliances and cozy up to tyrannical strongmen like Putin, Recap Tayyip Erdogan of Turkey, and North Korea's Kim Jung Un. Without an effective system of checks and balances, Trump will accelerate his intent on changing the world order. His July 25, 2019 phone conversation with Ukrainian President Volodymyr Zelensky had a dual purpose. In order to aid in his reelection campaign, Trump attempted to bribe Zelensky by holding up $391 million in military aid already promised to Ukraine until Zelensky publicly announced his intent to investigate Joe Biden and Hunter Biden. That would help Trump in his reelection bid, and although Trump initially tried to say it was for national security reasons, he was widely discredited—in fact, he was impeached for his lies. More to the point here, we believe that Trump's primary goal was to weaken Ukraine's position against Russia. Russia's gas pipeline under the Baltic Sea into Germany is scheduled to be completed in 2020. This will do significant damage to Ukraine's already weak economy and strengthen Russia for further incursion into Ukraine, followed by a potential for invasions into Poland and the Baltic states. Thanks in large part to Trump's betrayal of the Kurds in Syria; Russia has significantly increased its power and influence in the Middle East as well.

Political analyst and author Rachel Maddow, in her book, *Blowout,* focuses on the role of the oil and gas industry in politics around the globe: "When countries are 'captured' by oil and gas, governance suffers and the populations of these places suffer."[192] Maddow calls for the United States to "stop subsidizing the wealthiest business on earth, to fight for transparency, and to check the influence of the world's most destructive industry and its enablers. The stakes have never been higher. Democracy either wins this one or disappears." Maddow explains how the inner workings of the oil industry help explain Russia's role as an international bad actor, and how Putin uses Russian gas and oil to keep neighboring countries, like Ukraine, from becoming "strong, rich, stable Western-oriented democracies," and the Russian people themselves from demanding a democratic say in their own government:

> The solution was simple: use Russian gas and oil not only to make money for the Russian state but also to

---

192   Rachel Maddow, *Blowout: Corrupted Democracy, Rogue State Russia, and the Richest, Most Destructive Industry on Earth* (Crown, 2019).

keep neighboring countries corrupt and dependent. ... It reduced the expectations for democratic governance and the rule of law in those countries. It created a corruptly empowered political class invested in preserving the Russia-dependent system that enriched its practitioners and their families. It also created comfortable space for organized crime to flourish.[193]

To us it is obvious that Trump is supporting Putin's agenda. When Trump appointed Tillerson as his first Secretary of State, Kenneth Kimmel, president of the Union of Concerned Scientists, said in a UCS statement: "You wouldn't hire the CEO of a tobacco company to serve as the surgeon general. So why would you pick the leader of an oil and gas corporation to spearhead a position tasked with national security and global climate action?"[194]

Exxon/Mobil, and Tillerson himself, have contributed millions of dollars to GOP candidates since at least 2003. ExxonMobil has a culture of allegiance to money over any allegiance to America. Lee Raymond, who preceded Tillerson as ExxonMobil CEO, said of his corporate leadership role: "I'm not a U.S. company and I don't make decisions based on what's good for the U.S." (128)[195] In 2012 ExxonMobil was the largest corporation in the world measured by either revenue ($486 billion) or profit ($41 billion). In a May 3, 2012 article in the *Washington Monthly*, "What's Good For Exxon Is Not So Good For America" reporter Paul Pillar states "The clout, reach and mission of Exxon means that

---

193   Maddow, *Blowout*.
194   Kenneth Kimmell, "Secretary of State Pick Cements Governance By Oil Industry, Says Science Group", Union of Concerned Scientists, December 11, 2016, https://www.ucsusa.org/about/news/secretary-state-pick-cements-governance-oil-industry#.WFBVFKIrLBJ.
195   Steve Coll, *Private Empire: ExxonMobile and American Power* (Penguin, 2012).

it runs its own foreign policy." (129)[196] In 2006, Raymond received a "golden parachute" worth an estimated $400 million upon his retirement from ExxonMobil, adding to what he undoubtedly had accumulated before this windfall bonus. With that kind of money, it would seem you actually don't need to be tied to any one country—even though the corporate headquarters are in Texas. ExxonMobil claimed to accept the Paris Agreement global climate accord. However, the company's financial forecast conflicts with that claim, and instead reveals that ExxonMobil had no intention of complying with the Paris Agreement—or perhaps it was confident that the United States would leave the agreement.

We as a nation and as individuals need to work globally to reduce dependence on carbon-based energy sources and the attendant greenhouse gases. We must support the findings of the world's most learned scientists and economists to avoid the impending natural catastrophes we face if we don't make some drastic changes. As the earth warms, climate-related disasters include high-intensity hurricanes, floods, droughts, extreme precipitation, forest fires, and heat waves that pose rising dangers to life and property. Hurricanes become more intense and destructive as the warmer ocean waters feed more energy to the storms. Warmer air also carries more moisture for devastating rainfalls causing catastrophic flooding, while rising sea levels lead to a clear and present danger for low-lying areas throughout the world, including cities and agricultural regions. The cost of delaying action may well be the loss of cities including New Orleans, Miami, Tampa, Hoboken and Manhattan—and that's just some in the United States. Global warming, unless significantly lessened, will impact hundreds of millions of people.

---

196   Paul Pillar, "What's Good for Exxon is Not So Good for America", *Washington Monthly*, May 3, 2012, https://washingtonmonthly.com/2012/05/03/whats-good-for-exxon-is-not-so-good-for-america/.

Nothing Left for Your Children

> The cost of our success is the exhaustion of natural resources, leading to energy crisis, climate change, pollution and the destruction of our habitat. If you exhaust natural resources, there will be nothing left for your children. If we continue in the same direction, humankind is headed for some frightful ordeals, if not extinction.
> —Christian de Duve, scientist and author, 2010

Christian de Duve was a Nobel-prize winning scientist born near London to Belgian parents who fled to England in World War I. He was a medical doctor, a biochemist, endocrinologist and cell biologist. He is known for his discoveries about the internal workings of cells. His words of warning about humans' lack of good stewardship over our earth's resources appear in his 2010 book, *Genetics of Original Sin: The Impact of Natural Selection on the Future of Humanity*, in which he makes a case that evolution has made humans uniquely qualified to take actions and plan ahead for the common good over self-interest—but that sometimes we consciously choose not to.[197] We need to call out those who are choosing self-interest and take some responsibility, heeding the words and actions of teenage activist Greta Thunberg, who told the world leaders at the U.N. Climate Change Conference they were, "not mature enough to tell it like it is." This coming from a 16-year-old—whose generation is poised to suffer from global warming far more than those leaders will.

The Paris Agreement signed in 2016 is an agreement within the United Nations Convention on Climate Change framework, dealing with greenhouse gas emissions mitigation, adaptation,

---

[197] Christian de Duve, *Genetics of Original Sin: The Impact of Natural Selection on the Future of Humanity* (Yale University Press, 2010).

and finance. It brought together the vast majority of nations in a common cause to ambitiously undertake efforts to combat climate change and enhance support to developing countries in their efforts to also do so. As such, it charts a new course in the global climate effort. This Accord has a near universal membership. It has been signed by 197 countries and ratified by 185. Russia has not ratified it. President Obama signed America on in 2016. Trump withdrew the United States in June 2017, five months after he became president. The former chief of UN climate negotiations, Christiane Figueres, said the Trump administration has, "no understanding of the legal underpinning" of the agreement and that Trump "has no idea how an international treaty works," with his declaration that the United States was out of the agreement "as of today." Figueres explained, "In actuality withdrawing is complex and lengthy, taking four years to complete."[198]

Trump's rationale: "the agreement could ultimately shrink the gross domestic product by $2.5 trillion over a 10-year period." Just a note, that estimate is over twenty years, not ten, and it came from the conservative think tank The Heritage Foundation. Other analyses have described the potential economic impact as modest. The president's further justification for U.S. withdrawal from the Paris Agreement is that the U.S. would pay the cost and bear the burdens while other countries would get the benefits and pay nothing. This is yet another of Trump's "alternative facts" denying the truth. Our own government's analysis does not

---

198   Reported worldwide, for example see: Shanika Gunaratna, "UN Climate Negotiator Slams White House for Having 'No Idea' How Paris Agreement Works", CBS News, June 1, 2017, http://www.cbsnews.com/news/paris-agreement-climate-trump-united-nations/; and Mythili Sampathkumar, "Paris Agreement: Donald Trump Has 'No Understanding' of Deal, Says Former UN Climate Change Chief", *Independent,* June 2, 2017, http://www.independent.co.uk/news/world/americas/us-politics/paris-agreement-trump-climate-change-deal-un-chief-says-no-understanding-a7769941.html.

support this claim. In the first place, the climate is shared across the globe and alleviating global warming benefits all mankind; if the world doesn't meet this challenge, everyone is affected. Also, the United States is ranked eleventh out of forty-three countries in pledged contributions per capita (only nine of which are developing countries), but on a per capita basis, the U.S. emits more greenhouse gas than China (1.4 billion people) and India (1.3 billion) combined. China emits the most greenhouse gases in total tons, but the U.S. population is one-fourth of China's. Geoffrey Heal, a resource and environmental economist at Columbia University, said that staying in the Paris Agreement "would cost little and doing nothing would allow climate change to proceed and would be very expensive indeed." Heal added, "Remaining in the Paris Accord does not fully prevent climate change but it's a good start."[199]

The Paris Agreement calls for limiting the rise of global temperature to no more than 2°C by 2050. To do this, our government must be staffed with experts in the field: scientists, innovators, and policy experts who understand the regulations needed to achieve these goals. Trump has gutted the Environmental Protection Agency (EPA) of experienced scientists and staff. Trump has had more than 20 scientists removed from the EPA because their views on global warming are in disagreement with the president's proclamation. An additional number of scientists have left EPA in disgust and on their own volition. The American people are paying a heavy cost for the cynicism and greed of our politicians who appear more interested in the deep pockets of the fossil fuel industry. It's time to hold these reckless politicians accountable.

---

199   Margaret Hartmann, "What Quitting the Paris Climate Accord Will do to the U.S., and the Planet", *New York Magazine Intelligencer,* June 2, 2017, https://nymag.com/intelligencer/2017/06/what-quitting-the-paris-deal-does-to-the-us-and-the-planet.html.

Being Good and Decent People

> We must regain the conviction that we need one another, that we have a shared responsibility for others and the world, and being good and decent people are worth it.
>
> —Pope Francis, 2015

In our opinion, if the choice comes down to spending large sums of money to protect the planet from global catastrophe or doing nothing and letting the climate wreak havoc, we have to spend the money. Pope Francis' call for the people of the world to work together to care for our earth is a direct response to current ecological crises. He is calling on all of us to put aside differences to save ourselves and our home.[200] The earth is a responsibility and a gift. For Christians, it is an absolute God-given responsibility to exercise proper stewardship over the planet and all things therein: Since an overseer manages God's household, he must be blameless—not overbearing, not quick-tempered, not given to drunkenness, not violent, not pursuing dishonest gain. (Titus 1:7). We can do better to manage our earth, "God's household."

- Our food supply is being threatened by droughts and rising ocean temperatures.
- In Alaska the water is so hot that it is killing large numbers of salmon; if you go there you can see visibly the receding of the glaciers first-hand.
- Coral reefs of the ocean are dying off, and plankton, the beginning of the food chain, dramatically affected; the oceans phytoplankton are the planet's main source of oxygen (80 percent).

---

200   Pope Francis, "Laudato Si: On Care for Our Common Home", *The Vatican Encyclicals,* May 24, 2015, http://www.vatican.va/content/francesco/en/encyclicals/documents/papa-francesco_20150524_enciclica-laudato-si.html.

- Much of Australia was laid bare by uncontrollable wildfires.

There are so many effects that we don't have room to list them all here.

In 2018 the Nobel Peace Prize-winning Intergovernmental Panel on Climate Change released a harrowing report showing the world has just a few years left to move decisively towards renewable energy if we hope to achieve the globally agreed targets limiting warming to no more than 1.5 degrees Centigrade (3.2 degrees Fahrenheit) above the pre-industrial average temperature of the planet.[201] The public is disillusioned by long-standing congressional inaction. We'll never get anywhere without exploring new ideas and planning with a long-term vision for a future. The specific alternatives for achieving this vision must be ultimately worked out, and only then can we submit these alternatives to a rigorous benefit/cost analysis.

The Green New Deal offers a loose framework for addressing this crisis. The Green New Deal was first introduced in the 2016 presidential election by Green Party candidate Jill Stein. It does not lay out specific guidelines or the policies and proposals needed. Instead, it's a ten-year vision. No doubt, some of the proposals contained in the Green New Deal would be tough to implement and to transition to, and potentially extremely expensive. It committed to 100 percent renewable energy by 2030, costing approximately $20 billion. It would create a Renewable Energy Administration to create up to 20 million new green-certified jobs, which would cost an estimated $40 billion a year.

The Green New Deal proposed by Democratic progressives in Congress in 2019 is a bold new idea for improving energy efficiency, and limiting greenhouse gas emissions. Overhauling our

---

201   "Global Warming of 1.5 Degrees C: A Special Report", Intergovernmental Panel on Climate Change (IPCC), October 2018, https://www.ipcc.ch/sr15/.

transportation system is part of that plan as well as guaranteeing jobs and high-quality healthcare for all Americans. They are not specific proposals ripe for criticism or analysis, but rather a framework in which ideas can be incubated. The framework reflects the authors' version of our future and, importantly, it is based on the authors' and supporters' collective moral compass.

The Green New Deal is being criticized by conservatives as an indication of the new progressive socialism being expounded by some in the Democratic Party; but these critics are analyzing something that does not, in fact, exist. These proposals must be viewed as what they are: items on a yet-to-be-considered or worked-out wish list for making sure we have a planet to live on. More immediately, the first task for a new administration in 2021 must be to reverse decisions of the Trump administration so that we meet our "shared responsibility," and have the United States rejoin the Paris Agreement.

Trump's presidency has been like an earthquake that has reverberated across the globe, and the aftershocks continue to cause damage. We believe that our democracy would not survive another term. Climate change deniers are threatening basic human rights including the right to life, health and property. The president and his sycophants for the fossil fuel industry, in addition to most of his fellow Republicans in Congress as well as some Democrats do not want to do anything that will interfere with campaign contributions made by the industry that help fill their coffers. For the sake of their own profit, these elected representatives are putting people's lives and property at risk. Their counter argument is no more than a reflection of their greed and willful ignorance to ensure they can prolong the extraction of fossil fuels for at least as long as their own natural lives, and again, future generations be damned.

Many sincerely religious people take shelter and solace in their faith that God will protect us. That is not to be ridiculed, but respected. However, God granted us free will, to do what is right in Her or His eyes. We cannot exist as a nation primarily inhabited by pacifists. We survived world wars by confronting evil, not by being passive. We must approach the current crisis not with guns and bullets but with the gravity of a war nonetheless. The best weapon is citizen involvement. We must reclaim our democracy to heal our planet. Ordinary citizens have to find the time and energy to be involved.

CHAPTER 8

DON'T LET THE BASTARDS GRIND YOU DOWN

> Rebellion to tyrants is obedience to God.
> —Benjamin Franklin, founding father and statesman, 1776
>
> Illegitimi non carburundum.
> -Latin aphorism meaning "don't let the bastards grind you down"

DON'T LET THE BASTARDS GRIND YOU down: we live by these words. We ended the previous chapter by calling for immediate attention to our planet and identifying solution sets like the framework of the Green New Deal. Benjamin Franklin's suggestion for our new nation's Great Seal, "Rebellion to tyrants is obedience to God," justified acts of rebellion when done in the service of halting tyranny. Even if we can save the earth with action against climate change, we face a host of problems that are getting worse by the day under the rule of The Donald. We start this chapter by listing some of President Trump's more tyrant-like actions in his first three years in office:

- Proposing to ban Muslims from entering the United States.
- Hailing neo-Nazis as "good people."
- Conducting foreign policy via Twitter.
- Praising autocrats across the globe as good people and wonderful leaders.
- Alienating and insulting long-standing foreign allies of the United States.
- Withdrawing from the 2015 Iran nuclear deal.

- Engaging in and promoting blatant racism, misogyny and anti-LGBTQ actions and policies.
- Showing total disregard for the rule of law.
- Encouraging disdain and disregard for the First Amendment separation of church and state, as well as freedom of the press.
- Withdrawing from the Paris Agreement and promoting the falsity that climate change is a hoax.
- Promising a tax cut to help the middle class that in truth assisted the wealthy and worsened the growing income and wealth inequality.
- Increasing our national debt to $24 trillion, for which our children and grandchildren will pay.
- Neglecting to address critically needed repairs to our infrastructure.
- Failing to support any gun control legislation even in the aftermath of several mass killings.
- Attempting to extort the Ukrainian government to find or manufacture dirt on a political rival.
- Assigning his personal attorney Rudy Giuliani to conduct ad hoc foreign policy.
- Telling the Russian ambassador and Putin that he is not concerned about Russian interference in the 2016 U.S. presidential election because the United States does that, too.
- Publicly asking the governments of China and Ukraine to influence the 2020 U.S. election.
- Refusing to fill vacancies on the Federal Election Commission, leaving it without a quorum to do its job, including investigating election fraud and acting to ensure interference-free elections.
- Having recordings and transcripts of conversations placed

in highly classified repositories to hide what he has done from the American people.
- Dismissing a whistleblower as a partisan hack in order to bury the complaint by misusing the Justice Department and the White House Office of General Counsel.
- Intimidating potential witnesses who provided information to the whistleblower and saying they should be hung for treason.
- Violating his oath of office with blatant disregard for constitutional authority, ignoring legally issued subpoenas from the Legislative Branch and refusing to provide documents or allow persons to testify by falsely claiming executive privilege.
- Obstructing Congress, which again violates our rule of law.
- Engaging in conduct that is detrimental to our national security.
- Withdrawing a small contingent of troops from the Syria-Turkey border that were protecting our Kurd allies without consulting Congress *or* our allies, leaving the Kurdish people vulnerable to ethnic cleansing by Turkey.
- Attacking and attempting to dismantle U.S. government institutions.
- Firing Michael Atkinson, the intelligence community's Inspector General for informing Congress about the whistleblower complaint.
- Denying the danger of novel coronavirus pandemic labeling it a Democratic hoax and dangerously delaying our response.
- Lying about the United States' preparedness for COVID-19 and incompetently handling the response to the virus.
- Putting a change in the CARES Act adding a tax benefit to those who earn $1million or more per year.

- Firing Inspector General Glenn Fine who was responsible for oversight of the $2 trillion funding under the CARES Act.

This is only a partial list as of May 1, 2020. Forgive us for what we don't yet know. By the time of publication innumerable other unconscionable and damaging things initiated by Trump, whether directly or indirectly, openly or secretly, will have to be added.

The success of our system of government depends on men and women of good will working towards the good of the people by maintaining a civil discourse to debate differences based on facts and reaching reasonable compromises. We have lost that, hopefully only temporarily. The American government cannot function as intended without the rule of law and an effective system of checks and balances. That will not happen as long as Donald John Trump is president. We are on a slippery slope towards tyranny. Together we must climb back up the hill to an effective, fair-for-all, representative democracy.

Donald Trump is a symptom of a much more pervasive disease, but a symptom that in itself is life-threatening for our country as a democracy. Once a new president and new Congress are sworn in, we as a people must insist on legislation to take money out of politics. Elected officials must be made to represent the people and constituencies over wealthy special interest groups. Citizens must become better-informed voters who are armed with enough knowledge not to be swayed by impossibly simplistic promises and fear-mongering propaganda. There are millions of young people concerned about their futures and the future of our nation. Protests can be effective in bringing grievances to the fore, but increased involvement in research and the effective presentation of facts over multiple social media platforms is necessary. Young, eligible voters have traditionally had low voter turnout. Now is the time to change that. It is in everyone's self-interest to get involved in national concerns. The 2020 election will be a seminal point in determining if our democracy will continue with hope of a better future or a downhill slide toward tyranny. The electorate must take on this election as a deadly serious event. We must confront this Congress and this administration head-on to stop more erosion of our republic, and be armed with solutions and actions that might actually repair some of the destruction.

Unless the Republicans wrest the nomination away from Donald Trump for the 2020 election, we must be all be pragmatic and vote against Donald Trump. It is imperative that we elect a new leader. Ironically a large part of the reason Donald Trump got elected was because some segments of our population felt that their needs were not being served, and Trump promised to serve them what they asked for. The Democrat primary candidates proposed bold new programs aimed at our most pressing issues. Many of these ideas might prove to be godsends, exactly what is needed. Others may be only academic solutions to real world problems and need more thought and work before we know if they could even be useful. Some that are viable and much needed are perhaps too costly. Now, as a result of the coronavirus experience, we have a new perspective from which to address our nation's priorities. Thanks to this "Chosen One," the climb back up to some sense of normalcy and fairness is now far steeper. Politicians cannot continue to be allowed to promise everything and then to deliver virtually nothing. Therefore, the first and most essential rule of order: change our leadership.

Educate Yourself

Before elections, candidates for office promise the public what they'll do once elected. Then they sponsor and pass legislation in response to the hugely wealthy special interests. Finally, they often misrepresent what they did to a generally uninformed public. In this book we have attempted to explain in a straightforward, specific manner what the leaders in our society are doing in opposition to our best interests. We expose the detrimental effects and dangers posed by Trump's evangelical core voters. We warn that we must take the imminent threat to our democracy seriously, that the world is taking a frightening turn toward fascism. We outline the ominous threat of climate change and the raping of our economy by the ultra-rich.

As the problems and crises pile up with no end in sight, we feel the anger and frustration of not knowing where to go, or the most pressing issue, what to do—and that's while we also try to live our everyday lives. But the news keeps coming and the insanity keeps building. To this, we try to think of the words of Lao Tzu, a Chinese philosopher credited with founding the philosophical system of Taoism: "There is nothing better than to know what you don't know. Not knowing yet thinking you know… This is sickness. Only when you are sick of being sick can you be cured." So, here we offer a few examples of things that we've found promising and worthy of exploring: gun control policy and world news.

Gun Control: Do Some Research

Data from the *Gun Violence Archive* (GVA) shows that from January 1, 2017 through December 31, 2019, there were 417 mass shootings in the United States resulting in 459 deaths and 2,004 injuries; often with military-style assault weapons at times with magazines holding as many as 100 rounds of ammunition, and at schools, malls, theaters, houses of worship, and work locations. A mass shooting as defined by GVA is four or more people shot in one incident, not including the shooter, and occurs nine out of every ten days on average. In an August 19, 2019, *US News* article by Kenneth T. Walsh, he cited a recent NBC News/*Wall Street Journal* survey that found 89 percent of Americans favor expanded background checks for gun purchases. However, the only response from the Trump administration and the Republican Senate were promises, distractions, more promises, more distractions, and lots and lots of prayers. Our children have taken to the streets and led marches demanding action and fearful parents are buying their children backpacks with body armor; but these are not solutions to the problem of violence.

What we hear from the president are comments like, "The NRA leaders are good people. They agree something must be done." But nothing really happens, problems are ignored and the hateful rhetoric coming from the White House further encourages the crazies to come out and target "the invaders," people of color, "the 'fake news' media," and opposition politicians. And it looks like this is going to continue. According to NBC News, the NRA donated about $21 million to the Trump campaign in 2016, the highest amount the NRA has ever spent on a presidential candidate.[202] It was reported that the head of the NRA met with Trump again and may have offered more contributions to his 2020 run for office in exchange for Trump's promise to take gun control issues off the table. According to ABC News, the NRA admitted receiving some financial support from Alexander Torshin, a Putin ally. It was later reported that the FBI was investigating if several

---

202   Jon Schuppe, "NRA Sticking With Trump, Breaks Own Record for Campaign Spending", NBC News, October 12, 2016, https://www.nbcnews.com/news/us-news/nra-sticking-trump-breaks-own-record-campaign-spending-n665056.

millions of dollars were funneled to the NRA that made its way to the Trump campaign and other Republican candidates with money which came from Russia. However, Republicans on the Federal Election Commission blocked further efforts to investigate and the matter was closed. It seems like every time we turn around all roads lead to Russia.

World News: Pay Attention

On September 28, 2019, CNN anchor and political commentator Erin Burnett revealed that conversations between Trump and Crown Prince of Saudi Arabia Mohammad bin Salman have allegedly been hidden by some of the highest-ranking officials in the U.S. government at the direction of our president, more evidence that Trump has been running foreign policy in secrecy and without knowledgeable guidance.[203] For the sake of justice, we would like to know if their conversations had anything to do with the brutal murder of *Washington Post* journalist and U.S. resident Jamal Khashoggi. Despite the evidence pointing to the Saudi prince ordering the murder, Trump, for whatever reason, claims he doesn't believe U.S. intelligence agency information about this. We wonder why Trump chose to hide the conversation, and what else is being hidden.

We remember that Trump also met privately with Vladimir Putin and then ordered the attending interpreter's notes to be destroyed. Why? What was the purpose of that meeting? What was discussed? Why doesn't the president want anyone to know? It is now public knowledge that there are witnesses privy to Trump's conversation with the Russian ambassador that indicated that he (Trump) was not worried about Russian interference

---

203   Erin Burnett, "Erin Burnett OutFront," *CNN*, September 28, 2019, http://transcripts.cnn.com/TRANSCRIPTS/1909/27/ebo.01.html.

in the 2016 election because, his excuse went, the United States engages in the same kind of conduct. The Mueller Report and the House impeachment inquiry substantiated the allegation, which constitutes an admission by the president of his awareness that the Russians interfered in the election on his behalf. Moreover, Trump as yet has provided nothing to refute this, and in fact as late as October 2019 had publicly suggested to both Ukraine and China that they get involved with the 2020 U.S. elections.

Join Forces (even if you can't form your own PAC)

Many, many years ago, when the two of us were both still in school, we were introduced to the term "tyranny of data," which means being exposed to so much information that it becomes problematic to figure out what is really going on. When used as a political tool, it is often to cause so much confusion as to bury the truth. We recently heard the phrase "civic fatigue" as a way to define what has happened over the past three years. As individual citizens, our job is not to research each and every issue the nation is facing. Our elected officials are paid to do it or have the research done, and to present us with a clear and honest argument representing their beliefs about what is best for America. Whenever possible they should compromise and narrow their differences. That cannot be accomplished if we have a president that has a hidden, self-serving agenda and has been shown to lie to us, on average, more than fourteen times a day.

The smoke and mirrors and flak used by Trump and his cohorts are intended to sow confusion. Most members of the public would not describe themselves as political junkies who closely watch political news or impeachment hearings or conduct independent research for several hours each day to separate the wheat from the chaff. Most people have neither the time nor the inclination, and fair enough that they have other interests or needs on which to focus, and so rely on their elected officials to sort things out, to be honest, and to protect public interests. But that is not happening now, and the American public has been left vulnerable, now weakened by disease, and confused about what our purported leaders are doing and, more basically, who is in charge. We're not saying everyone needs to spend hours on the internet researching politics, but we are saying it is time for each of us to get some fortitude and take a stand.

It is telling that there are even evangelical Christians, like the editor of *Christianity Today,* breaking away from their comfort zones and umbrellas of conservative protection to align with social justice movements; they are decrying the absence of authentic Christianity in Trump's version of America. In addition, a group of politically savvy conservatives has launched a PAC, The Lincoln Project, aimed at stopping Trump's reelection. The group includes attorney George Conway (former advisor to Republican Senator John McCain), Steve Schmidt (former advisor to Republican Senator John McCain), John Weaver (former advisor to Ohio Governor John Kasich), former New Hampshire Republican Party Chairwoman Jennifer Horn, and pundit Rick Wilson. In a December 17, 2019, op-ed in the *New York Times,* Conway and others said: "Patriotism and the survival of our nation in the face of the crimes, corruption and the corrosive nature of Donald Trump are a higher calling than mere politics. As Americans we must stem the damage he and his followers are doing to the rule of law, the Constitution and the American character." We commend these patriots for their courage in speaking truth to the powerful. Our admiration is especially high for Conway, who is married to Trump White House insider Kellyanne Conway; it must be challenging trying to sleep with one eye open. Political strategist Reed Galen, listed as the group's treasurer, told the Associated Press that the

Lincoln Project represented "a shift from talk into action," and, "… a big turning point for the political season and for the president's reelection." We hope Mr. Galen is correct.

Find Your Moral Compass

We must reset our moral compass as a nation. Hitler and the Nazis eliminated freedom in Germany by quickly taking over the free press, ending fact-based decision making, removing independent judges from their judiciary, and packing the courts with Hitler partisans.

We must stop scapegoating. The Bible says in Exodus 22:21: "You shall not mistreat a stranger (foreigner) or oppress him, for you were once a stranger (foreigner) in the land of Egypt." We must talk openly and honestly with one another to understand different perspectives. The current extreme divisiveness in our country robs us all of the ability to share points of view and, in so doing, collectively end the stagnation in Congress and move forward. To do this we must rid ourselves of self-serving politicians and religious leaders.

The vulnerable in our society are not our enemies, yet they are being increasingly denigrated and used as political pawns to divert attention away from problems with the economy, income inequality, and a host of other domestic concerns and frightening foreign policies. Conflict provides an incubator for discord; there is a correlation between times of relative economic despair and an increase in prejudice and violence. Trump's hateful and bigoted rhetoric has set the stage, and there is no question that schisms among races are being exacerbated by Trump's rhetoric. With the current downturn in the economy displays of bigotry are likely to increase dramatically. The president's childish taunts and hateful rhetoric must go.

"The function of freedom is to free someone else," said author Toni Morrison.[204] We need to support one another and lift one another up. A simple way to show that you are a safe haven and willing to help individuals who may feel marginalized in the current political and social climate is to wear a lapel pin that would show solidarity with women, the LBGTQ community, immigrants, and people with disabilities, religious diversity, and people of color feeling uncertain of whom to trust. The pin movement arose as a show of solidarity against Brexit in the United Kingdom, with the notion that anyone against nationalistic, racist violence could identify themselves as a safe ally by wearing a pin prominently displayed. This "safe place" pin says to others: I see you, I understand, and you are safe here. With this pin you promise to others: if you need me, I'll be with you, all I ask is that you be with me, too; together we will be the strong arm of God. A variety of these "safety pins" can be found easily through a Google search.

America is not a theocracy. That argument was resolved for most western countries in the Enlightenment, and for us, by our founding fathers. Yet evangelicals have been extending their tentacles into our government as well as other governments around the world; evangelicals are the core of Trump's base. We need to stem that tide. Thanks in large part to Jeff Starlet, The Family is being brought out into the daylight. They are frightening and potent. It is fruitless to try to convince them of the error of their ways. And, we shouldn't try to engage them on their field of battle by intensifying the culture wars. They turn out the vote "religiously." Trump and his enablers rely on it. We can't diffuse this message with reason and logic alone. We must ensure that people of reason and logic get

---

204 David Anders Brodeur, "Toni Morrison in Her Own Words: 'The function of freedom is to free someone else'", *Boston Globe,* August 6, 2019, https://www.bostonglobe.com/arts/2019/08/06/toni-morrison-her-own-words-the-function-freedom-free-someone-else/OS8quuie2VF355fuKCwzDJ/story.html.

out to vote and make political change at the ballot box. Question political leaders and religious authorities, find out what they really stand for and what they truly believe.

Let's get that horse out of the hospital. Bring back reason, sanity and decency to our government, starting with the Executive Branch.

Don't Forget Our Past

There are some people who think we have had a president or two, that at times have acted as though they were not in line when God handed out common sense. As a nation we have had some chapters we'd probably rather didn't happen, or we'd like to forget i.e., slavery and the internment of Japanese-Americans. Nonetheless, we have survived and prospered as a nation. In the afterword to "The Rise and Fall of the Third Reich," historian William Shirer reminds us that memory can be an important ally in making sure catastrophes like this don't happen again.

Unless our leadership changes, fascism will continue to rise throughout the world. Trump's actions domestically and internationally have aided this resurgence. Europe's underestimation of the threat posed by Hitler's rise to power, and the world's attempts at appeasement, almost led to the end of democracy. World War II resulted in the death of an estimated 70 million people. Albert Einstein has been credited with saying: Insanity is; "doing the same thing over and over again, and expecting different results." The present threat is real. There is a parallel. Let's learn from history. We believe that the admonitions and warnings of our founding fathers should be reviewed by every American for they are truly on point in this troubling time. We also need to look to the future. Benjamin Franklin, one of our wisest statesmen, said:

> ... nothing is of more importance for the public weal than to form and train up youth in wisdom and virtue. Wise and good men are, in my opinion, the *strength* of a state: much more so than riches or arms, which, under the management of Ignorance and Wickedness, often draw on destruction, instead of providing for the safety of a people.[205]

The profound words of our founding fathers have never been more germane and precisely on point than they are today, more than 200 years later. For those of you who choose to continue to live in denial about the potential treachery of this president, there is not much anyone could ever do or say to convince you of the danger Trump poses. As Winston Churchill is reported to have said, "Evils can be created much quicker than they can be cured."

During the late 1940s and early 1950s the prospect of communist subversion seemed frighteningly real to many Americans. Wisconsin Senator Joseph McCarthy seized on this fear and went on his own witch hunt to ferret out communists in government and other sectors of society. This brought McCarthy to national prominence. He had literally no evidence or proof but spent nearly five years intimidating and bullying witnesses and ruining some people's careers and lives. After limited success trying in vain to expose communists working in the federal government, in 1954 McCarthy decided to take on the so-called communist invasion of the U.S. Armed Forces. This led to McCarthy's downfall. The televised Army-McCarthy hearings were seen by many as a shameful moment in American politics. Since November, 2016, we frequently think of the words of Joseph Nye Welch, Chief Counsel

---

205   Benjamin Franklin, "Letter to Samuel Johnson, 23 August 1750", *Founders Online*, National Archives, accessed January 20, 2020, http://founders.archives.gov/documents/Franklin/01-04-02-0009.

for the U.S. Army while it was under investigation for communist activities by McCarthy's Senate Permanent Subcommittee on Investigations, when Welch famously asked McCarthy: "Have you no sense of decency, Sir?" knowing that by then most observers were certain he did not. We ask this same rhetorical question of Trump and his underlings. Our answer: "No, they do not!"

As for those individuals who have been aware of any and all of the treachery by Trump and his minions and still allowed it to continue without intervening, they are culpable and should be dealt with accordingly. They are part of the conspiracy to suborn the lies and are in violation of the Constitution of the United States. They include the elected officials who have assisted this president in perpetuating deceit and illegal behavior, and are guilty of complicity. They are not worthy to serve as representatives in the halls of Congress or to hold any position of authority in this country. In the court of public opinion, they should be cited as being part of a conspiracy to defraud the people of the United States, be censured and voted out of office.

And Don't Let A Bastard Grind You Down

We found a quote attributed to Napoleon and immediately thought of Donald Trump: "In politics stupidity is not a handicap."[206] It wasn't because Trump is an emperor or great military leader (although he may want to be). Thinking about it, there's more than one way to take this adage. It could be that stupid people are not excluded from making it in politics, or it could be that the pretense of stupidity can allow someone in politics to get

---

206   Attribution unconfirmed. For context see: "Napoleon Bonaparte," *Brainy Quotes*, https://www.brainyquote.com/quotes/napoleon_bonaparte_110029; and Christian Oord, "Ten Famous Things Napoleon Bonaparte Never Said," *War History Online*, May 1, 2019, https://www.warhistoryonline.com/instant-articles/famous-things-napoleon-said.html.

away with things they might not otherwise. We have concluded that there are three plausible explanations for Trump's behavior, any combination of which provide some explanation for his actions—and reason to vote him out.

Option 1: Donald Trump Is, In Fact, a Moron

It may be possible that Donald Trump is, as Tillerson suggested, a "moron," and his actions are because he lacks adequate intellect, experience and sense needed to successfully carry out his duties as president of the United States. H.L. Mencken was an American journalist, essayist, satirist and cultural critic. Mencken, in "On Politics: A Carnival of Buncombe" said, "As democracy is perfected, the office of the president represents, more and more closely, the inner soul of the people. On some great and glorious day, the plain folks of the land will reach their heart's desire at last and the White House will be adorned by a downright moron."[207] That was published 100 years ago in the *Baltimore Sun* on July 21, 1920; Mencken now seems prophetic. While we still don't buy this explanation, if Tillerson's judgement is correct, Trump certainly is not the person we want in the Oval Office making decisions affecting the fate of mankind.

Option 2: Trump Has Narcissistic Personality Disorder and Needs some HELP

According to psychiatrist and scholar Fritz Redlich, Adolph Hitler had Narcissistic Personality Disorder (NPD), characterized by:

- Believing that you are better than others.

---

207   G. Jefferson Price, "Commentary: 'The White House Will Be Adorned by a Downright Moron'", Baltimore Sun, November 25, 2016, https://www.baltimoresun.com/opinion/op-ed/bs-ed-mencken-trump-20161119-story.html.

- Believing that others are jealous of you.
- Exaggerating your achievements or talents.
- Expecting constant praise and admiration.
- Believing you are special and acting accordingly.
- Failing to recognize other people's emotions and feelings.
- Expecting others to go along with your ideas and plans.
- Being jealous of others.
- Having trouble keeping healthy relationships.
- Setting unrealistic goals.
- Being easily hurt and rejected.
- Having a fragile self-esteem.
- Appearing as tough-minded and emotional.

Redlich concluded that even showing many symptoms of NPD, Hitler would not be categorized as mentally ill with this diagnosis because he knew what he was doing and chose to do it with pride and enthusiasm.[208] Glenn O. Gabbard, Clinical Professor of Psychiatry at Baylor College of Medicine in Houston, said, "Projection is more commonly found in personalities functioning at a primitive level as a narcissistic personality disorder or borderline personality disorder."[209] We are not mental health experts, certainly not psychiatrists, and in any case, even a good medical or mental health professional would not likely offer a diagnosis without personally and thoroughly analyzing a patient. However, we are concerned observers and, to us, even with our untrained eyes and ears, it appears our president shows numerous signs of NPD. Whether this is an accurate guess or not, it is clear to us that Trump's behavior fits the criteria of NPD enough to call into

---

208   See Redlich's extensive study: *Hitler: Diagnosis of a Destructive Prophet* (Oxford University Press, 1998).
209   Glenn O. Gabbard, ed., *Long-Term Psychodynamic Psychotherapy* (American Psychiatric Publishing, 2004).

question his stability, trustworthiness and fitness to be president of the United States. According to the experts, the following define NPD.

- NPD is: "a severe personality disorder, whose main symptoms are a great or complete lack of sympathy, social responsibility and conscience," according to the mental health resource PsychCentral.com. "Narcissistic manipulators are fake, fragile and they are cowards. They pretend to be strong, call others weak and sensitive, bully and abuse people, but if you challenge them about their lies or stand up for yourself, they immediately start playing the fragile victim. 'Look I'm being attacked!' 'You're the real bully!' 'They are so mean to me'." This is according to a blog post by mental health educator Darius Cikanavicius.[210]
- Projection is defined as, "placing your own negative traits or unwanted emotions onto others," according to Brandon Brewer of the Gooden Center residential drug and alcohol rehabilitation program in Los Angeles. It is blame-shifting.
- Wikipedia defines psychological projection as, "a defense mechanism in which the human ego protects itself against negative qualities in them by attributing them to others."[211]
- "The [NPD] trait of compulsive and pathological lying means that the narcissist will not be responsible or accountable for questionable actions. This ... trait can be used as projection which means falsely accusing others of the narcissist's crimes," explains Amy Adam in a reference article, "Pathological Lying: Narcissistic Personality

---

210 Darius Cikanavicius, "How Narcissists Blame and Accuse Others for Their Own Shortcomings", *PsychCentral*, last updated September 16, 2019, https://blogs.psychcentral.com/psychology-self/2019/08/narcissists-blame-projection/.
211 "Psychological projection," *Wikipedia*, accessed February 4, 2020, https://en.wikipedia.org/w/index.php?title=Psychological_projection&oldid=953895324.

Disorder", on *SelfGrowth*, an online self-improvement resource.[212]

Trump tells on average fourteen lies a day, and that's just the ones that we know about. He calls his adversaries liars, rude and treasonous. Is he mentally ill? We aren't qualified to make that call. We do think he is immoral and that we can make that call. In the Bible in Matthew 7:3-5, Jesus cautions against projection as a form of blindness to one's own hypocrisy:

> Why do you look at the speck of dust in your brother's eye and pay no attention to the plank in your own eye? How can you say to your brother, 'let me take the speck out of your eye' when all the time there is a plank in your own eye? You hypocrite, first take the plank out of your own eye, and then you will see clearly to remove the speck from your brother's eye.

Even if a diagnosis of NPD were to explain Trump's behavior, we still need more to explain the scope and level of his actions. None of these are good options, but the next one might be the most frightening, and also the one for which there is increasingly more evidence.

Option 3: Donald Trump Knows Exactly What He's Doing

We do not believe that "The Donald" is a moron. He may not be a seasoned political insider, but he's no dummy either, nor is he a stranger to the halls of power. We believe that even if Trump is suffering from a severe psychological disorder it would not fully explain all of his behaviors and actions. We believe that

---

212 Amy Adam, "Pathological Lying: Narcissistic Personality Disorder Traits", *SelfGrowth*, accessed December 20, 2019, https://www.selfgrowth.com/articles/identifying-narcissistic-personality-disorder-traits-excessive-entitlement.

Donald J. Trump has a plan and is working on the "long con" that he believes will vastly increase his own wealth and power. Is it possible that Trump has been working nefariously with Vladimir Putin on a grand plan to change the world order? The cost will be American democracy, morality, values, and integrity. If this proves to be the case, he is a traitor to America and guilty of treason, and a dangerous national security risk. What might look like seemingly inexplicable, nonsensical behavior by Trump has actually led to events that have benefitted Putin and Russia, and also Trump himself.

In "Trump: The Chosen One" we have cited many of the world's most intelligent and astute minds. We have used their words to help us define our nation's core values and characterize the imminent and ominous dangers facing our democracy. We sincerely hope these core values still ring true for a plurality of the American electorate. We pray that this plurality sheds the doldrums, casts off collective fear and anger, and mobilizes for fast-paced, dramatic change. It is our sincerest hope that the words we have written here can make some small impression on people of conscience. That we have gently reminded them of their duty to God and country; and inspire them to put aside partisan loyalties and think about our Constitution and the need to vigilantly and zealously protect the institutions that have served this nation, and the world, so faithfully for over 240 years. Under our nation's present circumstances, we fear that our blessings are in peril of vanishing into the cesspool.

The United States is a representative democracy. As our world has grown more complex and fast moving, we have become increasingly dependent on our elected officials to protect our interests and they are failing miserably. America is a diverse country. Our individual interests can vary dramatically. Governing is the art of compromise. Thomas Jefferson, in an 1824 letter to Louisiana Congressman Edward Livingston, wrote, "A government held together by the bands of reason only, requires much compromise of opinion, that things even salutary should not be crammed down the throats of dissenting brethren, especially when they may be put into a form to be willingly swallowed, and that a great deal of indulgence is necessary to strengthen habits of harmony and fraternity."[213] Jefferson and Livingston were corresponding about the city of New Orleans after the Louisiana Purchase, and differences of law and opinion. In the letter, Jefferson expressed a difference of opinion with much of Livingston's view, but that, "in one sentiment ... I particularly concur. 'If we have a doubt relative to any power, we ought not to exercise it'." Our democracy must occur in bright sunshine, it cannot be run in secrecy. When our politicians lie and cheat for their self-interest, they must be held accountable. When they assume powers not granted to them by law, they must be held accountable. They have to earn our trust. We cannot allow them to operate in the shadows. We must insist upon and enforce greater transparency.

The two articles of impeachment on which the president was indicted by the House were Abuse of Power and Obstruction of Congress. In the lead-up to the revelations for which Trump faced impeachment, he called for the execution of the whistleblower who revealed Trump's call with Ukrainian President Zelensky, along with the "traitors" (Trump's word) who gave information to the whistleblower. Calling whistleblowers traitors and spies, and suggesting they should be hung, is yet one more fear tactic that President Trump uses to intimidate anyone who challenges him or reports even potential wrongdoing. It is worth noting here that the main reason that China released information about the looming

---

213 Thomas Jefferson, "Letter to Edward Livingston, 4 April, 1824", *Founders Online*, National Archives, accessed February 2, 2020, https://founders.archives.gov/documents/Jefferson/98-01-02-4169.

danger of the novel coronavirus was because of the actions of a Chinese whistleblower.

Trump and Secretary of State Pompeo did everything in their power to keep people from coming forward to testify, going as far as putting out a memo ordering everyone in the State Department not to cooperate with or provide documents or testimony to the House committees engaged in the impeachment inquiry. That in itself constitutes an impeachable offense: obstruction of Congress. McConnell and Senate Republicans (with the exception of Mitt Romney) conspired with the White House to keep the truth from the American people, and to acquit the president of the high crimes for which there was clear proof of his guilt; they are now complicit in defrauding America and themselves guilty of breaching their oath of office. It is our position that anyone who assisted the president in any way with wrongdoing should be charged and dealt with legally with due process. As for Trump and Barr, McConnell and Nunes, Trump has already commented on how any traitor should be handled, and on that one thing we agree.

To die-hard Trump supporters we say: you are not only deceived, but the "Kool-Aid" you are drinking could be fatal to all of us. For the rest of us, we will not tolerate Trump's continual lies, deflection and obfuscation. We are mobilizing to defeat Trump in 2020 and must ensure that his successor is concerned with the nation's needs over his/her own. We must make our tax structure progressive and fair, increase wages, repair infrastructure, rejoin the Paris Agreement, re-establish relationships with foreign allies, pass legislation for much-needed gun control, address the evils of racism and bigotry, fix health care and bridge the extreme divisions in our society. This will not be as overwhelming as it sounds once we end the reign of this reality TV president.

On the last day of the Constitutional Convention of 1787, a decision was made about the form of government we would have. The story is that while leaving Independence Hall, Benjamin Franklin was asked by a woman in the crowd; "Well Doctor, do we have a republic or monarchy?" To which Franklin replied, "We have a Republic, for as long as we can keep it." Up to now we have managed to keep it through wars, disasters, depressions and other crises—at least until now, when we feel that this republic is the most jeopardized is has ever been. We find it incredulous that the party of Lincoln has closed its eyes to the duty to protect our nation's liberty and Constitution. We hope this book serves as an impetus to become more politically involved. In the meantime, we are confident there is more insanity to come, and so we leave you and our Executive Branch, Judiciary and Congress with this:

> *You'll know the tree from fruit it bears, and light that shines at dawn.*
> *Was love and light, His message brought, the reason He was born.*
> *For God is just; and we must too, be just, and follow He.*
> *A blind eye turned to what is wrong, may turn his wrath on thee.*
> *For God shall not be silent long, don't justify your way*
> *Don't close your eyes to evil works, and shun the light of day.*
> *In doing so, you seal your fate, lest freedom goes away.*
> *Let's not forget that God knows all the things that go astray;*
> *Is evil done for goodness sake, the place you want to go?*
> *If so, I fear we'll all be lost for God shall surely know*
> *Don't let your ideology keep you from doing right*
> *Don't think that God will need your help, for some religious fight.*
> *For if you do, you must not have a real good sense of He*
> *Presuming that you understand the way that things should be*
> *Our lives, our land, our liberty; God meant us to live free.*
> *Do not forsake the words of God nor ignore our liberty.*
>
> —James Henry Thurber 2020

EPILOGUE

WHERE ARE WE NOW, WHICH WAY IS OUT, ARE WE TOO LATE?

"Hell is the truth, seen too late."
—attributed to Thomas Hobbes, philosopher, Seventeenth Century

As we close this writing at the beginning of May 2020, we can see the events of the past three plus years now brightly illuminating the serious and immediate danger we face as a nation. We wonder if it is too late to have seen the truth, meaning we are in some kind of hell, in the words of Thomas Hobbes, a great political philosopher of the Enlightenment.[214] The revelations brought forth by the whistleblower from the U.S. intelligence community, the testimony of former U.S. Ambassador to Ukraine Marie Yovanovitch, and the recent release of court documents and public disclosures made after the trial, brought into clear focus the ongoing treachery of this President of the United States. Trump has been lying to the public from the beginning. He has been conspiring with allies in Congress to hide the truth from the American people. As the allegations increasingly became verified revelations, more and more people were purged from our government. It is now clear anyone coming forward to reveal what they have seen, heard, and know will not be protected by this Senate. For Trump's defenders we now know

---

214   The quote is commonly attributed to Thomas Hobbes, but lacks confirmation. We believe that this quote accurately reflects the nature of Hobbes and the ideas for which he is famous and highly regarded.

"they have no shame or sense of decency." We thought many would run and hide from the fallout. We thought they might sink into their own cesspool. They did not. Instead they doubled down on their sycophancy and subservience to their "chosen one."

Trump's underlings worked hard to discredit the whistleblower, not with evidence but with personal attacks on character, calling the whistleblower a partisan hack, hell-bent on getting rid of this president. But the allegations that were made by the whistleblower were deemed credible and urgent by Trump's own intelligence community inspector general (IG), Michael Atkinson, a Republican. Trump fired Atkinson on April 3, 2020. The IG's investigation provided a prima facie case of the allegations made against the president. The initial strategy voiced by congressional Republicans was along the lines of: we heard what he said, but he was just joking to get a rise of the Democrats. A few congressional Republicans actually said that with a straight face. Great muscle control—must have been painful! Mr. Atkinson was fired by the president.

We know that on October 17, 2019, Mick Mulvaney, Office of Management and Budget director and White House acting chief of staff, admitted that there was a quid pro quo presented to Ukraine, and confirmed this several times to reporters—who in turn seemed somewhat in disbelief over Mulvaney's public and repeated admission of this egregious wrongdoing. Mulvaney followed with the dismissive attitude of, "it is done all the time, get over it." Even this one event in the entire illegal, immoral episode of Trump's presidency cannot be normalized simply by bringing it into the open. Those who are questioning this and similar events are not in a deep state operation, nor a partisan witch hunt, nor just fourteen angry Democrats, nor the FBI gone rogue. Mulvaney did this on national television in front of everyone to hear and see, the president admitted to it, and his defense was a simple and disturbing one and went something like: "I didn't do anything wrong. and the Senate dismissed it."

The polls and news media showed the vast majority of Americans supported the impeachment inquiry. The allegations set forth in the whistleblower's statement, the testimony of the former Ukrainian Ambassador and the revelation of Trump's discussion with the Russian delegation were verified to be true by over a dozen witnesses. President Trump may very well go down in the annals of American history as being more despicable, more treacherous and more treasonous than Benedict Arnold. And, those that have come to his aid in obfuscating the truth should be listed alongside him. What has bothered us as much as anything else is that there are people within the highest echelons of our government who have known what has been going on in this White House from the beginning and have said nothing and were complicit in covering it up! They are absolutely without integrity or lacking any semblance of decency or honor. There are witnesses who have vindicated at least some of the White House personnel who were willing to come forward and expose what they have heard and seen. However, they have put themselves and families in jeopardy, threatened by a president that Republicans refuse to rein in.

After the ruse of an impeachment trial, the Republicans citing long-debunked conspiracy theories and specious arguments to justify Trump's actions the GOP-controlled Senate acquitted the president and in so doing set a dangerous precedent of effectively placing the president above the law. Given the present state of our democracy and the effectiveness of the Republicans in deliberating sowing confusion to conceal the truth over the past three years, this is problematic, to say the least. With the stresses and complexities of everyday life the public is looking for simple answers. The Republicans have been more successful than Democrats in providing soundbites because they do not feel constrained by an obligation to truth or even a modicum of integrity. Their playbook is simple: shield the president, obfuscate truth without regard to our democracy, and control the population by sowing divisiveness and appealing to fear and anger.

We believe that Congress had conclusive evidence of treason committed by Trump. By the White House not allowing key witnesses to testify and not responding to legally issued subpoenaed documents, Trump effectively precluded the possibility of a treason charge. The sham "trial" conducted by the GOP-led Senate was a circus, and not a very good one. The Republicans have effectively put Trump above the laws of our nation. It appears Trump is right on one point: his claim that if he shot someone on Fifth Avenue in Manhattan in front of a thousand witnesses and was recorded on videotape holding a smoking AK-47, the Senate would not convict him of wrongdoing. The GOP will continue to ignore the facts, pump in smoke and deflect with mirrors, and employ the blame game using falsehoods about Democrats and their motives for the impeachment.

The public was aware that the leader of the Senate, Mitch McConnell, had announced in advance that there would be a coordination of strategy between the White House and Senate Republicans for the Senate impeachment trial. We do not believe that this can sit well with most people. It is abundantly clear that many in Congress closed their eyes to this deliberate perversion of the truth. The blatant collaboration with the accused to ensure a specific outcome was deemed acceptable procedure by the Senate Republicans. Our Constitution demands a fair trial, which requires an honest review of and a presentation of all relevant evidence and witnesses. Polls revealed that more than 70 percent of the public wanted the Senate to review the documents that were subpoenaed by the House but were being withheld by the White House; and to call witnesses to appear before the full Senate in a public hearing.

However, McConnell made it abundantly clear that the calling of relevant and necessary witnesses, including Mulvaney, Bolton, Pompeo and others, would not happen—a guarantee that the truth of this matter, whatever it may be, would not see the light of day. Moreover, McConnell's declaration to coordinate with the White House to ensure the president's narrative, true or not, would continue unabated by any evidence, was fulfilled. The Republican strategy assumes that the public will accept that a fair trial was conducted without relevant documents, evidence and/or witnesses. The GOP is relying on the public being apathetic or very stupid. We want to believe their strategy will backfire on Election Day in 2020.

The House impeached President Trump on two charges: Abuse of Power and Obstruction of Congress. Speaker of the House Pelosi forwarded the articles of impeachment to Senate Majority Leader McConnell and awaited his response on how the Senate trial would be conducted. Senate Democrats wanted to subpoena four witnesses who all were current or former members of the administration believed to have direct knowledge of Trump's discussions with Ukraine about political investigations and military aid. They were Mulvaney and Mulvaney's senior advisor, Robert Blair; former National Security Advisor John Bolton; and, Associate Director of National Security at the Office of Management and Budget Michael Duffy. All four men were called to testify as part of the House inquiry but refused to appear. McConnell then announced he was working in "total coordination" with the White House to conduct this trial, that he wanted an expedited process without including witnesses, and that he intended to quickly move for an acquittal. The Democrats could not convince four GOP Senators to vote to call witnesses, the Senate "trial" was a sham, with the accused, President Trump, getting to set the rules over his own trial and the head of the Senate pre-determining the outcome. If the Republicans truly believe the president was innocent of wrongdoing, why didn't they allow witnesses to be called to prove it, in full view of the public?

As we predicted, once the president was officially acquitted by the Senate, he immediately claimed he had been vindicated and was even further emboldened. He has no constraints on his behavior and the checks and balances essential for our democracy have effectively been abandoned. Our remaining hope was for Trump to be entirely consumed by his reelection campaign so any future damage, on a national or international scale, is minimized; and that the public would ensure his defeat in 2020. Then came the devastation of the coronavirus exacerbated by Trump's lack of preparedness and feeble, self-serving response. Now, Trump has said he will personally disperse without oversight by an inspector general the $500 billion of the CARES Act designated for large corporations, and, he fired Glenn Fine the inspector general who was designated to provide legal oversight. We anticipate massive fraud. Follow the money!

We fear Trump is following the adage to "never let a good crisis go to waste," words attributed to politically motivated people throughout history, including Winston Churchill, political theorist Saul Alinsky, Chicago Mayor Rahm Emanuel, and even Machiavelli himself. Never one to miss an opportunity we believe that Trump is no doubt looking to make a massive profit from this particular American nightmare. Trump has clearly shown his lack of concern for the well-being and safety of hard-working Americans before. CNN unearthed Trump's 2006 declaration made in a Trump University audiobook: "I sort of hope the real estate market crashes. ... I'm excited for the housing market crash. I've always made money in bad markets."[215] In the economic crisis barely two

---

215   Jeremy Diamond, "Donald Trump in 2006: I 'Sort of Hope' Real Estate Market Tanks", *CNN*, May 19, 2016, https://www.cnn.com/2016/05/19/politics/donald-trump-2006-hopes-real-estate-market-crashes/index.html.

years later, 5 million Americans lost their homes and $13 trillion in family wealth was wiped out. But that did not seem to matter to The Donald if he could make money out of it.

The two most important elections in our nation's history were in 1864 during the Civil War and in 1940 prior to the United States entering WWII. The 2020 election is just as important; the very survival of our democracy and our way of life, are at stake. However, we are fearful that many Americans do not understand the gravity of this election. If Trump is reelected, we will have a lawless, unchecked president. As we write this, Senator and former Vice President Joe Biden is the likely Democratic nominee. Biden, whether he was your first choice for that ticket or not, offers us a stark and promising contrast to Trump in his statements and world view.

The Democrats were faced with a dilemma in 2019: they needed to present enough evidence and details to prove the gravity of Trump's wrongdoing, but in a way that the public would not be left numb by the weight of it. To simplify things, the House limited the impeachment charges to abuse of power and obstruction of Congress. Both charges were warranted, but, despite overwhelming evidence, Trump loyalists did not budge. Trumps' enablers claim that the impeachment inquiry was just politics, and the wrongdoing that was exposed and verified did not illuminate serious transgressions. In the public proclamations of the president's Chief of Staff, Mick Mulvaney: "Get over it!" We wholly disagree.

It is sad that our country can no longer trust its elected representatives to fulfill their duties under the Constitution without letting partisan politics get in the way. We are not attorneys but you do not need to be one to see that this is wrong. We are just citizens who are afforded an amazing privilege to be able to communicate our beliefs and feelings without fear of coercion or reprisal. Our Constitution gives all Americans that right; our fear is that eventually this may no longer be the case. Our freedoms are now being seriously challenged by the executive branch, and we fear this defiance of Congress and attacks on citizens "who step out of line" will continue with impunity while the Senate continues to go along with anything the president decides to do. It happened to Lt. Col. Vindman, his brother and others, and it will only be a matter of time until it will be the Supreme Court's turn to be defied and ignored. What will the court do should this president—or any other president—decide to do what Andrew Jackson did in the 1832 decision in *Worcester v. Georgia*? What can we do as citizens when Trump is allowed to defy subpoenas issued by the legislative branch, with half of its members too scared to challenge any wrongdoing and intimidated into being complicit in that decision? What will we do when Trump says that Chief Justice Roberts and the Supreme Court have made their decision now "good luck enforcing it"—an echo of President Andrew Jackson's sentiments?

The Abuse of Power charge by the House of Representatives was based on Trump's conspiring with Rudy Giuliani to withhold aid from the Ukrainian government to pressure Ukraine to announce an investigation into the debunked conspiracy theories about the Bidens. The actions amounted to using bribery tactics to manufacture a political narrative to conjure up dirt on a political opponent for use in the 2020 election. It was also an attempt to shift Russian election interference and meddling to the Ukrainians. John Bolton, the former national security advisor in the Trump White House, disparagingly referred to this scheme to hold up military aid to Ukraine in exchange for a promise from Ukrainian President Zelensky to announce an investigation of Joe and Hunter Biden, as a "drug deal." and wanted no part of it. It is now clear he knows the details and offered to appear as a witness before the Senate if subpoenaed after refusing to testify in the House. Trump and McConnell were no doubt confident that the prospect of Bolton's testimony was never going to come to fruition, and without four GOP senators who were willing to demand a fair trial with witnesses, it was not to be.

Without any Senate intervention upon the Executive Branch's circumventing the Legislative Branch's constitutional subpoena power authority, oversight may be forever rendered invalid. There was a whitewash of the truth and without the truth any hope of the public putting pressure on our representatives to do the right thing was lost. Without the ability to exercise the constitutional rights of checks and balances under Article 1 of the Constitution, what can be done if a president ignores the law he has sworn to uphold, declares an election invalid and claims himself supreme ruler? Will the people be forced into armed conflict in order to preserve our democracy? We shudder at the thought.

We have witnessed courageous and patriotic men and women, who attempted to bring forth what they believe to be the truth, berated, criticized, and accused of being traitors by the most powerful man in the world—the same man who suggested that "traitors should be hung." This powerful man is destroying their reputations and putting their lives and the lives of their families at risk for telling the truth as they know it; and the impropriety of it isn't even an afterthought for him or many others in Congress. These reckless and unconscionable actions by our executive branch will now have to be stopped by the people at the ballot box. We have little faith that our Supreme Court will intervene to stop this tyrannical president and correct the discourse plaguing the nation, or reset this out-of-control partisan division that is tearing our union apart. The Senate trial was a sham, and has let Pandora out of the box. It will be up to the voters to fix this.

Thomas Jefferson stated over 200 years ago: "I tremble for my country when I reflect that God is just; that his justice cannot sleep forever." Jefferson's words were part of his consideration of how to function as a nation with states and individuals holding drastically oppositional views, in this case about slavery. In fact, we think it is worth reading more of what Jefferson said here:

> ...and can the liberties of a nation be thought secure when we have removed their only firm basis, a conviction in the minds of the people that these liberties are of the gift of God? That they are not to be violated but with his wrath? Indeed, I tremble for my country when I reflect that God is just: that his justice cannot sleep forever.[216]

We are now a divided nation without the leadership needed to heal us back into unity. We are without a Jefferson or a Lincoln in the White House. We are losing our democracy through erosion of our principles. Our executive has acted as a self-interested tyrant who is sucking ever more power to his cesspool. We beseech all of our elected officials: **do not let this continue to go on unchallenged.**

Consider the words of Martin Niemoller, a Lutheran clergyman in Germany during the rise and rule of the Nazis who had fought as a soldier for Germany in World War I, and was a staunch nationalist who believed in God and his country. He later admitted to first aligning himself with the Third Reich's views about nationhood, but then realized during the course of World War II that the "not my problem" attitude was what allowed the horrors of the Holocaust to happen. He wrote his famous and poetic words as his personal apology for the cowardice of the German intellectuals and clergy (including himself) who looked away as the Nazis rose to power and purged the people whom they decided were not the right kind or not fully in support of Hitler:

---

216   Thomas Jefferson, "Notes on the State of Virginia, Query XVIII: Manners, 1781", *Teaching American History*, accessed May 1, 2020, https://teachingamericanhistory.org/library/document/notes-on-the-state-of-virginia-query-xviii-manners/.

> First, they came for the communists, and I didn't speak out because I wasn't a communist.
> Then they came for the socialists, and I didn't speak out because I wasn't a socialist.
> Then they came for the trade unionists, and I didn't speak out because I wasn't a trade unionist.
> Then they came for me and there was no one left to speak for me.[217]

Why do we think this can't happen here? They didn't think it could happen in Germany either. We all must live with the effects of our current situation. An honest House and Senate is by far the most important factors in the balance of power between the branches of government. We will therefore work to replace the corrupt ones. To do otherwise will be at the peril of the very Constitution and freedoms we hold so dearly.

We are all now consumed with the war against the pandemic We want this writing to serve as a reminder of all that has happened. Trump has assumed the mantle of a wartime president saving our nation from an unrelenting enemy, while abdicating his responsibilities as commander-in-chief as the carnage has continued to rise. The past few months have illuminated Trump's inadequacies. He has proven to be an ever-present danger. The worst of the virus is not yet behind us. However, we must start to pivot our attention to the election and Tuesday, November 3, 2020. In Texas Hold'em Poker parlance we need to go "all in" to save our nation. It may be our last chance.

---

217 Martin Niemoller (1892-1984); see https://en.wikipedia.org/wiki/First_they_came_... .